RISK, CAPITAL COSTS, AND PROJECT FINANCING DECISIONS

NIJENRODE STUDIES IN BUSINESS

Volume 6

Business is a broad field where science and business reality can and should meet to analyze and discuss old theories and to develop new ones, applicable for modern managers. One of the main objectives of the **Nijenrode Studies in Business** is to give a push to new developments in the multidisciplinary business area, to serve the profession as well as a wider audience.

RISK, CAPITAL COSTS, AND PROJECT FINANCING DECISIONS

Edited by

Frans G.J. Derkinderen
The Netherlands School of Business

Roy L. Crum
University of Florida

Martinus Nijhoff Publishing
Boston / The Hague / London

Distributors for North America:
Martinus Nijhoff Publishing
Kluwer Boston, Inc.
160 Old Derby Street
Hingham, Massachusetts 02043

Distributors outside North America:
Kluwer Academic Publishers Group
Distribution Centre
P.O. Box 322
3300 AH Dordrecht, The Netherlands

Library of Congress Cataloging in Publication Data

Main entry under title:

Risk, capital costs, and project financing decisions.

(Nijenrode studies in business; v. 6)
Based on a conference on financial management of
corporate resource allocations held at Nijenrode Castle, the
Netherlands, in August 1979, which was hosted by the
Netherlands School of Business.
Includes bibliographies.
1. Capital investments—Addresses, essays, lectures.
2. Corporations—Finance—Addresses, essays, lectures.
I. Derkinderen, F. II. Crum, Roy L. III. Series.
HG4028.C4R49   658.1'52   80-12003
ISBN 0-89838-046-4

CONTENTS

Introduction   vii

I RISK SPECIFICATION AND DEFENSIVE BEHAVIOR

1 Behavioral Risk Constraints in Investment Analysis
    O. Maurice Joy and F. Hutton Barron, University of Kansas   3
2 Risk Preference: Empirical Evidence and Its Implications
  for Capital Budgeting
    Roy L. Crum, University of Florida, and Dan J. Laughhunn
    and John W. Payne, Duke University   14
3 The Factor of Urgency in Corporate Capital Budgeting Decisions
    George W. Hettenhouse, Indiana University   37
4 Geographic Perspectives of Risk: A Financial Strategic Approach
    Frans G.J. Derkinderen, The Netherlands School of Business   54

II ESTIMATING THE COST OF CAPITAL

5 Estimating the Market Risk Premium
  Eugene F. Brigham and Dilip K. Shome, University of Florida   79
6 Growth Opportunities and Real Investment Decisions
  J.E. Broyles and I.A. Cooper, London Business School,
  Great Britain   107
7 A Multiperiod Cost of Capital Concept and Its Impact on the
  Formulation of Financial Policy
  A.I. Diepenhorst, Erasmus University Rotterdam, The Netherlands   119
8 Inefficient Capital Markets and Their Implications
  John M. Samuels, Tulane University and Birmingham University,
  Great Britain   129
9 An Investment Decision Model for Small Business
  Ernest W. Walker, University of Texas at Austin   149

III FINANCING THE INVESTMENT OF CAPITAL

10 On Working Capital as an Investment by the Firm
   Keith V. Smith, Purdue University   167
11 Capital Budgeting Proposals with Negative Salvage Values
   Sandor Asztély, University of Gothenburg, Sweden   186
12 The Cost of Financing to the Firm in Foreign Exchange:
   Some Empirical Results and Their Implications
   Harald Burmeister, IESE, Spain   204
13 Leasing: The Gulf between Theory and Practice
   Cyril Tomkins, Julian Lowe, and Eleanor Morgan,
   University of Bath, Great Britain   227
14 A Pragmatic Approach to the Estimation Problems Encountered
   in Lease-Purchase Analysis
   John D. Martin, Texas A & M University; Paul F. Anderson,
   Virginia Polytechnic Institute and State University; and
   Chester L. Allen, Stephen F. Austin State University   254

Epilogue   274

INTRODUCTION

The ending of the decade of the seventies and the dawning of the eighties can be characterized as a period of great uncertainty with prospects for economic-political instability. High inflation and fluctuating exchange rates in the developed Western world have served to strengthen the forces of disequilibrium in the financial markets, leading to an investment situation with several unusual but significant factors. Capital spending by business, leading to the creation of new jobs, has not been reduced substantially during this period of uncertainty, as happened in similar periods in the past. This is shown in part by the continuing low unemployment rates in evidence during the period, which are in contradiction to the trend exhibited in similar past periods. The expanding financing requirements resulting from high price inflation have led to an increase in the capital intensity of firms, and thus to enhanced sensitivity of their income streams to economic fluctuations. At the same time, the record high interest rates that companies have had to pay to acquire this inflated amount of capital have caused a deterioration in the safety or quality indicators by which the creditworthiness of the firms is judged. These developments tend to increase the stakes involved in business decision making. One important repercussion of this is that greater attention is now being focused on improving the quality of investment decisions. Central to this are the issues of financing methods and their costs, the underlying determinants of those costs, and the structural characteristics of capital budgeting analyses.

Focusing first on the heart of these issues, the required rate of return on capital has been developed in the literature as the aggregation of the pure rate of interest, a premium for the inflation expected over the period in question, and a premium to compensate the providers of capital for the risk inherent in the investment. Perhaps the most controversial conceptually, the issues of the meaning of risk in a capital budgeting framework, its impact on the cost of capital, and how it enters the analysis require exploration as a basis for assessing appropriate risk premiums. In this regard, two conceptions of risk presently coexist in the financial literature; they are fundamentally different and lead to a divergence of opinion as to how an appropriate risk premium should be estimated for use in a capital budgeting analysis. One viewpoint currently in vogue in many quarters is that the risk premium to be charged to a project should only reflect the extent to which that project would contribute to the risk of a diversified portfolio of securities. Thus the appropriate meaning of risk is in the capital market sense with the measure of systematic market risk being the beta coefficient of the project.

From a practical perspective, estimation of the correct value for the beta of a *capital budgeting project* has proven to be extraordinarily difficult, if not impossible in most cases. Also, most Capital Asset Pricing Model (CAPM) -based formulations are one-period models, while capital budgeting is inherently a multiperiod process. More basic, however, are other objections to this conception of the appropriate measure of risk by the opposing major school of thought. According to this other group, the vital question to ask is, Risk to whom? It is their conviction that for purposes of capital budgeting and corporate decisions, the risk to a capital market investor holding a diversified portfolio of securities is not unimportant, but neither is it of the greatest relevance. Rather, since the managerial decision maker has a vested and usually relatively undiversified interest in the continuing economic performance of a single firm—the one for whom he works—there is a strong motivation to view risk from the perspective of that more specifically defined sphere. Unfortunately, there is no single measure of corporate risk that is accepted as an adequate descriptor for all situations. In fact, many distribution-tied definitions of risk based on measures such as variance (or standard deviation), covariance, semivariance, or probability of loss, as well as distribution-free definitions such as implied by the various forms of stochastic dominance, have been suggested in the literature. Too often one gets the impression from reading this literature that the risk measure em-

ployed by a particular author is chosen more because of its mathematical properties for the purpose at hand than for its conformance to the manner in which
decision makers really behave. Suffice it to say, however, that this group of
scholars regards corporate risk—as opposed to systematic market risk—as the
basis for determining proper resource allocations within firms.

Regardless of the definition utilized, there are several ways in which risk is
taken into account in determining the economic viability of individual projects
(before portfolio issues come into play). An "appropriate" adjustment can be
made to the cash-flow stream to transform it into a financially equivalent
stream with other risk properties. This stream is then discounted at a rate that
reflects the required return for the stream's riskiness. Empirical studies seem
to indicate that a more usual procedure to adjust for risk in determining economic viability is to make "appropriate" adjustments to the hurdle rates employed to screen the individual projects. When this procedure is used, the hurdle
or discount rate is supposed to reflect the return required to compensate an
investor for the risk of the project. If this alternative procedure is to be employed as a first step toward determining the relevant risk-adjusted discount
rate (RADR) to be used for preliminary screening of projects, it is important
that the return required to compensate investors for the firm's presently existing
risk, or the current cost of capital, be estimated to serve as a market-derived
benchmark for comparative purposes. Thus a fundamental issue for improving
the quality of investment decisions is the determination of the required return
on equity for the company.

The problems associated with this endeavor are not inconsequential when
price data generated in an efficient market are available. However, when the
validity of these data is open to question because of inefficient capital markets
or when the data do not exist because the company is not publicly owned,
estimation problems are greatly magnified. The technique usually applied in
this situation is to try to find a "comparable" firm for which adequate market
price data are available to use as a proxy for the company in question. Another
approach is to assess (usually on an ad hoc basis) an equity premium to be added
to the firm's interest cost. While better than nothing, these estimates for the
required return on equity, even for large public corporations, are clearly weak
links in the capital investment process. In order to increase the quality of business decision making, then, a crucial step is to strengthen this part of the analysis
by developing more rigorous procedures for determining the cost of capital and
subsequently the relevant hurdle rate to be used for assessing the economic
viability of individual projects.

Turning to the numerator of the discounted cash-flow equation, there are
several ways that decision quality can be improved. Of obvious importance, and
yet often overlooked, is the requirement that all relevant cash flows for the

periods in question be included in the analysis. Some cash flows tend to be ignored at times because they are "mandatory" or because they represent joint expenses/revenues that cannot easily be associated with the conventional notion of an investment project. In other cases, there is a danger that opportunity costs or benefits—benefits not received or costs not incurred because of management action, or, more likely, management inaction—are neglected. It is also possible that assumptions implicit in the discounted cash-flow methodology will mask substantive ramifications of investment situations so that the decision maker is unaware that the firm is assumed to take actions that it would otherwise choose not to take, or may not even be permitted to take. Reinvestment of intermediate cash flows or financing of future shortfalls might come under this classification. What is called for by these potential sources of error or bias, then, is more careful attention to detail in defining the cash-flow stream for a project. With attention to these factors, enhanced decision-making quality will likely be forthcoming.

The considerations discussed above are some of the most significant, although not the only, factors that have a bearing on improving the quality of capital investment decisions. Because of their importance—indeed, because of the importance of the broad topic of improved decision making in today's world of increasing complexity and ever present change—the Netherlands School of Business hosted a conference on Financial Management of Corporate Resource Allocations in August 1979. Held at Nijenrode Castle in the Netherlands, this conference brought together over forty distinguished scholars and business executives from eleven countries to present research papers and to participate in round-table discussions. The fourteen essays selected for inclusion in this, the second volume to come out of that conference, represent a cross section of views on the subjects of risk, cost of capital, and project financing, considering the business environment of the 1980s. Thus they are attempts to come to grips with the main issues outlined above.

CONTENT OF THE BOOK

The first part of the book explores various issues and problems of defining and ascertaining what risk really means in a capital investment context. A common theme of the four papers in this section on risk specification and defensive behavior is that in an operational setting, risk is a multidimensional concept that cannot be captured adequately by either the concept of systematic market risk or corporate risk as conventionally defined in the literature. Joy and Barron approach the problem from the behavioral perspective and argue that current theories are not descriptively adequate. It is their contention that "failure risk" or "risk of ruin" plays a dominant part in managerial decision making that cannot be overlooked in models of choice. In their descriptive theory of risky decision making, failure risk serves as a strike-out rule that constrains the decision process. Only after this initial stage is passed can a project be evaluated by the more traditional methods.

Crum, Laughhunn, and Payne agree that risk of ruin plays a significant role in decision making, but go further to hypothesize that current perceptions of rational decision makers as uniformly risk averse are descriptively inadequate. They contend that a dominant characteristic of the decision-making process is the existence of a target or aspiration level for performance and that risk is defined by managers in relation to expected deviations of performance from the target. Extensive empirical studies have shown that expected failure to achieve this target will generally lead to the observance of risk-seeking behavior on the part of managers until risk of ruin comes into play. When possibly ruinous risk enters the picture, the decision maker tends to revert back to risk-averting behavior, although not necessarily to the extent that failure risk becomes an absolute strike-out rule. Similarly, for expected returns above the target, managers appear to be risk averse, as predicted by traditional theory. Thus, for descriptive reality, the twin notions of an aspiration level and a risk of ruin are required to structure a capital budgeting analysis in a sufficient manner.

Taking a different tack, Hettenhouse focuses attention not on the characteristics of decision makers in reacting to risk, but rather on specific characteristics of individual projects. Underlying his paper is the idea that social systems are not content with simply pricing and allocating risk properly, but rather that they openly try to change the risk attributes. That is, managers attempt to shape the risk profile of the firm so as to reduce the need to worry about unfavorable contingencies occurring in the future. Hettenhouse views an important component of this engineered flexibility in terms of what he calls urgency. He postulates that managers schedule projects for funding, or postpone implementation, on the basis of the time pressure or urgency of the projects. Thus when factors other than the traditional concept of profitability are suggested for explicit inclusion in capital budgeting analyses, a situation is created in which some form of multicriterion analysis is required. Hettenhouse presents a heuristic method for coping with the problems and discusses some of the mathematical programming variants that may be appropriate for this application.

Derkinderen expands upon this theme by asserting that distinct characteristics of the applicable problem class itself closely define the factors that are important for dealing effectively with the risk inherent in the decision context. Although this essay was not presented at the conference, its inclusion in this book is considered useful as it serves to round out the discussion of risk as a multiattribute concept. According to Derkinderen, to avoid the danger of making unjustified generalizations in defining the capital budget, a typological approach is needed to outline and structure suitable factors for shaping the risk profile of the company in the desired manner. The discussion is placed within the context of risk problems associated particularly with direct foreign investment decisions. Using a typological approach that is strategically grounded in the financial theories of the valuation of the firm, Derkinderen ascertains geographic-oriented aspects that are important for identifying, analyzing, and evaluating risk issues in preparing for investment decisions abroad. Thereupon, a followup method is developed to structure the geographic factors further and to reflect upon risk implications as they interact with other strategic considerations. He shows that resource allocations made on the basis of those decision rules are more consistent with the multidimensional perceptions of managers than are traditional approaches to risk analysis and project selection.

All contributions to Part I of the book tend to emphasize that corporate risk is relevant for making capital budgeting decisions. While none of the authors could be expected to advocate ignoring systematic market risk, all view the managerial decision-making process as richer than is admitted by advocates of the capital asset pricing model. Thus systematic risk alone is an inadequate concept for making *real asset* investments.

The second part of the book directs attention to one of the most significant difficulties in implementing a discounted cash-flow approach to capital budgeting: estimating an appropriate cost of capital. Brigham and Shome concentrate on situations in which the firm in question is large, publicly traded, and can be described as a mature company with normal growth possibilities. For firms that conform to this classification, it is assumed that an appropriate cost of capital is a predictable function of the risk premium demanded for the market portfolio. Based on the Gordon constant growth model, Brigham and Shome develop a methodology and estimate the market risk premium that is appropriate to use with the Capital Asset Pricing Model (CAPM) or other similar estimation methodologies. This, they believe, can be used as a basing point in the determination of the cost of equity for a firm.

Broyles and Cooper assert that the required rate of return on equity capital estimated by using the CAPM is inappropriate for use in capital budgeting analyses of growth prospects without modification. They show two ways in which capital budgeting procedures must be adjusted to take account of the options implicit in future opportunities for growth. The first adjustment, to the discount rate, applies a factor to the beta estimated from market values that reflects the extent of the growth opportunities facing the firm. The second adjustment, to the acceptance criterion, reflects the opportunity cost of project postponement, an omission in usual approaches that can substantially affect optimal real investment decisions by companies. Thus a linkage is formed between this paper and the one by Hettenhouse in the first part of the book.

Diepenhorst then explores the ramifications of the use of a perpetuity model to estimate a cost of capital to be employed in evaluating nonperpetual cash flows. For both perpetual and nonperpetual cash flows, he formulates a number of relations between the several uncertain cash flows, between their appropriate capitalization rates, and between the corresponding market values. From this analysis, conclusions are reached regarding the impact of financial leverage on the market value of the company and the firm's cost of capital, with and without corporate taxes.

The three papers presented so far in this section assume that an efficient market exists in which it is possible to price risk. The following two papers explore situations in which this assumption does not hold and market signals cannot be used to determine an appropriate cost of capital. Samuels contends that the existence of an inefficient capital market can lead to the adoption by companies of investment strategies and techniques that are different from those that are suitable in an efficient market. This occurs, according to Samuels, because on the one hand, the corporation has greater power to influence its own stock price in an inefficient market, and yet, on the other hand, there is a greater possibility that its price will move about in a manner not justified by the information available.

Walker then explores the situation in which there are no market data for the company because its stock is not traded in the market. He presents an investment model that employs the discounted cash-flow concept and does not require a single investment criterion. Not only does the model allow the manager to select the most desirable investment, it also "informs" the decision maker which financing mix is optimum for the project. This eliminates the necessity of the manager's knowing the firm's optimum capital structure prior to making the investment decision.

After the discussions of risk and the cost of capital, Part III focuses attention more directly on financing the investment of capital. In the first paper, Smith urges more explicit consideration of working capital investment in the capital budgeting process of the firm. It is his contention that since working capital can involve substantial amounts of money, any changes in working capital policies should be included as an explicit project and evaluated along with all other alternatives in the capital budgeting process. Only in this way can the financing available to the firm be allocated to the most profitable use.

Asztély considers an issue that is becoming more significant in today's world. Certain types of investments, such as those connected with mining operations, nuclear power plants, and waste disposal, lead to situations in which large negative salvage values are common. The discounted cash-flow methodology assumes implicitly that revenues over the life of the project will be sufficient to cover these back-end costs if the net present value is positive. Asztély maintains, however, that it is not enough to let the methodology mask the issue. It is his view that, for instance, future generations should not be charged with the cost of liquidating activities that satisfy present energy requirements. Thus he investigates different forms of apportioning future outlays to current revenues so that current consumers bear an appropriate burden of the cost and a large balloon payment is not required at the end of the project life.

Another financing issue that is of relevance in investment decisions, but that is often ignored, is the choice of a currency in which to denominate the financing instruments. According to Burmeister, the cost of a foreign exchange credit consists of the contracted interest rate (plus possible commissions, etc.) and the re- or devaluation (plus its tax treatment), if any, of the currency employed against the national currency. Current theory suggests that the firm does not have to make a choice as the cost of any currency is the same: A lesser interest rate is compensated for by a relative revaluation of the currency, and vice versa. Burmeister presents some empirical evidence to show that this is not an adequate description of reality and suggests that the choice of currency in which to denominate financing instruments should be approached systematically.

Changing the focus of the section slightly, the last two papers discuss a particular financing instrument that has received increased interest in recent years: leasing. Tomkins, Lowe, and Morgan argue that the existing academic literature does very little to help us to understand the development of leasing markets and lessee motivation to lease. They show that the financial leasing market in Great Britain is not one homogeneous unit, thus suggesting that there are different forms of lessee motivation. The paper concludes that there is little evidence to indicate that the tax issue is the main motivation for leasing and that very large or "big ticket" leases may be developing into a particularly creative form of international strategic management. Continuing the discussion, Martin, Anderson, and Allen then propose the use of two forms of sensitivity analysis to help cope with the problem of estimation error in lease-purchase problems. Thus, these last two papers in the book give a good synthesis of the "why" and the "how" of leasing analysis from the financing perspective.

Taken together, the fourteen essays included in this volume explore some vital issues that will become increasingly important in the years to come. To make good investment decisions in complex environments, prescriptive theories that better incorporate the necessary descriptive elements identified as important in these papers will have to be forthcoming.

I | RISK SPECIFICATION AND DEFENSIVE BEHAVIOR

1 BEHAVIORAL RISK CONSTRAINTS IN INVESTMENT ANALYSIS

O. Maurice Joy and F. Hutton Barron
University of Kansas

One of the important criticisms of the variance-covariance concept of risk is that it does not adequately describe manager's risk preferences and risk-evaluation procedures. Good examples of this kind of criticism are found in Mao [21] and in Machol and Lerner [20]. They argue instead for a kind of "failure risk" concept.

We offer in this paper a descriptive theory of decision making that employs failure risk that may be applied to investment decisions. The essential feature of this theory is that failure risk affects choice by excluding alternatives from further consideration. Descriptively, failure risk acts as a *constraint* or strike-out rule in the decision process. This point has not been explored extensively in the finance literature, although a recent paper by Libby and Fishburn [15] highlights this concept while reviewing the behavioral modeling of risk-taking literature. Another recent paper that bears directly on this issue is the Laughhunn and Sprecher [14] article, which integrates the probability of loss concept with capital asset pricing theory. The implications of these two papers for this article are discussed below.

3

In the next section, we establish the framework for decision making under risk that we employ. The following section briefly reviews the salient evidence regarding modeling failure risk as a constraint. We then discuss financial applications of the theory in the context of the standard Lorie-Savage [18] problems. The last two sections are concerned with posing questions and summarizing, respectively.

A FRAMEWORK FOR DECISION MAKING UNDER RISK

Risky decision problems may be characterized as having m disjoint alternatives[1] A_1, A_2, . . . , A_m; n disjoint states of nature S_1, S_2, . . . , S_n; and an $m \times n$ payoff matrix, U, whose entries are some index of desirability of the mn alternative state of nature pairs. Payoffs for the mn pairs are estimated by the decision maker, as are state probabilities. The payoff for the ith alternative should the jth state of nature occur is u_{ij}, and that state is expected to occur with probability p_j. The decision problem is to select a strategy, $f(Y)$, $Y = y_1$, y_2, . . . , y_m, where $y_i = 1$ if alternative i is accepted and $y_i = 0$ if alternative i is rejected.[2] If any number of axiom systems are accepted as a prescription for choice, then it is "rational"—that is, it is consistent with the axioms—to assign utilities to payoffs and, given the assignment of probabilities to states as well, to choose the strategy having the highest expected utility.

Given payoffs, or utilities for payoffs, and probabilities, the framework for risky decisions described above has been generalized in two ways:

1. The choice criteria or objective function is viewed as a member of a class of functions. In Barron and Mackenzie, the class of functions is represented "as linear functions of indices associated with each alternative (i.e., indices computable in terms of the entries in the payoff matrix)" [5, p. 61]. This class includes expected value, expected utility, subjective expected utility, and familiar criteria for decision making under uncertainty.
2. Choice is modeled as a chance-constrained optimization model by adding two components: T, tolerable (to the decision maker) level of outcome, and α, the probability of not realizing this tolerable level of outcome.

The choice process is viewed as first involving possible exclusion of some alternatives (due to the combination of T and α values), leading to a reduced set of feasible alternatives, followed by a selection of a preferred alternative from the set of feasible alternatives on the basis of some objective function. This formulation implies that while the decision maker will hazard the possibility that the actual or realized outcome may be less than the tolerable payoff, he will require that there be a probability bound on this undesirable outcome. We contend that the twin notions that failure risk is the probability of an intolerable outcome and that failure risk acts as an exclusion constraint form the basis for a behavioral theory of investment analysis.

The proposed decision framework has several attractive features. First, it is consistent with a general formulation of risky decisions [5] incorporating chance constraints. Second, it appears to be descriptive of what many investors and corporations perceive to be the essence of risky decision problems [20]. Third, it has offered parsimonious interpretations of many observed choice experiments that are difficult to explain in the traditional mean-variance framework [4]. In the next section, we develop the evidence and rationale for a chance-constrained model.

EVIDENCE FOR A CHANCE-CONSTRAINED MODEL OF RISK

The rationale for a chance-constrained optimization model is behavioral. The impetus for this formulation comes from two related developments: (1) the failure of objective function considerations alone both to predict choice behavior and to represent choice processes; (2) the corresponding adequacy of chance constraints in reflecting plausible information processing of perceived risk dimensions and multiple-decision criteria.

In discussing the inadequacies of objective functions alone, we consider a general objective function

$$\sum_{i=1}^{m} y_i I_i$$

and numerous laboratory studies of choice behavior. I_i is an index associated with alternative A_i and could be any of the usual decision criteria for decision making under uncertainty or any of the algebraic expectation models [22]. For criticisms of the former, see Luce and Raiffa [19]. Inadequacies of the expectation models are documented in numerous studies. For example, Lichtenstein, Slovic, and Zink [17] first had subjects make decisions under risk, then explained EV (expected value) to the subjects, and then additional decisions were made—decisions for which EV was supplied to the subject. Choices were far from optimal in an EV sense, both before and after EV was explained. Subjects later stated that EV was irrelevant or unimportant. Coombs, Bezembinder, and Goode [9] experimentally compared EV, EU (expected utility), SEV (subjective expected value), and SEU (subjective expected utility). They found SEU superior, failing in only 5 to 10 percent of the cases across two experiments. Other experiments [6, 11, 25] have tested, generally in a descriptive sense, individual axioms (usually the Savage axioms [23]) of SEU. Some general conditions under which individual axioms are frequently violated have been identified. Furthermore, violations persist, even after violations are explained [11]. Also, results of testing the necessary skills involved in applying SEU—viz., estimation of probabilities by students [13] and by trained scientists [26] and empirical specification of utilities by experienced managers [10] —are not encouraging.

An illuminating experiment by Lichtenstein and Slovic [17] has produced choices inconsistent with expected utility principles. Subjects, initially students, but later real-money gamblers in a Las Vegas casino, were offered objectively defined gambles, designated as gambles G_1 and G_2. As an example, gamble G_1 is win \$4.00 with probability .99, lose \$1.00 with probability .01; gamble G_2 is win \$16.00 with probability .33, lose \$2.00 with probability .67. A familiar response, and one that is entirely inconsistent with SEU maximization, is for the subject (1) to prefer gamble G_1 to gamble G_2 and (2) to require a higher selling price for gamble G_2 than for gamble G_1. An explanation for this preference reversal response pattern relies on information-processing heuristics. For an interpretive review, see Payne [22].

Finally, it might be argued that empirical data that are inconsistent with economic preference theory are artifacts of the experiments themselves. In a recent paper, Grether and Plott [12] systematically explore this possibility. Noting the large number of psychologically oriented studies that report the preference reversal phenomena mentioned above, they ask two questions: (1) Is the phenomenon relevant to standard economic theory? (2) Can it be explained by standard economic theory? Their answers are yes to the first question and no to the second. They do not have, however, alternative theories of optimization or preference to offer.

The second development focuses on the interpretive adequacy of constraints. Constraints, or more generally chance constraints, have been offered to explain observed choice behavior that is inconsistent with utility maximization [3], to reflect plausible information processes [5], and to allow for multiple criteria [24]. The implication of modeling risk as a chance constraint is that the constraint precludes alternatives. The constraint's role is to strike out alternatives.

One interpretive view of constraints is as follows: The decision maker scans all payoffs for all alternatives and focuses on a particularly obvious feature (e.g., smallest return) or calculates some overall index of "badness" (such as regret). Alternatives are then screened against either the obvious feature or the calculated (regret) level, one at a time. If an alternative fails—if the smallest return falls below an acceptable level or if regret is excessive—the probability of either occurrence is checked. If this probability is viewed as excessive, the alternative is excluded; if not excessive, the alternative is retained. Following this feasibility screening, alternatives are compared in an objective function sense and a best is selected. All experiments in Barron [3] were interpreted in this way. Similar interpretations were shown as possible in Barron and Joy [4]. Of course, there are other interpretations of the decision-making process. The decision maker may calculate desirability indices *first,* and then check for risk feasibility of the unconstrained optimal solution. Notice that in *either* scenario the risk constraint acts as a strike-out device.

Multiple-objective criteria imply multiple screens. Consistent with this theory, Schenkerman [24] formulates decision problems as a mathematical programming problem. Multiple criteria are expressed as (1) a single-criterion objective function, and (2) security or attainment levels as constraints. Reasons for this approach and against a sole optimizing criterion are that

> they [decision makers] may not appreciate the implications of utility. They may be wary about using expectation for nonrecurring events. They particularly may worry over adverse outcomes. . . . In fact, there is evidence that many decision makers are not completely satisfied with any single criterion. . . . Rather, a single criterion is accepted only after the establishment of certain *security levels.* [24, pp. 42–43]

In a recent survey article, Libby and Fishburn [15] discuss and interpret results from several empirical studies concerned with (among other things) defining (identifying) risk from the decision maker's standpoint. On balance, Libby and Fishburn interpret the available empirical evidence as supporting the concept of failure risk in a noncompensatory model. That is, failure risk acts as a constraint in the choice problem.

FINANCIAL APPLICATIONS OF THE THEORY

The decision framework, described earlier, is general in the sense that it is not restricted to applications that possess pecuniary payoffs. However, there have been several financial applications of this theory. Machol and Lerner [20] have argued for equation of risk with the probability of loss in the investment analysis problem. They also stress the importance of viewing risk as a chance constraint. Mao [21] cited evidence that corporate executives view risk as the probability of loss. Barron and Joy [4] have also used the chance-constrained probability of loss concept to interpret Mao's work and the results of a study by Alderfer and Bierman [1] in an investment selection laboratory study. Conrath [8] has also argued that chance constraints affect choice via exclusion of alternatives.

Having developed the concepts and rationale for the risky decision-making model, we next apply this model to three important investment problems.

There are three particularly commonplace investment problems that financial decision makers—corporate, governmental, and individual investors—continually face. These have been named the "accept-reject," "mutually exclusive ranking," and "capital rationing" problems [18]. Theoretical financial solutions, cum risk, to these three classes of problems are well known. In the accept-reject decision, a project is accepted (rejected) if its expected net present value is positive (negative). In ranking mutually exclusive projects, that project with the largest positive expected net present value is accepted. Under capital rationing, the decision maker solves an integer programming problem to find that group of projects that maximizes expected net present value subject to stipulated budget constraints.

It is clear that these solution procedures do attempt to account for risk in that expected net present-value calculation procedures typically make provisions for project risk by adjustment of either the discount rate or the expected cash flows. It is not so clear, however, that these solution procedures are consistent with the behavioral studies reported earlier.

Assume that payoffs are in terms of net present value (although our analysis does not require this). We next show how the chance-constrained probability of failure model fits these three investment problems.

The Accept-Reject Decision

This is the most pervasive decision in capital budgeting and is subsumed in both the mutually exclusive ranking and capital rationing decisions. There are two alternatives, only one of which may be chosen, and fractional projects may not be accepted. There are no budget constraints.

If we designate alternative 2 as the reject choice, the formal decision model is[3]

$$\text{Maximize} \quad y_1 \sum_{j=1}^{n} u_{1j} p_j + y_2(0)$$

$$\text{Subject to} \quad \Pr\{y_1 u_1 < T\} < \alpha$$

$$y_1 + y_2 = 1$$

$$y_1, y_2 \in \{0, 1\},$$

where u and T are in present value units and $u_1 = u_{1j}$ if state j occurs.[4]

The risk constraint requires that the probability that the realized net present value of the selected alternative falls below some minimum level, T, be less than some specified level, α. Operationally, the decision maker calculates the expected net present value of the project under consideration (alternative 1). If expected net present value is positive, the project is accepted provided the risk constraint is satisfied. Checking the risk constraint is a trivial calculation. Let β_1 be the probability sum for all those states for which u_{1j} is less than T. That is, let

$$\beta_1 = \sum_{j \in J_1} p_j,$$

where J_1 is the set of all states for which $u_{1j} < T$. If $\beta_1 \geqslant \alpha$, the project will be rejected. Thus a project with positive expected net present value will be unacceptable if its probability of "failure" is too large. The risk constraint serves to strike out the project from consideration even though it is acceptable on an expectation basis.

We might specify T as equal to zero, which defines failure as negative net present value. There are, of course, other specifications possible for T. An interesting aspect of negative T values is that it encourages project sharing; that is, it encourages dropping the no-fractional project requirement. When $T < 0$, a project that is unacceptable for risk-constraint reasons may be made acceptable by purchasing only a fraction of the project, assuming, of course, that fractional projects make sense. This is because reducing y_1 from unity reduces net present value associated with failure states without affecting the sign of the project's expected net present value. If, for example, the project's stakes are quite large, as in an oil exploration venture in Alaska, the net present value loss may be limited by sharing the venture with other companies.

The Mutually Exclusive Ranking Decision

In this problem the objective is to choose the best acceptable project (if any) among competing mutually exclusive projects. There are more than two alternatives (including the reject-all-projects alternative), only one of which may be chosen, fractional projects may not be accepted, and there are no budget constraints.

If we designate alternative m as the reject-all-projects choice, the decision model is

$$\text{Maximize} \quad \sum_{i=1}^{m} y_i \sum_{j=1}^{n} u_{ij} p_j$$

Subject to $\Pr\{y_i u_i < T\} < \alpha$ $i = 1, 2, \ldots, m$

$$\sum_{i=1}^{m} y_i = 1$$

$$y_i \in \{0, 1\} \qquad\qquad i = 1, 2, \ldots, m$$

The risk constraint serves as a strike-out rule just as it did in the accept-reject case. For project i, let

$$\beta_i = \sum_{j \in J_i} p_j,$$

where J_i is the set of all states for which $u_{ij} < T$. A project would therefore be selected only if it (1) has positive expected net present value that is (2) larger than any other feasible project and also (3) meets the risk constraint.

The Capital Rationing Problem

Here there are m alternatives, of which usually more than one may be chosen, fractional projects may not be accepted, and there are budget constraints. Adding behavioral risk constraints leads to the following decision model:

Maximize $$\sum_{i=1}^{m} y_i \sum_{j=1}^{n} u_{ij} p_j$$

Subject to $$\Pr\left\{ \sum_{i=1}^{m} y_i u_i < T \right\} < \alpha$$

$$\sum_{i=1}^{m} y_i c_{it} \leqslant b_t \qquad t = 1, 2, \ldots, N$$

$$y_i \in \{0, 1\}$$

The objective is to choose that group of projects with maximum expected net present value that satisfies the risk and budget constraints. Other similar models have been proposed that also account for risk attitudes in the constraint set (see, for example, [20]). Solution algorithms for this model are typically not trivial. One possible method uses a combinational solution technique similar to that of Barron [2]. First, solve the model ignoring the risk constraint, and then check the optimal solution for feasibility. If feasible, the problem is solved; if not, a possibly large number of 0-1 linear programming problems must be solved.

OTHER ISSUES

Although we contend that the existent empirical evidence supports the failure risk concept presented here, that concept is, as yet, an ad hoc notion. The Laughhunn-Sprecher [14] contribution is to show that if the risk-free interest rate is accepted to be the disaster (failure) rate of return level, then the failure risk concept is consistent with the capital asset pricing model, which is an equilibrium pricing model. Unfortunately, it is unclear that the risk-free interest rate is a universally appropriate failure level standard.

There are other unresolved issues also. It is unclear, for example, whether the failure risk concept is a project-specific or portfolio concept. That is, does the failure constraint apply to projects individually, or to groups of projects? Laughhunn and Sprecher favor the former, but it seems fair to say that the issue has yet to be resolved. The question of whether or not managers and investors aggregate failure risk across investments has not been addressed empirically.

Other unresolved problems exist, which, like the two just discussed, are of a "technical" nature. By technical, we mean here that even if the failure risk theory is accepted as generally valid, there still are problems relevant to its interpretation, implementation, and justification. Perhaps more important, however, are issues that question the fundamental validity of the failure risk theory. Certainly, the evidence pertaining to it today is not voluminous (particularly in realistic finance settings), is not the usual kind of empirical evidence found in finance studies, and is small-group oriented. The issue of whether observed behavior in individual or small-group settings can be extrapolated to large-group (market) settings is a crucial one.

CONCLUSIONS

Financial theory emphasizes the variance-covariance risk concept with lesser attention given to other risk concepts and/or dimensions. However, several reported experiments indicate that risk is perceived as a constraint in the decision-making model. More specifically, risk is described as a "failure constraint." And this descriptive theory of failure risk appears to be germane to more than just financial theory. On the basis of this evidence, we have proposed investment decision models that directly incorporate these behavioral risk concepts. The distinguishing feature of this theory is its portrayal of risk as a chance constraint in the decision process. In this theory, risk acts as a strike-out rule that precludes some alternatives from consideration. Although the effect of this theory is to make even the simple accept-reject and mutually exclusive investment problems chance-constrained programming problems, solution procedures for these two classes of problems are trivial. Application of the model to the capital rationing case may result in problems that are not so easily solved.

NOTES

1. One being the "do nothing" or "no commitment" alternative.

2. Requiring (0, 1) binary values for y_i acknowledges that neither fractional alternatives $(0 < y_i < 1)$ nor multiples of alternatives $(y_i > 1)$ may be purchased and that alternatives may not be sold short $(y_i < 0)$. If the decision maker accepts only a single alternative, exactly one $y_i = 1$; if several alternatives can be accepted, more than one $y_i = 1$.

3. Positing the objective function in terms of expected value makes the model an "E"-type chance-constrained programming model discussed by Charnes and Cooper [7]. Some behavioral theorists have argued that a more descriptive objective relates to satisficing. These objectives may be expressed as a "P" model (see [7]) that either maximizes the probability of attaining some objective or, alternatively, minimizes the probability of not attaining some objective. The choice of the objective function may be important for behavioral reasons, but we choose not to focus on that issue in this paper.

4. T and u values may also be stated in units other than net present value. They have previously been defined in units of rate of return [8, 21] and regret (regret for a state, *ex post,* being maximum possible payoff for that state minus actual payoff) [4].

REFERENCES

[1] Alderfer, C.P., and Bierman, H., Jr. "Choices with Risk: Beyond the Mean and Variance," *Journal of Business* 43 (July 1970).

[2] Barron, F.H. "A Chance Constrained Optimization Model for Risk," *OMEGA* 1 (June 1973).

[3] Barron, F.H. "The Potential Adopter's Decision Rule: A Constrained Optimization Model of Decision Making under Risk and Uncertainty," Ph.D. dissertation, University of Pennsylvania, 1970; see *Dissertation Abstracts* 31, No. 10 (1971).

[4] Barron, F.H., and Joy, O.M. "A Behavioral Model for Risky Decisions," *Journal of Business Administration* (Fall 1972).

[5] Barron, F.H., and Mackenzie, K.D. "A Constrained Optimization Model of Risky Decision," *Journal of Mathematical Psychology* 10 (February 1973).

[6] Becker, S.W., and Brownson, F.O. "What Price Ambiguity? Or the Role of Ambiguity in Decision Making," *Journal of Political Economy* 72 (1964).

[7] Charnes, A., and Cooper, W. W. "Deterministic Equivalents for Optimizing and Satisficing under Chance Constraints," *Operations Research* 11 (January–February 1963).

[8] Conrath, D. W. "From Statistical Decision Theory to Practice: Some Problems with the Transition," *Management Science* 19 (April 1973).

[9] Coombs, C. H.; Bezembinder, T. G.; and Goode, F. M. "Testing Expectation Theories of Decision Making without Measuring Utility or Subjective Probability," *Journal of Mathematical Psychology* 4 (1967).

[10] Dyckman, T. R., and Salomon, R. "Empirical Utility Functions and Random Devices: An Experiment," *Decision Sciences* 3 (April 1972).

[11] Ellsberg, D. "Risk, Ambiguity, and the Savage Axioms," *Quarterly Journal of Economics* 75 (1961).

[12] Grether, D. N., and Plott, C. R. "Economic Theory of Choice and the Preference Reversal Phenomenon," *American Economic Review* (forthcoming).

[13] Kahneman, D., and Tversky, A. "Subjective Probability: A Judgment of Representativeness," *Cognitive Psychology* 3 (July 1972).

[14] Laughhunn, D. J., and Sprecher, C. R. "Probability of Loss and the Capital Asset Pricing Model," *Financial Management* 6 (Spring 1977).

[15] Libby, R., and Fishburn, P. C. "Behavioral Models of Risk Taking in Business Decisions: A Survey and Evaluation," *Journal of Accounting Research* 15 (Autumn 1977).

[16] Lichtenstein, S., and Slovic, P. "Reversals of Preference between Bids and Choices in Gambling Decisions, *Journal of Experimental Psychology* 89 (1971).

[17] Lichtenstein, S.; Slovic, P.; and Zink, D. "Effect of Instruction in Expected Value on Optimality of Gambling Decisions," *Journal of Experimental Psychology* 79 (1969).

[18] Lorie, J. H., and Savage, L. J. "Three Problems in Rationing Capital," *Journal of Business* 28 (October 1955).

[19] Luce, R. D., and Raiffa, H. *Games and Decisions.* New York: John Wiley & Sons, 1957.

[20] Machol, R. E., and Lerner, E. M. "Risk, Ruin and Investment Analysis," *Journal of Financial and Quantitative Analysis* 4 (December 1969).

[21] Mao, J. C. T. "Survey of Capital Budgeting: Theory and Practice," *Journal of Finance* 25 (May 1970).

[22] Payne, J. W. "Alternative Approaches to Decision Making under Risk: Moments versus Risk Dimensions," *Psychological Bulletin* 80 (1973).

[23] Savage, L. J. *The Foundations of Statistics.* New York: John Wiley & Sons, 1954.

[24] Schenkerman, S. "Constrained Decision Criteria," *Decision Sciences* 6 (January 1975).

[25] Tversky, A. "Intransitivity of Preferences," *Psychological Review* 67 (1969).

[26] Tversky, A., and Kahneman, D. "Belief in the Law of Small Numbers," *Psychological Bulletin* 76 (1971).

2 RISK PREFERENCE:

Empirical Evidence and Its Implications
for Capital Budgeting

Roy L. Crum
University of Florida

Dan J. Laughhunn and John W. Payne
Duke University

Finance is a subject that must inevitably deal with decisions that involve choices from risky alternatives in a wide variety of settings—for example, choices of investment portfolios or selections of capital assets. In order to develop normative and predictive models for choice problems such as these, assumptions about the risk preference of individual decision makers have been necessary. The traditional assumption made about risk preference is that individuals are uniformly risk averse. In its strongest form, the assumption of risk aversion has been translated into the proposition that individuals choose between risky alternatives on the basis of mean and variance (or semivariance) and that individuals are averse to risk as measured by variance (or semivariance). In a weaker form, the assumption of risk aversion implies that the utility function of individuals is concave in terminal wealth.

On the other hand, the possibility of risk-seeking behavior has been suggested in the economics and psychology literature for some time, dating at least as early as the classic paper by Friedman and Savage [10]. These authors utilized a mixture of a convex segment (risk seeking) and two concave segments (risk aversion)

14

in a single utility function to explain the simultaneous purchase of insurance and gambling by the same individual. Several other papers have subsequently appeared dealing with the possible existence of risk-seeking behavior, as well as the conditions under which such behavior can occur [16, 23, 29, 34, 43].

While these ideas regarding risk-seeking behavior have existed for some time, the possibility of this form of behavior has not been addressed in the literature of finance. When discussing risk preferences, the common practice is to acknowledge the possible existence of risk-seeking behavior, but then to summarily dismiss the possibility on the grounds of its being inappropriate for further consideration as a legitimate concern of finance. Typical of this approach is the following comment by Sharpe [37]:

> No fundamental law of nature requires all investors to be risk averse. In fact, a single investor might be averse to risk concerning decisions likely to result in one range of outcomes but actually prefer risk decisions likely to result in outcomes in another range. For analyzing *major investment decisions,* such cases are of relatively little importance. The remainder of this chapter deals with individuals who are risk averse. [P. 196, emphasis added]

While admitting the possibility of risk-seeking behavior, at least under certain circumstances, Sharpe proceeds to ignore it and implies that it is only in trivial choice problems that such behavior arises (e.g., when gambling for small stakes). By implication, he suggests that risk-seeking behavior has no important role to play in the development of financial models that focus on decisions that can be considered "significant" to a decision maker. The basis for Sharpe's position appears to be empirical evidence about risk preference of individuals, although none is provided or referenced.

Apart from the issue of its descriptive reality, the assumption of uniform risk aversion is appealing because it is analytically convenient. Its use in finance leads to models that are analytically tractable and capable of generating closed-form solutions. The analytical value that derives from the assumption, coupled with an absence of referenced empirical support for it, raises the question of whether descriptive reality in terms of risk preference has been compromised merely to gain analytical tractability.

The purposes of this paper are to review the literature dealing with risky choices in order to assess how well the assumption of uniform risk aversion— in both its specific and its general form—is supported by the available empirical evidence and to report on a series of exploratory studies conducted by the authors that were designed to measure risk preferences of managers. Implications of the results from these exploratory studies, as well as results from earlier studies, for the development of financial models are then discussed, particularly for normative models that are designed to aid in the capital budgeting process of business firms. The issue of the appropriate tradeoff between descriptive reality of risk-preference assumptions and analytical tractability for capital budgeting models is also examined in light of available empirical evidence.

RISK AVERSION: MEAN-VARIANCE DOMINANCE

The predominant assumption about risk preference in the finance literature is that decision makers are risk averse and base their choices on the mean (μ) and variance (σ^2), or standard deviation (σ), of risky alternatives. In this circumstance, risk aversion implies that individuals dislike σ^2 or σ and, other things being equal, prefer to make either of these two equivalent indexes of risk as small as possible. Given this specific assumption of risk aversion, individuals will make choices from available risky alternatives that are consistent with (μ, σ) dominance and that are (μ, σ) efficient in the sense of Markowitz [30].

The mean-variance formulation of risk aversion is a fundamental assumption underlying the development of the capital asset pricing model developed by Lintner [26] and Sharpe [36], a model that has been a primary focus of finance research in the last several years. This formulation of risk aversion can be justified on the basis of either a presumption that utility functions are suitably restricted quadratics or that all probability distributions for risky alternatives are capable of complete description for decision purposes by two independent parameters. In cases where portfolio models, rather than models for evaluating single alternatives, are being developed, Feldstein [5] has shown that even more restrictive assumptions on the form of probability distribution are necessary.

Criticisms of the quadratic utility function as the basis of support for the mean-variance formulation of risk aversion are well known. At a theoretical level, a quadratic utility function has been justifiably criticized because it can, at best, only be used to represent preferences for a restricted domain of return since a quadratic function eventually exhibits negative marginal utility of return. A quadratic utility function has also been criticized because it implies increasing, rather than decreasing, risk aversion in the Pratt sense [33].

Additional evidence about the inadequacy of quadratic utility functions comes from empirical studies that have attempted to measure utility functions of individuals. A summary of these studies is provided in a recent paper by Fishburn and Kochenberger [8]. None of these empirical studies indicates a single instance for which an individual's utility function was adequately represented by a quadratic function, except possibly in a very restricted domain of return. The consensus of both theoretical and empirical research is that, if based on the supporting assumption of a quadratic utility function, risk aversion as embodied in mean-variance analysis should not be taken very seriously.

However, the other supporting basis for the mean-variance form of risk aversion—that all alternatives have probability distributions that are completely described by two independent parameters—is equally suspect. There is no compelling reason to believe that all risky alternatives confronting an individual decision maker will be of the requisite two-parameter variety, particularly in capital budgeting situations. For example, subjective probability judgments of managers for the various inputs (e.g., sales and price) necessary for evaluating a proposed capital project need not be of the two-parameter variety. Such judgments may generate probability distributions that do not match any standard distributional form or may involve distributions that require third moments in order to capture skewness. The central limit theorem is not powerful enough in this circumstance to ensure that the overall probability distribution of return will be normal, or even approximately so, since net cash flows in various time periods are typically correlated in some fashion.

In spite of these types of objections to risk aversion of the mean-variance type, an argument could be advanced that such a construct is useful because it can explain or predict actual choices of individuals when they are confronted with decisions that involve risk. On this score, however, empirical evidence indicates that mean-variance analysis does a very poor job of explaining actual choice behavior.

In one of the earlier studies of choice behavior under conditions of risk, Slovic [39] found that observed preferences could not be explained by using variance as an index of risk. These findings have since been replicated in several other studies. Alderfer and Bierman [1], for example, found that an extremely large number of subjects in three different experiments made choices that were inconsistent with mean-variance dominance. In the three experiments, 89 percent, 71 percent, and 34 percent of the individual participants made choices that were inconsistent with this form of risk aversion. Conrath [4] and Greer [14], in studies of choice behavior by business executives, obtained similar results and found a substantial degree of inconsistency between mean-variance dominance and the expressed preferences for risky alternatives. In another study of business executives, Fidler and Thompson [6] investigated a series of potential factors that can influence executive preferences for risky alternatives and found that variance was of little importance in explaining preference patterns when compared to other factors.

In the largest empirical study conducted to date of executive behavior under conditions of risk, Bassler et al. [3] asked over 400 top-level U.S. and Canadian business executives to develop preference orderings for nine hypothetical investment opportunities in which they could choose to invest 10 percent of their wealth. The amount of wealth involved was approximately $20,000 on average. The probability distribution of return for all investment alternatives was normal; several properties of each distribution were computed (including mean and variance) and provided to the executives for decision purposes. Out of the total of 463 usable preference orderings, just 91 (or 19.7 percent) were consistent with choices based on mean-variance dominance.

This study was followed by a subsequent study by MacCrimmon, Stanbury, and Wehrung [27] that involved forty top-level business executives from the United States and Canada. These executives were presented with three different sets of five alternatives and were asked to rank-order the sets based on preference and also to choose the most preferred alternative from among the best of the three individual sets. Only one out of the forty executives had preference rankings that were totally explained by mean-variance dominance. This finding led the authors to conclude that

> the mean-variance rule . . . still seems to be a common investment heuristic. To the extent that this model is intended to be descriptively valid, we have presented data showing that it reflects the preference of very few business executives. [P. 29]

Further empirical evidence about the general inadequacy of risk aversion in the form of mean-variance dominance has been developed by the authors on two separate occasions. On the first occasion, thirty-six business managers were asked to choose the most preferred risky alternative from three that were made available. Eight such choices were made by each manager. Of the thirty-six sequences of preferred alternatives observed, only three were consistent with choices on the basis of mean-variance dominance. This process was repeated on a second occasion with thirty-nine business managers. For this replication, only one out of thirty-nine decision sequences was consistent with mean-variance dominance.

Collectively, these empirical studies provide consistent and strong evidence to indicate that the mean-variance dominance form of risk aversion is a completely inadequate construct to explain the risky choice behavior of individuals, including business executives. Some papers have sought to rectify some of the apparent defects of mean-variance analysis while simultaneously retaining the assumption of risk aversion. Markowitz in his pioneering work explored target semivariance (S_t) as a preferred alternative to variance because it allows for a common target return (t) when evaluating risk across alternatives and because it includes only deviations below this target. Markowitz finally selected variance rather than target semivariance because of its computational advantages and general familiarity.

Target semivariance has been subsequently incorporated into a reformulation of the capital asset pricing model by Hogan and Warren [18] and into a normative model for use by firms when making capital budgeting decisions by Porter, Bey, and Lewis [32] and by Hoskins [20]. The general assumption about risk preference in these papers is that individuals are risk averse when S_t is used as the index of risk and choices are made from risky alternatives on the basis of (μ, S_t) dominance.

Very few studies exist concerning the extent to which (μ, S_t) dominance provides an improved description of actual choice behavior as compared to (μ, σ) dominance. For those studies that do exist, the evidence is mixed. Hoskins [19] found that the use of target semivariance as an index of risk made it possible to explain most of the decisions that Greer [14] could not explain on the basis of mean-variance dominance. Fidler and Thompson [6] also concluded that target semivariance was a more important index of risk than variance when explaining the preference of business executives. But other studies have found little or no support for the (μ, S_t) form of risk aversion.

Bassler et al. [3] found that (μ, S_t) dominance does little better than (μ, σ) dominance in explaining the preferences of business executives. In the two studies conducted by the authors mentioned earlier, no support was identified for (μ, S_t) dominance. In both replications of the experiment, involving thirty-six and thirty-nine business managers, respectively, not one decision sequence was consistent with choices on the basis of (μ, S_t) dominance.

These empirical findings do not, of course, provide any substantive basis to dispute the general assumption that individuals are risk averse. But, as a collection, they do provide strong evidence to indicate that the specific form of risk aversion that is embodied in (μ, σ) dominance or (μ, S_t) dominance is incapable of representing risk preferences of individuals, particularly business executives. In fact, neither of these two forms of risk aversion appears to be even a reasonable first approximation for explaining behavior of individuals when confronted with risky choices.

RISK AVERSION: CONCAVITY OF THE UTILITY FUNCTION

The assumption of risk aversion also appears in the finance literature in the less restrictive form of an assertion that utility functions of decision makers are concave. The concavity assumption is strong in the sense that the utility function is presumed to be uniformly concave for the entire domain of monetary return, however measured. This effectively rules out convexity, or risk-seeking behavior, from the entire domain of the utility function. Concavity of the utility function ensures that a decision maker will be risk averse and that an alternative with a certain return of x will be preferred to any risky alternative with an expected value of x. This assumption about risk preference is intuitively appealing since it implies that the marginal utility of additional monetary return declines as monetary return increases.

Risk aversion in the form of uniform concavity of the utility function has been widely used in the finance literature, for example, to develop the rationale for second-degree stochastic dominance models [15] and for third-degree stochastic dominance models [42]. Such models are used to prescreen risky alternatives into an efficient set, which is subsequently analyzed by the decision maker in order to make a final choice, and an inefficient set, which can be discarded on the basis of being inferior to alternatives in the efficient set. Dominance models constructed on the basis of the uniform concavity assumption have appeared in many studies; see, for example, Levy and Sarnat [24] and Porter, Bey, and Lewis [31]. Uniform concavity of the utility function has also been used as a necessary property when searching for a plausible utility function to describe risk preferences of decision makers; see, for example, Spetzler [40].

The study by Spetzler supports the assumption of uniform concavity of utility functions. Spetzler found that all the executives in a sample of thirty-six from one company exhibited preferences that were consistent with uniform concavity throughout the entire domain of returns tested. This domain included both profit gains and losses. In another study, Green [13] estimated utility functions for four middle managers in a chemical company, using percent return on investment as the argument of the utility function. The utility functions for these individuals provided no evidence of risk-seeking behavior. All utility functions were consistent with the assumption of uniform concavity, particularly for rates of return below 20 percent. For rates of return above 20 percent, the utility functions were approximately linear, indicating risk neutrality in this region.

The predominance of risk-averse behavior was also found in a study reported by Gordon, Paradis, and Rorke [11]. These authors constructed a portfolio game to investigate decision rules used in making risky choices. This game was played by thirty-four graduate students. The general conclusion made about risk preference after administering the game to the students was that

> none of the experiment's participants behaved like risk lovers as long as their wealth was large enough to provide some expectations of a livelihood under risk aversion behavior, and everyone deprived of that expectation became risk lovers. [P. 110]

Results of this study provide support for the position that risk-averse behavior is the norm for individuals and is replaced by risk-seeking behavior only under very unusual circumstances. Risk-seeking behavior was observed only when an individual was reduced to a wealth position that was considered inconsistent with future viability at an acceptable level of consumption.

These studies are exceptions, however, since several other studies provide support for the existence of risk-seeking behavior, at least in some circumstances, and generally provide support for a mixture of risk seeking and risk aversion by the same individual. Swalm [41] interviewed one hundred business executives and provided summary data and estimated utility functions for thirteen of them. Of the thirteen utility functions summarized, which were developed using dollar return as the argument, eleven exhibited convexity for selected regions of dollar return. One of these executives had a utility function that was convex for both dollar gains and dollar losses with a drastic change of slope at a zero dollar return. Nine of these executives had utility functions that were convex for losses, but concave for gains. The remaining executive had a utility function that was concave for losses, but convex for gains.

Grayson [12], in a study of managers in the oil industry, also found risk preferences to be a mixture of risk-seeking and risk-averse behavior. In four out of nine reported cases, Grayson found a mixture of risk seeking and risk aversion in the domain of losses; in five out of nine cases, managers were also risk seeking in the domain of gains.

Halter and Dean [17] provided empirically based utility functions for an orchard farmer, a grain farmer, and a college professor. The orchard farmer exhibited a linear utility function for both gains and losses, while the grain farmer exhibited risk-seeking behavior for losses and a mixture of risk seeking and risk aversion for gains. The college professor exhibited a utility function consistent with risk seeking for losses and risk aversion for gains.

A mixture of risk-seeking and risk-averse behavior, rather than uniform risk aversion, was also noted in the study mentioned previously by MacCrimmon, Stanbury, and Wehrung [27]. In this study, 53 out of the 120 preference orderings observed were consistent with uniform risk aversion, 16 out of 120 were consistent with uniform risk seeking, and 51 out of 120 were consistent with both risk seeking and risk aversion. Barnes and Reinmuth [2] imputed utility functions to two contractors for use in competitive bidding situations. For both contractors, the utility function was convex for losses. For one contractor, the utility function was also convex in the region of gains, while the utility function was linear in this region for the other contractor.

Finally, Fishburn and Kochenberger [8], using some of the empirical data from decision makers that were reported in these earlier studies, employed statistical estimation techniques to assess the degree of fit for two-piece Von Neumann–Morgenstern utility functions. The assumption underlying this study was that the utility function above a target return can have a different shape, and hence can reflect a different risk preference, when compared to the utility function below a target return. Linear, power, and exponential functions were employed, both for returns below and above target. Data from twenty-eight decision makers were employed for estimation purposes in both the region of gains and region of losses measured from the target return. For the twenty-eight data sets examined, the most predominant form of risk preference was consistent with a convex function (risk seeking) below the target return and a concave utility function (risk aversion) for returns above the target. Thirteen out of twenty-eight data sets were consistent with this pattern of risk preference, with the power function being the best-fitting function both below and above target. Only three out of the twenty-eight decision makers exhibited a utility function that was consistent with the conventional view of risk preference — that is, uniform concavity for returns both above and below the target return. For just below target returns (losses), 67 percent of the best-fitting utility functions implied risk-seeking behavior.

These empirical findings suggest that a mixture of risk seeking and risk aversion may be a more realistic view of behavior under conditions of risk, as compared to assuming that individuals are uniformly risk averse or that individuals depart from risk-averse behavior only under unusual circumstances.

The existence of risk-seeking behavior for losses measured from a target level of return and its rationale have been recently reexamined by Kahneman and Tversky [21]. These authors provide a substantial amount of empirical evidence to support the position that the utility function will be convex for losses and concave for gains, with gains and losses measured relative to a target return. They labeled the mixture of risk seeking for losses and risk aversion for gains, respectively, as the reflection effect and argued that a pure reflection of risky alternatives about the target return will generally reverse preference orderings. The explanation for this type of reversal in preference orderings is attributed by Kahneman and Tversky to the tendency of individuals to overweight outcomes that are certain relative to outcomes that are merely probable. These authors also argue that individuals evaluate risky alternatives in terms of gains and losses, measured from a target return, rather than in terms of final states of wealth.

The consensus of all these studies is that an assumption of uniform risk aversion is not a tenable representation of the risk preference of individuals. The overwhelming weight of existing empirical evidence indicates that this assumption, in either its strong or its weak form, is grossly inadequate from a descriptive viewpoint.

As an alternative, empirical evidence indicates that there is no single characterization of risk preference that is comprehensive enough to describe all individuals. Differences in risk preference among individuals are to be expected. However, the evidence also reveals that a majority of individuals exhibit a mixture of risk-seeking and risk-averse behavior, with the range of returns where these two risk preferences are the predominant modes of behavior being intimately connected with the notion of a target return. For returns below target, a large majority of individuals appear to be risk seeking; for returns above target, a large majority appear to be risk averse.

These results suggest the need to develop methods for estimating the risk preference of individuals in such a way that both risk-averse and risk-seeking behavior are admissible and measurable, while simultaneously allowing explicit recognition of the target return concept. A model with these properties has recently been developed by Fishburn [7].

ADDITIONAL EXPERIMENTAL EVIDENCE

Fishburn Model

Fishburn has investigated the properties of a mean-risk dominance model, denoted an $\alpha - t$ model, for choices among mutually exclusive alternatives that have uncertain returns. In this model, he suggested that the risk of an alternative be defined in terms of two characteristics: (1) an aspiration level or target level of return and (2) the relative consequence of falling short of the target return by various amounts. Formally, the risk of an alternative, denoted A, is a probability-weighted function of returns below target given by

$$R(A) = \int_{-\infty}^{t} (t - x)^{\alpha} \, dF(x),$$

where $F(x)$ is the probability of receiving a return not exceeding x, t is the target return, and α is a nonnegative parameter to measure the importance of returns below the target. Both α and t are parameters that are unique to a decision maker.

In the $\alpha - t$ model, the risk of an alternative is combined with its mean return to determine preference. Given any two alternatives A and B, having mean returns $\mu(A)$ and $\mu(B)$, respectively, A is preferred to B if, and only if,

$$\mu(A) \geqslant \mu(B)$$

and

$$R(A) \leqslant R(B)$$

with at least one strict inequality holding.

The general form of this preference model is a familiar one and belongs to the broad class of dominance models. Based on the specification of α, the $\alpha - t$ model includes as special cases some of the mean-risk dominance models that have been investigated by others. For example, $\alpha = 0$ implies that probability of loss is the appropriate index of risk, whereas $\alpha = 1$ and $\alpha = 2$ imply that expected opportunity loss and target semivariance are appropriate.

The important point for this paper, however, is the interpretation that Fishburn gives to α. According to Fishburn, the magnitude of α relative to 1.0

serves to delineate the importance of returns below target. If the main concern of a decision maker is failure to achieve the target return without particular regard to the amount that return falls below the target, then a value of α in the range $\alpha < 1.0$ is appropriate. On the other hand, Fishburn argues that a value of α in the range $\alpha > 1.0$ implies that the decision maker regards small deviations below target as being relatively harmless when compared to large deviations.

An alternative way of thinking about the parameter α is in terms of the relative importance of two basic dimensions of an uncertain alternative: probability of losing and amount of loss, where losing is defined to be a return below t. An $\alpha = 0$ indicates a focus solely on the probability of losing, with no concern for the magnitude of losses. At the other extreme, $\alpha = \infty$ indicates a focus solely on the largest amount to lose, with no concern for the probability of losing.

In terms of a classical utility function, Fishburn demonstrates that the risk preference of a decision maker when returns are below target is completely described by the magnitude of α relative to 1.0. If $\alpha < 1$, the decision maker will have a convex utility function for returns below target (consistent with risk seeking), whereas if $\alpha > 1$, the utility function will be concave in this region of return (consistent with risk aversion).

Experimental Procedure

The procedure developed to measure risk preference was based on the $\alpha - t$ model and was designed to estimate the parameter α, integrating into the procedure some of the ideas suggested by Fishburn. An interactive computer program was designed to visually display a series of pairs of alternatives from which to choose. Each pair of alternatives consisted of one uncertain alternative, with two possible returns and associated probabilities, and one sure thing. The value of the parameter t was always set at $t = 0$ by virtue of instructions given to the participants, so that stated returns for both alternatives in each pair could be interpreted as gains or losses. The expected value of return was always the same for both alternatives in each pair.

For example, an individual could be presented with the following initial choice problem:

Choice of:

A	or	B
-$20 with $p = .5$		-$10 for sure
$0 with $1 - p = .5$		

This pair of alternatives involves A, which has a .5 probability of losing $20 and a .5 probability of losing nothing, versus B, which will result in a loss of $10 for sure. The initial choice problem was always designed as suggested by Fishburn, so that the certain loss for the sure-thing alternative was $t - d$, where d is a noticeable difference from t. The first uncertain alternative always involved a loss of $t - 2d$ with .5 probability and t with a .5 probability. In the above example, $d = \$10$.

Suppose an individual chose alternative A in the initial problem. This would indicate that $\alpha \leqslant 1.0$ and that the individual would prefer to risk losing $20, with .5 probability, in order to have the option of achieving the target return, also with .5 probability, rather than be guaranteed a below-target return. The individual who had such a preference might then be presented with the following choice problem:

Choice of:

A	or	B
–$10 for sure		–$20 with $p = .95$
		$180 with $1 - p = .05$

Again, $\mu(A) = \mu(B)$. In this case, however, the loss of $20 with alternative B is almost certain, and so the individual might prefer alternative A with the smaller amount to lose. If this were the case, the individual would then be presented with a series of further choices involving various values of p until the individual indicated indifference between the sure loss of $t - d$ and the uncertain alternative having $t - 2d$ loss with probability p and a return of $t + d(2p - 1)/(1 - p)$ with probability $1 - p$, where $p \geqslant 1/2$. When the indifference probability p_0 was determined, α was given by $\alpha \cong \log(1/p_0)/\log 2$. If the uncertain alternative was preferred to the sure loss for all $p < 1$, then $\alpha = 0$.

In the case in which an individual expressed preference for alternative B in the initial choice problem, the value of d was determined by presenting choice pairs involving two uncertain alternatives. The first uncertain alternative had a relatively small probability p (i.e., $p \leqslant .25$) of returning $t - 2d$ and probability $1 - p$ of returning t, while the second had even chances of returning $t - d$ and $t + d(1 - 4p)$. When the indifference probability p_0 was determined, α was given by $\alpha \cong \log (1/2p_0)/\log 2$. If the even-chance alternative was preferred for all $p > 0$, then $\alpha = \infty$.

Subjects. Two groups of business personnel participated in the computer exercise. The first group was composed of thirty-seven middle managers who were attending an executive development program (EDP) at the Duke Graduate

School of Business Administration. The second group consisted of fifty business personnel who were in the two-year Executive M.B.A. Program at Duke.

Results. The first group of managers was asked to express preferences for two different series of uncertain alternatives, one series with d = $10 and one with d = $20. Twenty-nine of the thirty-seven managers provided usable responses for both series of alternatives. Table 1 presents the α values computed from responses for each of those subjects for the two values of d. These data reveal a large range of α values across individuals, with a range from 0.1 to 5.64 and some variations in α values for the same individual for the two values of d. However, only three individuals had a variation in α values that was so large that risk seeking ($\alpha < 1$) was indicated for one value of d and risk aversion ($\alpha > 1$) indicated for the other. The data also provide no support for some of the commonly employed risk indexes: probability of loss ($\alpha = 0$), expected opportunity loss ($\alpha = 1$), and target semivariance ($\alpha = 2$). Noninteger values of α are predominant.

The most striking feature of the data in Table 1 is the implication for the prevalence of risk-seeking behavior. Forty-eight of the fifty-eight values of α (85 percent) are below 1.0. Eliminating the individuals providing mixed signals about risk preference, twenty-two out of twenty-nine individuals (75 percent) exhibited preferences consistently compatible with risk-seeking behavior. In contrast, only three out of twenty-nine individuals (10 percent) were consistently compatible with the conventional assumption of risk aversion. Given the

Table 1. Values of α for EDP Participants

Subj.	d-Value 10	d-Value 20	Subj.	d-Value 10	d-Value 20	Subj.	d-Value 10	d-Value 20
1	.44[a]	1.00	11	.44	.36	21	1.86	.12
2	.44	.16	12	5.64	.17	22	.04	.08
3	.23	.18	13	.39	.44	23	.97	.16
4	.78	.44	14	.01	.08	24	.39	.63
5	.50	.44	15	2.03	2.93	25	1.98	1.84
6	.48	.41	16	.60	.63	26	.15	4.84
7	.44	.33	17	.27	.39	27	1.86	2.43
8	.29	.32	18	.22	.23	28	.23	.23
9	.44	.39	19	.77	.76	29	.19	.54
10	.50	.50	20	.39	.39	$\bar{X}$	.79	.74

[a] An α value < 1.0 implies risk seeking, and an α value > 1.0 implies risk avoidance.

exploratory nature of this study, statistical tests were not employed to explore significance of these results.

The second group, consisting of Executive M.B.A. students, was asked to respond to three sets of uncertain alternatives, with d = $10, $20, and $100. Forty-six of the fifty students provided data for all three sets of alternatives. Table 2 presents the α values for each of these subjects. The findings clearly replicate those for the first group, including the large variation in α values across individuals, coupled with some variation for the same individual for different values of d. For the Executive M.B.A. students, 118 out of the 138 values of α (85 percent) are below 1. Eliminating the individuals who provided mixed signals about risk preference, thirty out of forty-six individuals (74 percent) consistently exhibited risk-seeking behavior for returns below target. Only one

Table 2. Values of α for Executive M.B.A. Students

	d-Value				*d-Value*		
Subj.	*10*	*20*	*100*	*Subj.*	*10*	*20*	*100*
1	.51	.47	.53	24	.45	2.05	.23
2	1.94	.04	.04	25	.51	.94	.53
3	1.65	.04	.43	26	.45	.40	.45
4	.23	.12	.16	27	3.64	.06	.04
5	3.26	.32	.25	28	.32	.26	1.97
6	3.31	.10	3.56	29	3.64	3.64	3.64
7	.97	.04	.43	30	.40	.48	.45
8	.66	.65	.67	31	.41	.30	.42
9	.09	.09	.08	32	.32	.42	.35
10	2.15	.23	.34	33	.43	1.95	.04
11	.45	.64	.51	34	.07	.06	.07
12	.17	.04	.04	35	.27	.06	.04
13	2.46	.07	.07	36	.62	.51	.51
14	.32	3.64	.32	37	.41	3.62	.86
15	.42	1.54	2.84	38	.16	.07	.04
16	.19	.18	.18	39	.04	.04	.07
17	3.64	.33	.34	40	.17	.28	.24
18	.40	.32	.40	41	.42	.21	.30
19	.31	.13	.15	42	1.79	.34	.32
20	.58	.51	.40	43	.04	.04	.04
21	.28	.45	.40	44	.54	.15	.04
22	.51	.51	.04	45	.89	.82	.79
23	.17	.18	.16	46	.32	.35	.32
				$\bar{X}$	.89	.60	.52

out of forty-six individuals (2 percent) exhibited risk-averse behavior for all values of d.

Taken together, the results from the two groups indicate that a substantial majority of the individuals (fifty-two out of seventy-five, or 70 percent) made choices from alternatives involving primarily below-target returns in a way that is consistent with the classical definition of risk seeking. Risk aversion for returns below target was observed only in a relatively few instances. These results are consistent with the finding noted earlier by Fishburn and Kochenberger [8] that 67 percent of the below-target utility functions they estimated were convex.

In summary, our results, as well as those of other researchers, indicate that the general statement that decision makers are risk averse, at least as classically defined, must be modified. A substantial majority of decision makers appear to prefer an uncertain alternative over an equivalent sure thing when the outcomes involved are primarily below target.

IMPLICATIONS FOR CAPITAL BUDGETING MODELS

Incorporation of assumptions about risk preference in financial models often involves a tradeoff between resulting analytical tractability and descriptive reality of the assumptions. The available empirical evidence just reviewed indicates that the literature of finance, by focusing exclusively on risk aversion, appears to have gone significantly too far in the tradeoff of giving up descriptive reality in order to gain analytical tractability. As a consequence, the resulting models are based on a view of risk preference that is grossly inconsistent with the behavior of individuals under conditions of risk.

The inconsistency may be viewed as relatively unimportant for predictive financial models, such as the capital asset pricing model, because such models are designed to predict aggregate market behavior of such phenomena as equilibrium stock prices. Tests of the adequacy of such models possibly hinge more on predictive ability than on the reality of underlying assumptions, including that related to risk preference. Achieving financial models that are analytically tractable and predict reasonably well may be sufficient compensation for empirically inferior assumptions with respect to risk preference of individuals. Even in this context, however, it is not obvious whether a more realistic risk preference assumption would or would not improve the resulting predictive capability of such models. This question deserves further empirical investigation.

However, in the context of normative capital budgeting models that are designed for implementation by firms in order to aid the decision process, the conclusion about the appropriate tradeoff between tractability and descriptive reality of assumptions is unjustified. Realism of the assumption about risk preference takes on additional importance in this context since it is essential that the model reflect, as closely as possible, the risk preference of the decision maker or decision-making group. Without the necessary correspondence—to the satisfaction of the relevant decision maker—normative capital budgeting models will simply be avoided, no matter how analytically tractable. Avoidance of formal capital budgeting models that explicitly incorporate risk dimensions is prevalent. Various papers [9, 22, 35] have reported on the limited use of models that explicitly incorporate risk into the decision-making process of firms. Firms apparently favor using relatively simple methods for handling risk—for example, payback, adjustment to the discount rate, and sensitivity analysis. This practice continues in spite of the fact that the financial literature contains a large number of analytical models that are designed to formally incorporate risk into the decision process. A variety of explanations can be provided for the reluctance of decision makers to implement formal risk models.

The empirical evidence reported in this paper would indicate that a major reason for lack of interest may be that the available models do not capture the essence of risk as defined by decision makers. When this occurs, it is not likely to matter how elegant or analytically tractable the model is. Analytical tractability ought to assume a secondary role in the development of normative capital budgeting models. A preferred approach would be to construct models based on a realistic assumption about risk preference and then to search for ways of obtaining solutions, even if solutions involve approximations. An approximate solution to a model that is based on a realistic risk preference assumption is more likely to be implemented than is an exact solution to an analytically tractable model that is considered too contrived by the ultimate user.

Available empirical evidence suggests several useful properties about the risk dimension in capital budgeting models that have an increased application potential. One important property is that capital budgeting models that do not allow for individual differences in risk preference are not likely to have much impact. Empirical studies have been unanimous in the conclusion that individual differences among decision makers are pervasive. This finding suggests that armchair theorizing about appropriate definitions of risk, as well as methods of incorporating risk into models, is incomplete and that a more thorough empirical knowledge of risk preference for the specific user group ought to be the starting point in modeling efforts. Few, if any, of the capital budgeting models now available in the financial literature have these origins, even though some appear to have been at least motivated by previous discussions with business executives.[1] Most models simply conjecture a plausible or intuitively appealing definition of risk. As a consequence, it is not too surprising to find that available models have been based on the empirically inadequate assumption of risk aversion in various forms.[2]

While empirical evidence amply demonstrates the need to recognize individual differences and to incorporate such differences into capital budgeting models, the evidence also provides some useful information about the common features of risk preference that can serve as a useful benchmark in the search for more realistic models. This information will be summarized here in terms of empirically supported properties of utility functions and is drawn from a variety of different studies. In the following discussion, a utility function for monetary consequences, denoted $U(\cdot)$, is presumed to exist for the appropriate decision-making group.

Domain of the Utility Function

A common view of finance is that the appropriate domain of the utility function is terminal or ending wealth. In this view, an individual is presumed to integrate initial wealth (W) with the payoff from an uncertain alternative (X), so that X is preferred to its rejection when $EU(W + X) > EU(W)$, where $EU(\cdot)$ denotes expected utility. This implies that the individual considers the utility of X to be determined by the terminal wealth to which it leads.

Recent empirical evidence provided by Kahneman and Tversky [21] indicates that individuals do not integrate a random return X with initial wealth, but instead focus attention on X itself along with the characteristics of its probability distribution. The appropriate domain of the utility function appears to be a change in wealth position, rather than terminal wealth, which incorporates beginning wealth with the return from an uncertain alternative. With this characterization, an individual prefers an uncertain alternative X to its rejection (a status quo alternative that yields a zero return with certainty) when $EU(X) > EU(0)$.

Evaluation of alternatives in terms of changes in wealth is attributed to the isolation effect by Kahneman and Tversky. In order to simplify the process of choosing between alternatives, individuals tend to eliminate characteristics that alternatives have in common so that differences between alternatives can be effectively isolated. In the above example, W would be eliminated from consideration since it is common to both X and the status quo alternative.

Use of terminal wealth as the appropriate domain of a utility function may explain why finance has ignored risk-seeking behavior since, in this case, only the nonnegative terminal wealth domain $(W + X \geq 0)$ needs consideration. Any value of negative terminal wealth implies ruin and can be ignored. In the nonnegative domain, terminal wealth tends to confound the problem of risk preference by allowing initial wealth to mask the importance of gains and losses measured from the initial wealth position.

Importance of a Target Return

The utility of changes in wealth for an uncertain alternative tends to be measured from a reference point t, which can refer to the current wealth position (implying $t = 0$) or to an aspiration level that serves as a goal or target for the individual. This pattern of behavior has been noted in several empirical investigations by Mao [28], Siegel [38], and Kahneman and Tversky [21]. Reference point t serves to delineate the domain of the utility function into a region of gains ($x \geq t$) and a region of losses ($x < t$), where x denotes a change in wealth. The loss region is typically classified as the region of pure risk, since variations of wealth changes in this region provide prospects of falling below target t. Most real prospects that will confront an individual decision maker will be composed of both possible gains and possible losses—that is, they will be speculative risks.

The importance of a target return t in the conception of risk by individuals places a restriction on the class of risk indexes that are feasible for consideration in capital budgeting models. Inconsistency with this restriction, for example, would rule out variance and semivariance measured relative to the mean, as well as any other measure of risk that does not use a standard benchmark for measuring return variation across alternatives.

Risk Preference

The predominant (although not universal) form of utility function is consistent with a mixture of risk seeking and risk aversion, coupled with a marked difference in slope characteristics for returns above and below target:

1. Above t, the utility function is concave, indicating risk aversion.
2. Below t, the utility function is convex, indicating risk seeking.
3. At any given distance below t, the utility function is substantially steeper than it is at the same distance above t.
4. At t, the utility function need not be differentiable.

These properties and their rationale in psychological terms are discussed in detail by Kahneman and Tversky [21].

Ruin Considerations

When returns from an uncertain alternative fall below t by a large enough amount, ruin considerations can enter the decision process. In this case, ruin is the value of return that would cause a significant alteration in the financial viability of the decision maker—for example, bankruptcy or severe cash-flow difficulties. This implies that the utility function has the characteristic that $U(x) = -\infty$ for $x \leqslant r$, where r is the ruin value of return for the individual decision maker. This characteristic suggests that ruinous loss enters the decision process in a noncompensatory fashion—that is, as a risk so undesirable to the individual that it will be screened out without any possibility of a tradeoff with desirable characteristics of the uncertain alternative.

A Composite View of Risk

Taken together, all of the above properties imply a utility function with a general graph as shown in Figure 1, with $U(t)$ set arbitrarily at zero. This form of utility function implies that capital budgeting models need to involve a two-step risk-evaluation process. In the first step, ruin considerations dictate that alternatives be eliminated from further consideration if they involve a chance of ruinous loss, no matter what other desirable characteristics they might possess. In the second step, the alternatives that satisfy the ruinous loss constraint will be evaluated by use of a tradeoff process that is based on the probability distribution of each uncertain alternative and the characteristics of the utility function. This tradeoff process will incorporate the existence of risk-seeking behavior for returns below target, coupled with risk aversion for returns above target.

This general view of the process by which risky alternatives are evaluated is supported by results from a recent literature survey by Libby and Fishburn [25]. These authors, after an extensive review of the business and psychological literature, concluded that

> the evidence tends to support a model where probability of ruinous loss acts as a constraint and risk of below-target return is traded off with expected return to determine preference. . . . In this model, two types of risk operate in determining preference. First, any project presenting a significant possibility of ruinous loss is immediately removed from consideration. The disastrous results of ruinous loss apparently cannot be counterbalanced by possible gain, regardless of how large. The second type of risk—risk of non-ruinous loss or below-target return—is then combined with the mean to determine the preferred alternative among the remaining projects. [P. 29]

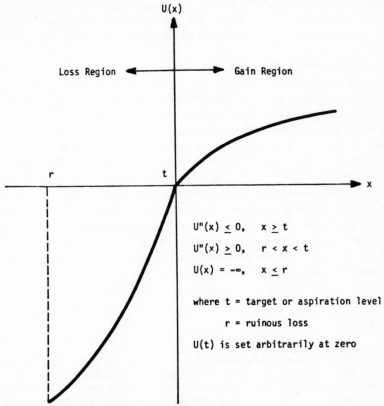

Figure 1. Predominant Form of Utility Function

To our knowledge, there is no capital budgeting model now in the literature that has been constructed on the basis of these characteristics of risk preference. Judging from surveys of industrial practice and empirical evidence, such models would appear to have much more promise from an implementation viewpoint than those already existing.

CONCLUSIONS

This paper has investigated the empirical basis for the conventional assumption in finance that individual decision makers are uniformly risk averse, both in the specific form of (μ, σ) or (μ, S_t) dominance and in the general form of uniform concavity of the utility function. The available empirical evidence from other studies and the results of the exploratory studies reported in this paper show the assumption of uniform risk aversion to have no basis and to be inconsistent with choice behavior of individuals under conditions of risk to a very significant degree.

Empirical evidence suggests that a reformulation of assumptions about risk preference is necessary for use in developing capital budgeting models with increased application potential. In this reformulation, individuals will be assumed to evaluate uncertain alternatives in terms of gains and losses relative to a target return, rather than in terms of terminal wealth, and will generally exhibit a mixture of risk-seeking and risk-averse behavior. An allowance for individual differences in risk preference will also be necessary. This pattern of behavior, when coupled with the existence of ruinous loss, implies that capital budgeting models need to be more concerned with incorporating risk in terms of a two-stage process whereby risk of ruinous loss serves as a constraint to eliminate inferior alternatives and, subsequently, the risk of below-target return is traded off with desirable characteristics of return distributions. This latter tradeoff generally involves risk-seeking behavior for returns below target and risk-averse behavior for returns above target.

NOTES

1. Models with at least some empirical basis include those of Mao [28], and Porter, Bey, and Lewis [32] and Hoskins [19], who have extended his work, and Conrath [4].

2. An exception to the use of risk aversion has occurred with models based on probability of loss as an index of risk. Under certain circumstances, probability of loss is consistent with risk-seeking behavior. See Fishburn [7].

REFERENCES

[1] Alderfer, C.P., and Bierman, H. "Choices with Risk: Beyond the Mean and Variance," *Journal of Business* (July 1970).
[2] Barnes, J.D., and Reinmuth, J.E. "Comparing Imputed and Actual Utility Functions in a Competitive Bidding Setting," *Decision Sciences* (October 1976).
[3] Bassler, J.F.; MacCrimmon, K.R.; Stanbury, W.T.; and Wehrung, D.A. "Multiple Criteria Dominance Models: An Empirical Study of Investment Preferences," Working Paper No. 500, University of British Columbia, November 1977.
[4] Conrath, David. "From Statistical Decision Theory to Practice: Some Problems with the Transition," *Management Science* (April 1973).

[5]   Feldstein, M.S. "Mean-Variance Analysis in the Theory of Liquidity Preference and Portfolio Selection," *Review of Economic Studies* (January 1969).

[6]   Fidler, Eduard, and Thompson, Gerald. "An Experiment on Executive Decision Making," Management Science Research Report No. 407, Carnegie-Mellon University, July 1977.

[7]   Fishburn, Peter C. "Mean-Risk Analysis with Risk Associated with Below-Target Returns," *American Economic Review* (March 1977).

[8]   Fishburn, Peter C., and Kochenberger, Gary A. "Two-Piece Von Neumann–Morgenstern Utility Functions" (forthcoming).

[9]   Fremgen, J.A. "Capital Budgeting Practices: A Survey," *Management Accounting* (May 1973).

[10] Friedman, Milton, and Savage, L.J. "The Utility Analysis of Choices Involving Risk," *Journal of Political Economy* (August 1948).

[11] Gordon, M.J.; Paradis, G.E.; and Rorke, C.H. "Experimental Evidence on Alternative Portfolio Decision Rules," *American Economic Review* (March 1972).

[12] Grayson, C.J. *Decisions under Uncertainty: Drilling Decisions by Oil and Gas Companies.* Boston: Harvard Business School, Division of Research, 1959.

[13] Green, P.E. "Risk Attitudes and Chemical Investment Decisions," *Chemical Engineering Progress* (January 1963).

[14] Greer, Willis J. "Theory versus Practice in Risk Analysis: An Empirical Study," *Accounting Review* (July 1974).

[15] Hadar, J., and Russell, W.R. "Rules for Ordering Uncertain Prospects," *American Economic Review* (March 1969).

[16] Hakansson, Nils. "Friedman-Savage Utility Functions Consistent with Risk Aversion," *Quarterly Journal of Economics* (August 1970).

[17] Halter, A.N., and Dean, G.W. *Decisions under Uncertainty.* Cincinnati: South-Western Publishing Company, 1971.

[18] Hogan, W.W., and Warren, J.M. "Toward the Development of Equilibrium Capital Market Model Based on Semi-Variance," *Journal of Financial and Quantitative Analysis* (January 1974).

[19] Hoskins, C.G. "Theory versus Practice in Risk Analysis: An Empirical Study – A Comment," *Accounting Review* (October 1975).

[20] Hoskins, C.G. "Capital Budgeting Decision Rules for Risky Projects Derived from a Capital Market Model Based on Semivariance," *Engineering Economist* (Summer 1979).

[21] Kahneman, D., and Tversky, A. "Prospect Theory: An Analysis of Decision under Risk," *Econometrica* (March 1979).

[22] Klammer, T. "Empirical Evidence of the Adoption of Sophisticated Capital Budgeting Techniques," *Journal of Business* (October 1972).

[23] Kwang, N.Y. "Why Do People Buy Lottery Tickets? Choices Involving Risk and the Indivisibility of Expenditure," *Journal of Political Economy* (October 1965).

[24] Levy, H., and Sarnat, M. "Alternative Efficiency Criteria: An Empirical Analysis," *Journal of Finance* (December 1970).

[25] Libby, Robert, and Fishburn, Peter. "Behavioral Models of Risk Taking in Business Decisions: A Survey and Evaluation," *Journal of Accounting Research* (Autumn 1977).

[26] Lintner, John. "The Valuation of Risk Assets and the Selection of Risky Investments in Stock Portfolios and Capital Budgets, *Review of Economics and Statistics* (February 1964).

[27] MacCrimmon, K.R.; Stanbury, W.T.; and Wehrung, D.A. "Wall Street Wagers: At Variance with Risk Theory," unpublished paper, University of British Columbia, May 1978.

[28] Mao, J.C.T. "Survey of Capital Budgeting: Theory and Practice," *Journal of Finance* (May 1970).

[29] Markowitz, Harry. "The Utility of Wealth," *Journal of Political Economy* (April 1952).

[30] Markowitz, Harry. *Portfolio Selection.* New York: John Wiley & Sons, 1959.

[31] Porter, R.B.; Bey, R.P.; and Lewis, D.C. "An Empirical Investigation of Stochastic Dominance and Mean-Variance Portfolio Choice Criteria," *Journal of Financial and Quantitative Analysis* (September 1973).

[32] Porter, R.B.; Bey, R.P.; and Lewis, D.C. "The Development of a Mean–Semi-Variance Approach to Capital Budgeting," *Journal of Financial and Quantitative Analysis* (November 1975).

[33] Pratt, John W. "Risk Aversion in the Small and in the Large," *Econometrica* (January–April 1964).

[34] Rosett, R.N. "The Friedman-Savage Hypothesis and Convex Acceptance Sets: A Reconciliation," *Quarterly Journal of Economics* (August 1967).

[35] Schall, L.D.; Sundem, G.L.; and Geijsbeek, W.R. "Survey and Analysis of Capital Budgeting Methods," *Journal of Finance* (March 1978).

[36] Sharpe, William F. "Capital Asset Prices: A Theory of Market Equilibrium under Conditions of Risk," *Journal of Finance* (September 1964).

[37] Sharpe, William F. *Portfolio Theory and Capital Markets.* New York: McGraw-Hill Book Company, 1970.

[38] Siegel, Sidney. "Level of Aspiration and Decision Making," *Psychological Review* (July 1957).

[39] Slovic, P. "The Relative Influence of Probabilities and Payoffs upon Perceived Risk of a Gamble," *Psychonomic Science* (October 1967).

[40] Spetzler, Carl S. "The Development of a Corporate Risk Policy for Capital Investment Decisions," *IEEE Transactions on Systems Science and Cybernetics* (September 1968).

[41] Swalm, Ralph. "Utility Theory–Insights into Risk Taking," *Harvard Business Review* (November–December 1966).

[42] Whitmore, G.A. "Third-Degree Stochastic Dominance," *American Economic Review* (June 1970).

[43] Yaari, M.E. "Convexity in the Theory of Choice under Risk," *Quarterly Journal of Economics* (May 1965).

3 THE FACTOR OF URGENCY IN CORPORATE CAPITAL BUDGETING DECISIONS

George W. Hettenhouse
Indiana University

The process for evaluating capital investment decisions in a managerial context has received considerable attention in the roughly twenty-five years since its popularization in the literature of economics and finance. It is now in such a stage of sophistication that its basic tenets of discounting and risk adjustment are in daily use by a majority of practicing financial managers. Capital investment theory, however, is essentially normative in its focus; by accepting projects with returns greater than the cost of capital, the classical profit-maximizing behavior of microeconomics is applied to corporate investment decisions. The development of the positive aspects of the decision process—how the realities of uncertainty, organizational size, internal politics, and corporate strategy should be integrated into the theory—has received far too little attention. Rather, the analytical focus has remained for the most part on tangible benefits and costs. Intangibles are generally not formally considered; the major exception, of course, is in the area of uncertainty, where management's subjective

The helpful comments of Wolfgang Bühler, University of Dortmund, West Germany, are gratefully acknowledged.

estimates of the future are often converted into probability distributions for further analysis. The explicit treatment of risk and uncertainty represents an appropriate first step in an attempt to operationalize the normative theory.

Extensions of the normative model have, in general, been focused on two dimensions:

1. The measurement question as applied to both returns and capital costs
2. Differences between corporate practice and the normative model

Under extension 1 would be included the vast body of literature applied to the measurement of the cost of capital, the implications of capital structure on capital costs and extensions of the capital asset pricing model (CAPM) to both the measurement of capital costs, and the desirability of individual investment projects.[1] These extensions are for the most part refinements of the normative theory, rather than adaptions to incorporate differences between theory and practice.

Under extension 2 would be included the literature that revolves around the problem of capital rationing, the use of strategic hurdle rates, subjective risk adjustments, and multiple-goal formulations of the investment decision problem. The thing that distinguishes these refinements is that they are, by and large, not firmly anchored in economic theory. Rather, they are attempts to provide an analytical structure to problems that exist in practice, but are generally assumed away in theory.

Most corporate investment decisions are subjected to a matrix of constraints not formally considered in the theory. Foremost among these is an almost permanent condition of capital rationing; this situation exists for reasons other than the classical argument concerning a discontinuity in the supply curve for capital. In practice, firms are capital-rationed in order to budget and manage growth within physical limits imposed by personnel and resource availability, as well as within policy limits established by management under the rubric of strategic planning. Methods for allocating scarce capital resources to investment projects vary across firms, but observed practice would suggest:

1. Projects with positive NPVs are commonly rejected or postponed.
2. Return-based rankings are seldom done, but even if they are, such rankings are only one factor in the capital allocation process.
3. Product line, market objectives, and productive capacity and efficiency goals, while not incompatible with NPV goals, are generally heavily weighted in the decision process.

In general, therefore, it is the firm's long-run strategic plan that ultimately determines the allocation of capital resources.[2] Some firms have a formal corporate plan against which to measure project desirability; for others, the plan is implicit in the actions of the top executive group. In either case, a Weingartner-type programming solution to maximizing total NPV subject to budget constraints would have little more than curiosity value.[3]

These remarks are not meant to suggest that firms suboptimize or are slow to incorporate management science techniques into the decision process. Rather, managers envision their decisions to be multidimensional and in many cases do not consider the academic models sufficiently robust to be particularly helpful. The fact that academic models have become operational in such areas as portfolio management, option trading, and cash management suggests that it is the models, not the managers, that have shortcomings. In the capital investment area, our models have simply not captured the essence of the managerial decision process. Until they do, they are likely to remain on the academic bookshelf.

A reasonable question at this stage might well be, Why should the academic community work to extend the model: Why should the business community not alter its practice to make it more consistent with economic theory? There are two possible responses here. First, some of the impracticalities of the model result from measurement difficulties and other potentially solvable problems whose solution would permit greater application while retaining the basic elements of the economic theory. The second response would argue that a modern business is an entity with multiple goals and purposes; while many of these objectives have an economic orientation, there are also noneconomic or social goals of significant importance. It is to the first type of response that this paper is addressed; it is these potentially solvable, but nonetheless economic, considerations that stand between theory and practice. Whether the gap between practice and a more robust economic model, addressed in the second response, is sufficient to prevent the model's eventual applicability must remain untested.

The initial steps in modifying the economic model to correspond more closely with practical realities require that the academic community suggest new dimensions to the decision model. Through a process of evolution, portions of these various modifications should become a part of the economic model, thus broadening its appeal to practicing managers. This paper represents an early step in that direction; a commonly invoked intangible consideration, the factor of urgency, will be investigated as a possible addition to the decision process.

THE URGENCY DIMENSION

One factor that is commonly used in the practical decision process, but that has neither a theory base nor a good decision heuristic, is the question of urgency. Managers schedule projects for funding (or postpone implementation) on the basis of their perceived time pressure or urgency. The decision process here is almost totally subjective and in some instances is capricious or political.

Projects having an urgency dimension can be of two types: those that have an appreciable revenue stream (even though the NPV is negative) and those in a nonrevenue category. Projects without revenues would include things like facility upgradings (aesthetics, parking lot upgrading) and voluntary efforts in excess of current regulatory requirements in the areas of health, safety, and environmental pollution. The ranking of projects on an urgency dimension is compounded by mixing nonrevenue projects with profit-enhancing investment; rate of returns (or NPVs) cannot be used to assign priority to such investment. No good measures of relative urgency have yet been developed. It is important to stress at this point that the problem of urgency is much broader than the simple question of doing something now vis-à-vis doing the same thing later. Rather, project urgency captures a variety of pressures, some economic, others less tangible, to do something as part of the capital budget. These pressures may build or diminish as a function of time, but considerations other than timing serve to initially create project urgency.

This paper will investigate the various aspects of the urgency question and suggest several possible decision frameworks in which urgency considerations could be made more explicit. It is not the intent of this paper to provide a definitive structure for treating a multiple-objective investment decision process; rather, the role of the discussion is to urge further inquiry into this and other practical problems that surround the capital investment decision process. The urgency dimension that is the basis for the discussion serves only as an example of the practical complexities of decisions that are not adequately handled in the normative decision process.

TYPES OF URGENCY-BASED PROJECTS

For discussion and analytical purposes, it is helpful to categorize urgency-based projects into three types:

1. Projects having a formal "regret function" or cost of postponement. This is the most definitive category of project from an analytical standpoint. Revenues and costs are able to be estimated and a NPV (positive or negative) calculated. For this class of project, it is possible (and desirable) to calculate ΔNPV, the change in NPV that would result from delaying the project for one year. By calculating the ratio ΔNPV/investment, an index of urgency is created. Positive values indicate that postponement is desirable; negative ratios signal the degree of urgency involved in each

project. For negative ratios, the index could be used like a profitability index, with investment scheduled first for the largest negative values.[4]

Projects of this type are quite common. Negative changes in NPV could be caused by the actions of competitors during the delay period, inflation in construction costs or factor inputs, and erosion in goodwill, either external or internal to the firm. Positive changes in NPV or a postponement signal could result from predicted improvements in process or product technology, significantly higher product prices in the future, or significant reductions in uncertainty during the delay period.

Consider, for example, the situation of the natural resource company (or country) during the decade of the 1980s. The key strategic question for such decision units is the rate at which they extract product and put it on the market. NPVs from rapid extraction and sale now are likely highly positive. Postponement of the developmental effort to a later date could, however, result in a combination of demand, process technology, and distributional efficiency that would argue in favor of delay. The issue, then, is not whether to develop the field, but when to develop it and at what rate to extract product. To both decisions, the factor of urgency is central.

2. Projects that represent "insurance against calamity." Investment in this type of project provides some degree of protection against some probabilistic loss of unknown size in the future. Investments in anticipation of or compliance with regulatory requirements are an example here. To commit capital investment now may eliminate or reduce the likelihood of a complete shutdown at some time in the future. Like any purchase of insurance, the NPV is difficult to calculate and, except under the most pessimistic of assumptions, likely to be negative. In such decisions, the firm assesses the magnitude of the possible loss and the price and extent of insurance coverage in order to arrive at a strategy of self-insurance and purchased insurance appropriate for its capital position and risk-aversion tendencies. The key question in such decisions is when to commit the funds.

It is increasingly argued that the best way to cope with the demands of governmental regulation and activist groups is to meet them halfway. Although such a strategy may possibly lower settlement cost, the earlier expenditure may be more costly in NPV terms than postponement, considering again the prospects for future changes in attitudes, prices, and technology. In any case, the key question here is when to commit capital; there is generally little discretion as to the ultimate expenditure of funds. The decision is further complicated by myriad intangible factors that surround the decision; how does one value the impact of a critical news story in either the print or electronic media, for example?

3. Nonrevenue projects that are ultimately funded on the basis of intangible factors. Projects of this type are purely discretionary and are easy to delay when funds are short. Included here would be landscaping, office construction or remodeling, and parking lot improvements. While almost everyone would agree that such expenditures are necessary, they are virtually impossible to justify in NPV terms without substantial creativity in translating intangibles into dollar benefits. Such projects, therefore, are scheduled for investment on a mostly political basis, recognizing that every dollar committed to such investment worsens corporate ROI.

TREATMENT OF THE URGENCY FACTOR IN PRACTICE

Even casual observation of corporate practice would show that projects in all three of the above categories are routinely funded. While urgency is often listed among the items to be considered in recommending project funding, the degree of urgency is not generally treated in an explicit manner. Rather, capital budgeting procedures are organized in such a way that urgent, but inferior or negative, NPV projects can be funded.

There are several types of procedures in use that permit managerial discretion. One common method is to budget corporate funds by project type and then to allocate funds to various organizational units. In this way, competition for funds remains within homogeneous project types; once a sum has been set aside for facility improvement and remodeling, for example, the poor NPV consequences of such investment are irrelevant to the decision process. Concepts like divisional equity, corporate politics, and compatibility with long-run corporate plans become the paramount decision criteria. The presumption in making the initial allocation to a low NPV class of projects is that the NPV consequences of profit-based investment decisions are adequate to ensure a net positive NPV for the capital budget as a whole. Not surprisingly, the extent of corporate funds allocated to type-three nonrevenue projects is highly dependent on corporate profitability and the immediate EPS impact of the capital budget. When profitability is lagging or when the capital budget is disproportionately committed to projects with startup losses (product introduction, facilities construction, etc.), discretionary investment without positive NPVs is often postponed.

A second system in common usage is a decentralized decision process in which a total package of funds is allocated to each decision unit for it to disburse as it sees fit. Since urgency is a relative phenomenon, it becomes a more important decision criterion to a decentralized unit than it is to a centralized decision unit. At the divisional level, nonrevenue projects are scheduled for funding or postponed on the basis of urgency vis-à-vis the profitability consequences of alternative uses for funds. Once again, if profitability is high or if the NPV consequences for a sizable portion of the capital budget are particularly healthy, the nonrevenue project has an enhanced probability of funding. If, on the other hand, the decision unit is operating with an ROI deficiency against its target rate, the threshold for accepting urgency-based projects is generally raised.

Irrespective of the organizational methods used to allocate capital to projects, there is a major interaction between the organization's strategic plan and the type of projects described above. Decisions with regard to urgency-based projects, therefore, are made at multiple organizational levels. Specifically, the desired risk exposure from type-two projects would likely be discussed and resolved at the corporate level, with only top management participating in the decision. The timing aspects of type-one projects would generally be discussed and resolved as part of the long-run planning process for each organizational unit; participation here would include top management and divisional managers. Nonrevenue projects of the third type would likely be left to the plant manager's discretion, perhaps with divisional approval.

The traditional academic solution to the capital rationing problem—some type of constrained optimization formulation—does not fit this decision environment for several reasons. As discussed above, the capital allocation process is a sequential process taking place at different organizational levels; present models implicitly assume a single-level decision framework. In addition, the decision criteria that apply not only are broader than NPV maximization, but also interact with one another. A goal programming formulation of the capital rationing problem would permit the consideration of multiple criteria, but is not particularly adept at handling intangible factors and is not structured to capture the feedback properties of the profitability-urgency tradeoff. Current models, therefore, are not presently in use and are unlikely to be called into service in their present form.

FACTORS AFFECTING THE DEGREE OF URGENCY

To enhance understanding of the urgency dimension with the goal of generating interest in more robust model formulation, the discussion will next consider some of the major determinants of project urgency. These factors are not intended to be mutually exclusive and are normally found in combination with one another. Each, however, captures a slightly different dimension of the whole question of project urgency. Degree of project urgency is related to:

1. The potential response of competition. When the actions of competitors would combine to diminish market opportunities and the resulting NPV, the potential expenditure is subject to the pressure of urgency. The more narrow the time window for managerial action, the greater the urgency dimension.

2. The prospects for product technology. There are a variety of possibilities here. It may be that recent technological change presents the market opportunity discussed above. Alternatively, near-term prospects for technology improvement may either encourage postponement of new-product introduction to reduce risk of obsolescence or raise in importance the expansion of manufacturing and distribution facilities to handle an impending new product.

3. The prospects for process technology. Pending technological change here most often encourages management to delay process change or replacement to gain future cost advantages. Once the technology is introduced, there may be argument for further postponement to permit refinements to be introduced or to take advantage of learning curve properties in its introduction.

4. Impending price changes or potential shortages in a factor market. In inflationary times it is not uncommon to do something earlier than necessary to avoid price increases. Similarly, when potential shortages of labor or material are in prospect, project urgency is obviously created. Unfortunately, the immediate past suggests that both effects are likely to be crucial to the decision environment of the future, particularly with regard to energy resources.

5. The rate of uncertainty resolution. Managers often wait as a way of reducing the uncertainty attaching to a decision; if this is the situation, a project would have a lowered urgency rating. It should be noted that this factor is not independent of the others in this list; each of the other tradeoffs also has an uncertainty dimension. In fact, items like competitive actions and technology may be the major contributors to the uncertainty.

6. The importance of the project or product to the company's business plan. This importance may relate to either the strategic plan itself or to its interim achievement goals. A project may have little NPV merit on its own, but may still be considered urgent because of the role it plays vis-à-vis the corporate plan. As long as corporations measure performance against a plan, project congruency with the plan will serve to reduce the importance of NPV considerations. In many cases the interactions alluded to prevent measurement of a "stand-alone NPV."

7. The politics of the organization. Certain managers and/or profit centers simply must receive some level of investment regardless of the return picture. Even if the ultimate decision is divestment or abandonment, political equity introduces a dimension of project urgency. As discussed earlier, this dimension is often solved in an implicit fashion by organizing the investment decision process in a decentralized fashion.

8. The impact of the project on intangibles. Attributes such as product quality, labor relations, and corporate image are largely intangible, but often dominate NPV considerations in the decision process. Since these intangibles are difficult, if not impossible, to value objectively, they normally show up in the urgency dimension of the decision; such considerations serve to broaden the concept of project urgency.

There are probably other factors that are relevant to the urgency dimension. The point to be realized from this discussion is that urgency is a "real" decision variable and is a multidimensional consideration. It is clearly broader than simply a matter of project timing. These multiple facets add to the difficulty of incorporating the urgency dimension into the decision process.

POSSIBLE DECISION MODELS

To incorporate the factor of urgency into the corporate decision process in a more formal fashion would require some type of a formalized decision model. There are possibilities to consider, ranging from a simple subjective heuristic to one of the several types of constrained optimization models commonly found in the literature. The discussion to follow will not offer a preferred solution to the problem; rather, the advantages and disadvantages of several possibilities will be discussed, leaving to the reader the choice of a conclusion or a continued search for a more appropriate model.

The applicability of various decision models depends on two things: the extent to which the decision maker desires a generalized model and the extent to which the decision maker requires an optimizing model. Like most decision processes, the greater the desire for a generalized optimizing structure, the more extensive and compromising must be the assumptions and the decision structure. If too extensive, the offered solution may take its place alongside other academic models. Less ambitious models, on the other hand, may aid the decision maker, but may not contain the theoretical rigor necessary to ensure that their use is indeed compatible with overall financial goals. In such cases, there is always the possibility that the offered model would be worse than no model at all.

Level 1: Nonglobal, Nonoptimizing Models

As earlier discussion indicated, it is often possible to consider that subset of
urgency-based projects involving postponement decisions in strictly NPV terms.
Type-one projects, having a formal "regret function," would be included in this
category. The decision maker is able to calculate a ΔNPV from project postponement and then act on the information so gained. When there are multiple
projects of this type, the ΔNPV$/I$ urgency index referred to earlier can be calculated and used as a basis for scheduling projects for funding. In this category,
explicit treatment of the urgency dimension has improved the information
available to the decision maker. Further, the new information is compatible
with the NPV criteria suggested in the literature for making value-maximizing
investment decisions. The difficulty with this method, of course, is that it is
limited to the subset of projects having formal regret functions and, even then,
to changes in intangible benefits or costs. The intangibles that are often important to the urgency decision are not explicitly considered.

Level 2: Nonglobal, Optimizing Models

The information gained from analysis of the regret function can easily enter the
multiperiod linear (integer) programming solution method commonly offered to
solve the capital rationing problem. Postponable projects become available for
investment in one of several decision periods. The regret function permits a
restatement of NPV and I in each decision period; a mutually exclusive constraint prevents the project from being accepted in more than one period. As in
any programming solution, projects are considered in a value-contribution-
opportunity-cost framework; the advantage here is that the shadow price on the
capital constraint implicitly establishes a cutoff for project postponement. The
more severe the capital rationing, the higher the ratio ΔNPV$/I$ will have to be to
avoid project postponement.

The practicability of this solution method is suspect, not because of the
added urgency dimension, but because of the lack of robustness of the method
generally. If anything, the proposed change serves to increase its applicability
to the decision process. This tool will likely remain on the shelf for the simple
reason that it requires too great a compromise with decision reality. The model
presumes that all investment decisions are made at one point in time, at one
organizational level, and with one dominant decision objective (maximize
NPV). Further, it generally assumes away risk differences in constructing the
project portfolio and presumes that budget constraints are absolutely fixed in

size over time. Until these divergences from decision reality are incorporated into the model, its usefulness in dealing with the urgency question will remain unproven.

Level 3: Global, Nonoptimizing Models

A common approach to dealing with decision complexity is to establish a decision heuristic. The advantage of such an approach is that it permits the decision maker(s) to approach the decision in an organized and consistent fashion over time. The problem with heuristic models, however, is that they are often only remotely related to an accepted theoretical construct. Their use, therefore, results from convenience and the perceived benefits of consistency, rather than from demonstrated profit enhancement.

The appendix to this paper presents an example of a hypothetical decision heuristic to treat the factor of urgency. The decision maker is confronted with a series of dimensions that are relevant to project urgency and is asked to categorize the project on each of these dimensions. The urgency dimensions involve both tangible and intangible considerations; they are not independent of each other. Once a project is rated on each dimension, the urgency ratings are totaled to obtain a total urgency factor for the project. In the example shown in the appendix, the decision maker is given the opportunity to assign differential weights to the importance to each factor; weights would likely not be project-specific but would be established in advance for all investment opportunities rated in a particular decision unit.

The urgency-point total enters the decision process as an additional consideration to NPV. While a second decision dimension is clearly incompatible with economic theory, it is certainly not incompatible with the decision process as viewed by corporate management. The only question in their minds is whether the additional information aids an already multidimensional decision process.

There are, of course, plenty of objections that can be raised with the suggested heuristic. The factor weights and point assignments are quite arbitrary. The additivity of factor points to gain a point total can be similarly questioned on the basis of an unknown dependency structure and an incompatibility of the tangible and intangible factors underlying the analysis. Lastly, the structure is more conducive to manipulation than is the NPV calculation; to argue that the latter is objective, however, is to admit to considerable naiveté. The above difficulties are not unique to this decision dimension, but rather are found in almost any decision heuristic. Admittedly, heuristic models cannot be dismissed on such grounds; they must be rejected on the basis of a fair trial in the decision process.

Level 4: Global, Optimizing Models

Recent advantages in financial model building have admitted the possibility of constrained optimization in an environment with more than one decision objective. Goal programming permits the decision maker to consider an optimizing problem with multiple decision goals and an explicit goal priority. While the goal programming structure is a more accurate depiction of the decision environment than either an L.P. or integer programming formulation, it suffers from a practical difficulty of specification. The decision maker must specify each goal *a priori* and weight deviations from each goal in a systematic fashion. For anything but the simplest of problems, it is difficult to achieve internal consistency of goals and weights. Not surprisingly, most users of goal programming prefer to make successive modifications of goals, weights, and physical constraints before selecting a preferred solution.

Multiobjective linear programming avoids the problem of *a priori* specification of goals and weights by specifying multiple-objective functions subject to multiple environmental constraints. This new decision model locates a set of efficient solutions for the decision maker. The "best" solution is selected by the decision maker by evaluating the tradeoffs available. The goals and deviation weights specified *a priori* for goal programming are used implicitly for selecting a preferred solution to the multiobjective linear program. The disadvantage of this method lies in its computational inefficiency and the potential for an exceedingly large number of efficient solutions to complex problems.

The urgency objective may be combined with the traditional NPV objective, and other objectives if desired, using either of these two methods. The problem, again, revolves around the need for specifying a numerical value to the urgency dimension. The obvious candidate is an urgency heuristic similar to the example described earlier. If such a heuristic, acceptable to managers and compatible with NPV and other dollar-denominated values, can be developed, then these more sophisticated models would be applicable to the urgency problem. Without such acceptance, of course, urgency evaluation must remain subjective and intangible for all projects lacking a formal regret function.

CONCLUSIONS

The factor of project urgency, like many other practical considerations that enter the corporate decision process, has not been adequately evaluated as an impact to the capital investment decision. It, along with many other practical considerations, is either ignored as incompatible with the microeconomic structure on which the decision process is based or is lumped together with other intangible considerations. The limited acceptance of anything but the most basic decision models may have as its cause the cavalier treatment of such intangible factors.

This discussion paper has considered one such factor, that of urgency, from a variety of viewpoints. It is not meant to be definitive in its treatment or offered solution. Rather, it is intended to encourage additional work on the incorporation of intangible factors into the decision process. Such effort may require compromise with economic theory to become operational. The ultimate question is simply: Which is to be preferred—a theoretically correct, but practically inapplicable model, or a practical model with some theoretical deficiencies? While the answer depends in large part on the question of degree, it is the contention of this paper that an improved decision framework is sufficiently meritorious to deserve more attention in financial research.

APPENDIX: A SAMPLE METHOD FOR CALCULATING THE HEURISTIC URGENCY FACTOR

Step 1. Consider each of the factor descriptions shown in Appendix Table 1 and rate them on a scale from 0 to 2 in terms of their importance to corporate goals.

Step 2. Assign points for the project under consideration on each of the factors listed. Point assignment should be in accordance with the following scale:

Points	Description
4	Project results highly sensitive to delay on this dimension; delay would worsen desirability considerably.
3	—
2	Project results moderately sensitive to delay on this dimension; delay would worsen desirability moderately.
1	—
0	Project results insensitive to delay on this dimension; delay would have no impact on desirability.
-1	—
-2	Project results moderately sensitive to delay on this dimension; delay would improve desirability moderately.
-3	—
-4	Project results highly sensitive to delay on this dimension; delay would improve desirability considerably.

Step 3. Multiply point totals by the scale factor for each item. Sum algebraically to obtain the urgency factor total for the project.

Appendix Table 1. Sample Rating Form

Factor Description	Factor Scale[a]	Points Assigned[b]
Market opportunity – the extent to which delay may result in actions of competitors	———	———
Product technology – the extent to which delay has an impact on future product technology	———	———
Process technology – the extent to which near-term technological change will result in process obsolescence or cost inefficiencies	———	———
Price sensitivity – the extent to which delay will expose the firm to price escalations in excess of the inflation rate	———	———
Uncertainty resolution – the extent to which delay will resolve uncertainty surrounding future costs and/or benefits	———	———
Strategic plan consistency – the extent to which the project is important to realization of plan objectives	———	———
Internal goodwill – the extent to which delay would worsen organizational and/or employee morale	———	———
Product goodwill – the extent to which delay would worsen product quality or market image	———	———
Regulatory pressure – the extent to which delay would risk exposure to fines, shutdowns, and image damage	———	———
Total urgency points (algebraic sum of products of factor scale times assigned points)	———	

[a]Range is 0 to 2, from unimportant to critical; average importance is 1.
[b]Range is +4 to –4; see scale.

NOTES

1. To attempt a listing of citations here would be impractical. A chronological perusal of academic journals or financial textbooks would give the reader an appreciation of the studies made in these areas.

2. See, for example, the article by Donaldson [7], in which it is argued that strategic considerations should dominate cost of capital in resource allocation decisions.

3. The now classic article by Weingartner [33], showing the application of linear programming methods to the solution of the capital rationing problem, is one of the first examples of the use of management science techniques in broadening the applicability of the normative model.

4. Many financial researchers have already pointed out the potential for inconsistent rankings using profitability index. If projects differ greatly in size and the budget limit is completely inelastic, the ranking of projects by profitability index for funding may result in a lower aggregate net present value than would result from a programming-type solution. This same caveat would apply, of course, to the urgency index.

REFERENCES

[1] Bacon, P.W. "The Evaluation of Mutually Exclusive Investments," *Financial Management* (Summer 1977), pp. 55–58.

[2] Baumol, W.J., and Quandt, R.E. "Investment and Discount Rates under Capital Rationing—A Programming Approach," *Economic Journal* (June 1965), pp. 317–329.

[3] Bernhard, R.H. "Mathematical Programming Models for Capital Budgeting—A Survey, Generalization, and Critique," *Journal of Financial and Quantitative Analysis* (June 1969), pp. 111–158.

[4] Bower, R.S., and Jenks, J.M. "Divisional Screening Rates," *Financial Management* (Autumn 1975), pp. 42–49.

[5] Brigham, E.F. "Hurdle Rates for Screening Capital Expenditure Proposals," *Financial Management* (Autumn 1975), pp. 17–26.

[6] Carleton, W.T. "Linear Programming and Capital Budgeting Models: A New Interpretation," *Journal of Finance* (December 1969), pp. 825–833.

[7] Donaldson, G. "Strategic Hurdle Rates for Capital Investment," *Harvard Business Review* (March–April 1972), pp. 50–58.

[8] Elton, E.J. "Capital Rationing and External Discount Rates," *Journal of Finance* (June 1970), pp. 573–584.

[9] Fogler, R.H. "Ranking Techniques and Capital Rationing," *Accounting Review* (January 1972), pp. 134–143.

[10] Hastie, K.L. "One Businessman's View of Capital Budgeting," *Financial Management* (Winter 1974), pp. 36–44.

[11]   Hatsopoulos, G.N.; Gyftopoulos, E.P.; Sant, R.W.; and Widmer, T.F. "Capital Investment to Save Energy," *Harvard Business Review* (March–April 1978), pp. 111–122.

[12]   Hawkins, C.A., and Adams, R.A. "A Goal Programming Model for Capital Budgeting," *Financial Management* (Spring 1974), pp. 52–57.

[13]   Keown, A.J., and Martin, J.D. "An Integer Goal Programming Model for Capital Budgeting in Hospitals," *Financial Management* (Autumn 1976), pp. 28–35.

[14]   King, P. "Is the Emphasis of Capital Budgeting Theory Misplaced?" *Journal of Business, Finance, and Accounting* (Spring 1975), pp. 69–82.

[15]   Lee, S.M., and Lerro, A.J. "Capital Budgeting for Multiple Objectives," *Financial Management* (Spring 1974), pp. 58–66.

[16]   Lerner, E.M., and Rappaport, A. "Limited DCF in Capital Budgeting," *Harvard Business Review* (September–October 1968), pp. 133–139.

[17]   Lockett, A.G., and Gear, A.E. "Multistage Capital Budgeting under Uncertainty," *Journal of Financial and Quantitative Analysis* (March 1975), pp. 21–36.

[18]   Lorie, J.H., and Savage, L.J. "Three Problems in Capital Rationing," *Journal of Business* (October 1955), pp. 229–239.

[19]   Lustig, P., and Schwab, B. "A Note on the Application of Linear Programming to Capital Budgeting," *Journal of Financial and Quantitative Analysis* (December 1968), pp. 427–431.

[20]   Merville, L.J., and Tavis, L.A. "A Generalized Model for Capital Investment," *Journal of Finance* (March 1973), pp. 109–118.

[21]   Myers, S.C. "A Note on Linear Programming and Capital Budgeting," *Journal of Finance* (March 1972), pp. 89–92.

[22]   Petty, J.W.; Scott, D.F., Jr.; and Bird, M.M. "The Capital Expenditure Decision-Making Process of Large Corporations," *Engineering Economist* (Spring 1975), pp. 159–172.

[23]   Sartoris, W.L., and Spruill, M.S. "Goal Programming and Working Capital Management," *Financial Management* (Spring 1974), pp. 67–74.

[24]   Schwab, B., and Lustig, P. "A Comparative Analysis of the NPV and Cost-Benefit Ratios as Measures of the Economic Desirability of Investments," *Journal of Finance* (June 1969), pp. 507–516.

[25]   Sealey, C.W., Jr. "Financial Planning with Multiple Objectives," *Financial Management* (Winter 1978), pp. 17–23.

[26]   Thompson, H.E. "Mathematical Programming, the Capital Asset Pricing Model, and Capital Budgeting of Interrelated Projects," *Journal of Finance* (March 1976), pp. 125–131.

[27]   Trivioli, G.W. "Project Investment Analysis and Anticipated Government Mandated Expenditures," *Financial Management* (Winter 1976), pp. 18–25.

[28]   Wacht, R.F., and Whitford, D.T. "A Goal Programming Model for Capital Investment Analysis in Nonprofit Hospitals," *Financial Management* (Summer 1976), pp. 37–47.

[29]   Weingartner, H.M. "The Excess Present Value Index – A Theoretical Basis and Critique," *Journal of Accounting Research* (Autumn 1963), pp. 213–224.

[30]   Weingartner, H.M. *Mathematical Programming and the Analysis of Capital Budgeting Problems.* Englewood Cliffs, N.J.: Prentice-Hall, 1963.

[31]   Weingartner, H.M. "Capital Budgeting of Interrelated Projects: Survey and Synthesis," *Management Science* (March 1966), pp. 485–516.

[32]   Weingartner, H.M. "Criteria for Programming Investment Project Selection," *Journal of Industrial Economics* (November 1966), pp. 65–76.

[33]   Weingartner, H.M. "Some New Views on the Payback Period and Capital Budgeting Decisions," *Management Science* (August 1969).

[34]   Weingartner, H.M. "Capital Rationing: N Authors in Search of a Plot," *Journal of Finance* (December 1977), pp. 1403–1431.

[35]   Zeleny, M. *Linear Multiobjective Programming.* New York: Springer-Verlag, 1974.

4 GEOGRAPHIC PERSPECTIVES OF RISK:

A Financial Strategic Approach

Frans G.J. Derkinderen
The Netherlands School of Business

Empirical evidence increasingly suggests that traditional finance theory is operationally inadequate, or at least underdeveloped from the managerial point of view, since several crucial features of the capital budgeting decision process are not incorporated in conventional models. In recent years, however, there have been indications of a growing academic interest in methodological adaptation to narrow differences between theory and corporate practice. Along this line of thought, an exploration of risk from the perspective of enhanced realism for corporate decision making is indicated. In this respect, adequate managerial applicability to promote effective capital budgeting is of vital importance. Such an approach should develop operational risk concepts and verify that they are not incompatible with the basic tenets of economic theory. A prerequisite for providing effective structure to problems that exist in practice is an appreciation of the fact that managers appear to envision their decisions to be multidimensional. This insight dictates that an analysis or investigation of risk issues should give sufficient attention to their interaction with other key strategic factors.

Of significance for the practical decision process, and of readily apparent topical interest, is one set of features that increasingly requires management attention in the risk perspective. These refer to geographic-oriented factors that are important for identifying, analyzing, and evaluating risk problems associated particularly with foreign direct investment decisions. This paper is directed toward specifying and structuring such geographic factors in order to focus effectively on their risk implications from the manager's standpoint. This is accomplished in a context that is basically compatible with the generally accepted body of elementary economic and financial concepts. Developing a financial-strategic approach to the "where" issue regarding internationalization, this method will be applied to a problem situation in which reduction of the overall riskiness of the firm is required. Using this approach, the impact of crucial geographic factors on the risk problem under discussion will be highlighted in a decision framework that promotes proper selection of the applicable country for direct investment. In this way, the risk implications of geographic aspects can be explored and evaluated while reflecting upon the interaction of key factors in strategic perspective. So doing, useful information can be offered as an aid to management during the multidimensional decision process under review.

Before such a method can be used, though, it is necessary to explain the analytical procedure. Thus, in the next section, there is a discussion of "preplanning" as an entrance to an evaluation of the firm's strategic posture. This forms the introduction to a typological approach to derive meaningful recommendations that are strategically sound. With this methodology, attention is turned to the problem situation of interest: which country to enter to reduce the overall riskiness of the company.

INTRODUCING STRATEGIC GUIDANCE
BY PROJECT SET PREPLANNING

Decisions that are not grounded firmly in the firm's strategy cannot lead consistently to the desired outcomes. A methodology designed to aid management in developing a sound resource allocation strategy and in monitoring the appropriateness of and adherence to this strategy is called *preplanning*. Preplanning refers to the process of determining the direction of movement of the company's strategic posture, including appropriate actions that need to be taken to move in the intended direction, supplemented, if possible, by a rough, but situationally conditioned, indication of the magnitude and rate of change of this movement as far as it is concerned with the full project set.[1]

This determination has two dimensions. The first part of preplanning is concerned with an analysis of the company's current strategic posture in terms of strengths, weaknesses, and the ability of the firm to respond appropriately to opportunities and threats as they tend to arise. The second part concentrates attention on identifying actions that can be taken to improve the strategic posture and to render the company better able to capitalize on opportunities and to meet adverse contingencies.

Preplanning as defined here is the logical starting place or the initial identification phase in the decision process upon which all business activity is predicated. It is also in harmony with recent developments in managerial theory. The trend in management today is to concentrate attention on those variables that can be forecast with reasonable reliability and further to develop timely and built-in relevant capabilities to maintain the flexibility to respond as appropriate to that which at present is less foreseeable. The talk now is about strategic *management* rather than strategic *planning*.[2] Attention is shifting from the long range back to the intermediate, and sometimes, albeit temporarily, even to the short-run perspective. This is supplemented with the promotion of capabilities to find relevant strategies and to ensure as far as possible the flexibility both to act when opportunities of a perceived type arise and to cope with adverse contingencies.

The nature of today's business environment, its greater complexity and change, has encouraged the shift of early emphasis from planning to preplanning. Increasingly, the problem encountered by management is lack of enough reliable data upon which comprehensive plans can be based. Even such techniques as scenario analyses are of little help since what may turn out to be, *ex post*, the most critical factor is often difficult to ascertain *ex ante* for use in setting elaborate plans. This reality must be dealt with explicitly in allocating scarce resources of the company.

An analysis of the current strategic posture of the firm is the appropriate platform upon which the development of the new project set can effectively be based. Thus it is advisable to start the preplanning process by giving consideration to this current posture. Additionally, starting from this departure point helps to prevent the analysis from leading to irrelevant generalizations.

The strategic posture of the company can be ascertained in a useful way through comparative analysis with an appropriately defined external benchmark or reference firm. Such a reference firm is a company, preferably of similar size and product mix and operating in the same industry(ies) or in a related activity field, that is classified as sound by the financial world in terms of the characteristics required not only to survive, but also to thrive in the environment under review.[3]

The reference firm is used as a benchmark to facilitate a relative analysis of the strategic strengths and weaknesses of the company under study. Since by definition the financial world (market) has classified the reference firm as sound, an analysis of relative strengths and weaknesses of a company along several dimensions can give management an idea of the strategic areas in which it needs to improve to become more attractive to the financial community. This analysis may also reveal areas of perhaps hidden strengths that can be exploited to achieve a better competitive position.

Using a carefully defined reference firm is better than relying on an arbitrary industry average for orientation since adequate similarity is vital for strategic comparisons—provided that the financial markets have passed judgment on the benchmark as a sound firm. Comparisons can also be made according to several essentially qualitative factors through an analysis relative to the reference firm, whereas such assessments would remain undefined using an industry average as a benchmark.

These strategic comparisons involve the explicit consideration of several environmental and internal variables with, as a by-effect, a tendency to increasing complexity. The usual definition of strategy indicates that an analysis in diverse perspectives is necessary to focus attention on the most salient facets of important strategic issues. Although individual relative comparisons are fairly easy to make in isolation, when considered together, it is rather difficult to structure them in a manner that ensures the extraction of the maximum amount of strategically significant and applicable information. Thus a structuring and summarizing device is required to reduce the complexity without destroying essential data.

This device should consolidate the information into a framework that is meaningful to management. In this way, the aggregated information portrayed by the summarizing factor(s) is stated in terms of concepts that can at once be identified with broad strategic attributes of paramount importance for developing the project set. The number of aggregating strategic factors should be kept at a minimum consistent with retention of the essential data contained in the individual comparisons. In the following, such a device is highlighted as the Potential And Resilience Evaluation, or PARE, method.[4]

POTENTIAL AND RESILIENCE EVALUATION
OF THE FIRM'S PROJECT SET

Going back to the underlying financial theories of the valuation of the firm,[5] the present value of a company is a function of its cash-flow stream in perpetuity capitalized at a rate of return sufficient to induce investors to hold the stocks and bonds of the firm. The perpetual cash-flow stream implies that the cash throwoff from the current project set is important, *but so is the ability of the firm to find and exploit profitable projects in the future.* The all-encompassing capitalization rate is designed to compensate investors for the variability of the cash flow, *as well as for another component that may be only indirectly linked with variability of cash flow:* the chance that, for whatever reason, the firm will experience financial stress which, in the limit, means it will have to cease operations and liquidate, or, in other words, become bankrupt. As described below, the PARE method is consistent with and follows directly from the above considerations with respect to the valuation of the firm and has several distinct advantages over the traditional concepts of return and risk.

To assess the company's ability to attain its strategic objectives, a corporate planner focuses attention in the first instance on the *Potential* of the firm. Potential refers to the ability of the company to generate and utilize attractive return possibilities for both the present and the future.

Opportunities is the designation given to projects that possess Potential. The existence of present and expected future opportunities gives a primary indication of the ability of the firm to remain competitive in the marketplace. Adequate opportunities are also an essential determinant of the market value of the company. Hence, opportunities are the first *strategic element* identified as important for project set development.

According to the valuation models mentioned above, identification of opportunities is necessary, but not sufficient, to describe the Potential of the firm in an appropriate way. A parallel consideration is the likelihood that such opportunities can be feasibly exploited by the company as deemed advisable. This involves a determination of whether the firm has the resources readily available for use in exploiting the opportunities according to its strategic plans. This capability to act is referred to as the *action range* and depends not only on the company's financial competence, but also on available managerial talent, manpower, technical and marketing knowhow, and organizational and logistical flexibility. Without the capability to exploit opportunities in a timely manner, the Potential of the firm cannot be realized. Hence, action range is the second strategic element identified as important for project set preplanning. By considering both opportunities and action range together in the form of Potential, a richer concept than return emerges that is consistent with the theories of valuation and is more operationally meaningful for developing the portfolio of projects.

An evaluation of the Potential of a company is based upon the planner's assessment of the two strategic elements for Potential—opportunities and action range—relative to the reference firm. It should be recognized that these two elements are distinguishable, but not separable, in evaluating the corporate Potential. In the preparatory phase of the strategic evaluation process, explicit attention to these factors in the indicated order is essential. During this process, management will have to combine its assessments of opportunities and action range to arrive at a strategically meaningful identification of the company's Potential relative to the reference firm. Without explicit attention to these strategic elements—opportunities and then action range—during this critical phase, the danger of an uncritical lumping together is too manifest.

In the second instance, the company's ability to withstand environmental threats and hold steady in the face of unfavorable contingencies has to be identified. This protective ability of the firm to cope with adversities associated with its projects, to handle contingencies, and to recoup to its original, if not to a better, position for future action, is referred to as the corporate *Resilience.*

The first key determinant of Resilience is the uncertainty to which the relevant cash flows are exposed in the sense that the realized return from the investments may be less than the expected return. This, the third strategic element, is referred to as the *risk* of the company, and it is approached through management's assessment of the vulnerability of the firm's cash flow to contingent setbacks.[6] However, risk alone is not sufficient to describe adequately the concept of Resilience. A parallel consideration to risk is the capability of the company to marshal resources to ensure survival in the event of adverse developments. This is referred to as the firm's *endurance* and is the fourth important strategic element.

The probability of a very low cash-flow outcome is not a sufficient indication of "bankruptcy risk" except in a *ceteris paribus* sense. This is true since suffering an extremely low cash-flow outcome at a time when endurance is high may have less serious bankruptcy implications than the occurrence of a "better" or higher cash-flow outcome when endurance is very low. Endurance thus refers to the company's capability to cope with unfavorable contingencies when beset with difficulties.

An evaluation of the Resilience of a company is based upon the planner's assessment of the two strategic elements for Resilience—risk and endurance— relative to the reference firm. It is important to imagine that in reflecting on the corporate Resilience, risk and endurance are distinguishable, but not separable. During this important reflection phase, the danger of an uncritical consolidation is manifest unless there is adequate preparation that pays explicit attention to these strategic elements in the correct order—risk and then endurance.

Resilience as determined in this way is, as a useful expansion, consistent with the valuation theory concept that underlies—or requires compensation for an investor to endure—the determination of the capitalization rate. It incorporates the idea of the variability or the distribution of possible cash-flow outcomes, including the likelihood of low values. Also, it includes a consideration of the resources and capabilities that the company can marshal to offset or overcome adverse cash-flow events. Thus both vital components of bankruptcy risk are explicitly taken into account.

Just as the four strategic elements were condensed into two comprehensive characteristics or *Key Strategic Factors*—Potential and Resilience—that reflect the underlying information in main lines, it is desirable to compress further the information into a single survey of the strategic posture of the company relative to the reference firm. Condensing the information into a single or grand indicator facilitates directional guidance for assessing the company's posture. In this way, the firm's overall attractiveness is also considered according to the financial markets in which the leading investment banks are of particular relevance from the corporate point of view.

The grand indication can be achieved by use of a comparative analysis or PARE chart for classification as shown in Table 1. The chart has only two positions—strong and weak—for each Key Strategic Factor. However, a similar posture should also be permitted in a relative analysis. Such a position can be plotted on the solid line that separates the cells of the chart, thus preserving directional indications for improvement. If either of the company's Key Strategic Factors is similar to those of the reference firm, any strategic issues in that perspective will not be so prominent, and so attention is focused mainly on the more salient postures.

Note that the reference firm plots in the center of the chart by this convention. Thus PARE position I dominates the reference firm, PARE position IV is dominated by the reference firm, and in PARE positions II and III, there are mixed indications (but for different causes).

For maximum strategic benefit, it is advantageous to expand the PARE chart to include the specific cause(s) for the firm's falling into a given PARE category. Referring to the expanded PARE chart shown in Table 2, it is seen that there are sixteen PARE classes into which the company can be placed—one for PARE I (no key problems with any of the strategic elements relative to the reference firm), three for PARE II (Potential problems), three for PARE III

Table 1. PARE or Comparative Analysis Chart

| | | Resilience | |
		Strong	Weak
Potential	Strong	I	III
	Weak	II	IV

Table 2. PARE or Comparative Analysis Chart (Expanded)

		Strong: No "R" Problems	*Resilience Problems* Weak — Mainly Risk	Weak — Mainly Endurance	Weak — Both Risk and Endurance
Strong: No "P" Problems		I	IIIa	IIIb	IIIc
Potential Problems **Weak**	Mainly Opportunities	IIa	IVa	IVb	IVg
	Mainly Action Range	IIb	IVc	IVd	IVh
	Both Opportunities and Action Range	IIc	IVe	IVf	IVi

PARE posture I: The company has neither Potential nor Resilience problems relative to the reference firm and is in a dominant position.
PARE posture II: The company has Potential problems relative to the reference firm, but has no problems with Resilience.
PARE posture III: The company has Resilience problems relative to the reference firm, but has no problems with Potential.
PARE posture IV: The company has problems with both Potential and Resilience relative to the reference firm.

(Resilience problems), and nine for PARE IV (difficulties with both Potential and Resilience).[7]

This expanded comparative analysis chart serves a purpose that is more than a matter of cosmetic embellishment. The important distinctions between the two strategic elements that interact to determine each of the Key Strategic Factors enrich the analytical power of the PARE tool of management. By showing that the outward manifestations of problems with Potential or Resilience (or in a conventional analysis in terms of return and risk) may be caused by fundamentally different, predominantly internal deficiencies, more attention is devoted explicitly to the source of the problem. There is great danger with an analysis that ignores this strategic differentiation because reacting to Potential and Resilience (or return or risk) in their aggregated form may be akin to treating outward symptoms rather than root causes. Attacking symptoms rather than the more fundamental underlying deficiencies can lead to an exacerbation of the real problem.

The ramifications of a firm's falling into a particular class according to the expanded PARE chart can be radically different from its placement in another class, even if both placements indicate difficulties with the same strategic factor. For a company with a Resilience problem, eliminating or rejecting high-risk projects can be suboptimal if the reason for the difficulty is rooted in the short-term endurance dimension. Similarly, a firm can have many promising opportunities and yet still have a Potential problem if it cannot obtain the specialized talent required to exploit the opportunities successfully. It should be obvious that these subtle, but important, distinctions have to be included in the project set preplanning process. However, the danger of errors of omission is great if they are not included explicitly in the analytical framework in a strategically structured way. All sixteen PARE classes enhance the ability to differentiate between often crucial situations whose corrections require a very specific set of actions.

Identification of the PARE position of the company under analysis relative to the reference firm can be conducted in the above strategically structured manner by typifying the company's current posture. Hereafter, this current position is referred to as the *departure situation*. With the aid of this tailored method, strategically applicable preplanning suggestions for actions can be derived. This approach will minimize the danger of situationally unjustified generalizations.

Defining the departure situation less comprehensively tends to blur or to dimensionally reduce the amount of unambiguous information that can be gleaned from such an analysis. This information is vital for giving clear signals about how the firm can effectively react to the challenges of the environment.

The primary focus of this typification methodology is on the medium or short term, without, however, losing too much long-run sight. The predominant long-range aspects are directed more toward identification of particularly advantageous types of projects or geographic areas and timely development of relevant capabilities of the firm.

Suggestions based on the PARE analysis for actions that will exploit opportunities or defend against threats or other ways to strengthen the posture of the company should result in a comprehensive overall strategy. One can evaluate the project set with respect to the four strategic elements by reflecting on the implications of the recommendations in the PARE perspective. Using these reflections, preplanning suggestions can be derived that contribute to an increase in Potential, Resilience, or both, while not decreasing either.

GOING ABROAD TO REDUCE RISK

The previous typification, though rather comprehensive, is sometimes still too general to give recommendations for all relevant dimensions, considering the various problems that a firm may encounter. Especially for determining detailed actions for strategic improvement and the associated implementation issues in case of a particular problem, a followup is needed.

Such followup analysis is demonstrated in this paper with the help of an example case dealing with a company considering further international expansion. The example is a firm that is situated in PARE position IIIa—having weak Resilience because of mainly risk problems. Thus there are no substantial problems with respect to opportunities, action range, and endurance, but the risk level is relatively high. Further analysis is required to ascertain and to specify the right actions, including implementation suggestions, to improve the unfavorable posture. Thus the root causes of the firm's risk problem first have to be examined.

In the case under review, it is assumed for the purpose of demonstration that there is evidence that the risk problem is probably, in particular, geographically oriented. To identify proper action, an in-depth typification in geographic perspectives forms a prerequisite.

The first question to be answered in this respect is: How are the firm's current strategic business units (SBUs) spread over the discernible geographic areas? SBU stands here for a segment of the firm as the smallest self-contained business for which a strategy can be defined. In this respect, it is useful to distinguish between the firm's "core SBU"—the activity from which management expects the highest discounted net cash flow—and its "noncore activities." As a measure for each SBU to determine the spread under discussion, cash flow is normally regarded as the most salient factor to consider, and so it will be used for this purpose. To enable more depth in the analysis, a distinction will be made between the firm's "main" geographic area—the area pertinent to the activity or activities under review from which management expects to realize the highest present value of the associated cash flow—and its "other" geographic areas.

The SBUs of the company in the example case are assumed to operate in eight different geographic areas (A through H) and the total net cash flow is distributed among them—for instance, according to the following percentages: A38, B16, C8, D6, E8, F16, G4, and H4.

The next question to be answered is: What other characteristics of the geographic areas covered by the firm's current SBUs are most relevant? A selection of other important geographic attributes leads to the following list:

Economic circumstances, meaning the assessment by management of the overall economic climate in the geographic areas under study (glossary of this paper, item 3)

Environmental change, referring to management's assessment of the impact of environmental change on the project's return (glossary item 4)

Inflation impact on profitability, which deals with the impact of inflation on the net cash flow of the firm's activities (glossary items 7 and 8, respectively, for costs and revenues)

Investment climate, referring to management's evaluation of the attitude toward business in the geographic area under consideration (more specifics included in glossary item 9)

Geographic risk, which deals with management's perception of the geographically oriented risk (political, economic, sociological, etc.) as far as it impacts the net cash flow of the projects executed in the area under analysis (glossary item 11)

Cash-flow transferability, referring to the extent to which host governments place restrictions on the movement of generated profits to other units of the firm outside the host country (glossary item 2)

Geographic cash-flow variability, which is the perceived extent to which the cash flow from the projects within the geographic area under study tends to fluctuate as approached by the coefficient of variation of the cash flow over the most recent five-year period (glossary item 13)

Geographic cash-flow growth rate, which indicates the annual compound rate of growth in net cash flow available to the firm from the geographic area under study (glossary item 5)

Geographic market growth rate, which refers to the annual compound rate of increase in total demand for the products or services provided by the firm's activities within the area under study (glossary item 6)

Accessibility for cash-flow anticipation, which deals with the extent to which management has confidence in its ability to forecast accurately the expected future cash flow from the SBUs in the geographic area under analysis (glossary item 1)

Some of the factors mentioned are partly overlapping and thus are not independent of each other; however, it is very difficult to compose a set of mutually exclusive variables without encountering the danger of neglecting some important aspects. Each factor, however, captures both a different and a significant dimension of the overall problem under review. Management can rate on a five-point scale each of these factors for all eight geographic areas pertinent to the current SBUs in the example case. For example, as is mentioned in the glossary item concerned, environmental change may be evaluated according to the following classification categories: radically favorable, ongoing favorable, no appreciable impact, ongoing unfavorable, and radically unfavorable.

As a reference point, the country is chosen, from all countries in which the company or its reference firm is active, that has an average or median value with respect to the attribute under consideration. The reference country may sometimes be different for various attributes, depending upon the specific nature of the factor under discussion.

To each classification category pertinent to the aspect under review, a value on a Likert-type continuum with an equidistant symmetrical scale from 1 to 5 is assigned; 1 corresponds to the most favorable rank, in terms of impact on cash flow, and 5 is the most unfavorable. If management assesses the characteristic of a country under study as identical to the corresponding attribute of the relevant reference country, a score of 3 is assigned to that characteristic. In this way, one can compute a weighted average score for the firm as a whole for each factor by multiplying the cash-flow distribution percentages pertinent to the relevant geographic areas with the scores associated with the appropriate rank. This is demonstrated for "geographic risk" in the example case under the assumption that the geographic-riskiness rank for the eight areas has been assessed as follows: B, E, and H "very high 5"; A and F "high 4"; D "medium 3"; G "low 2"; and C "very low 1." These risk scores are weighted according to the already mentioned cash-flow distribution percentages among the area that leads to the firm's average score:

$$\frac{(16 + 8 + 4)5 + (38 + 16)4 + 6 \times 3 + 4 \times 2 + 8 \times 1}{100} = 3.9.$$

For the company in the example case, the average score on geographic risk as a whole is rather high, 3.9, compared to the median score of 3.0. In this manner, the firm's average score can be determined for all attributes that are considered to be important for further typification of the geographic analysis. For the company in the example case, the values in Table 3 were assessed and computed for the previously mentioned characterization factors.

This way of characterizing the firm's attributes by means of scores has the advantage of giving further insight into the current situation and its strengths and weaknesses, keeping in mind that 3.0 is the median value. Empirical evidence from interviews and consulting experience supports the contention that managers perceive this characterization method as useful in preparing effectively multidimensional decisions, particularly if barely tangible aspects are also involved.

It has been assumed that a high score for each attribute corresponds to an unfavorable impact on net cash flow. Thus from Table 3 the following conclusions can be drawn: The company is apparently concentrated in geographic areas in which the economic circumstances are worse than average, in which the investment climate is not very good, and for which the risk characteristics are rather unfavorable. Also, the perceived change in the business environment is expected to be less favorable than average. The positive factors, such as cash-flow transferability and cash-flow growth rate, do not outweigh the negative ones. Four factors are considered to be similar to their respective counterparts in the reference country.

The firm should certainly change the geographic spread of its activities, provided that such a change is strategically adapted to the specific situation under review. Considering the firm's strategic posture, this spread of interests should be risk-reducing, provided that the corresponding returns are sufficiently rewarding. This consideration has important implications with respect both to

Table 3. Average Scores for the Example Firm

Characterization Factors	Score
Economic circumstances	4.0
Environmental change	3.6
Inflation impact	3.0
Investment climate	3.7
Geographic risk	3.9
Cash-flow transferability	2.8
Geographic cash-flow variability	3.0
Geographic cash-flow growth rate	2.5
Geographic market growth rate	3.0
Accessibility for cash-flow anticipation geographically	3.0

the activity chosen for expansion abroad and the countries in which such internationalization should be effected. On the one hand, the company in these circumstances has to refrain from radically new activities, since the lack of experience would bare too great a risk in itself. Therefore, it is recommended that the expansion abroad be in terms of an extension of the core business or an activity closely related to it. On the other hand, to effect further internationalization, countries should be chosen that have favorable characteristics regarding their ability to improve the unhealthy risk position at hand.

One should take care that the intended international expansion for the purpose of risk reduction will not have a damaging impact on the firm's favorable departure position according to the other three strategic elements. In the next section this "where" problem will be investigated in more detail.

THE "WHERE" PROBLEM FOR RISK REDUCTION

In preparing for the selection of countries, one should gather information about salient characteristics of the areas that are viable candidates. This process preceding the location decision is called *geographic specification*.[8] For this specification, the ten geographic attributes that were already dealt with in corporate perspective have also to be considered in analyzing the pros and cons of the candidate countries. Additionally, however, this group of factors should be supplemented by some characteristics that reflect the impact of the intended internationalization on the strategic elements opportunities, action range, and endurance.

The overall identification revealed that there are no problems with these other strategic elements, but it is necessary to protect that favorable position so that the risk problem will not be replaced by, for instance, an action range problem. In this context, management must choose key attributes for these strategic elements that are useful as a relevant signal for preventing unfavorable developments. It is assumed that in the example firm, two additional factors have been identified as being particularly useful for this safeguarding function:

- A geographically oriented version of the operating profitability/operating risk feature for monitoring the opportunities dimension (glossary items 10 and 12, respectively)
- Capital requirements for the geographic area under review for scanning action range, as well as endurance problems resulting from the scarcity of capital

Regarding the company in the example, further expansion abroad is appropriate for mitigating the firm's risk problem. It is assumed that the strategic position under study cannot be improved substantially by timely retrenchment of the most vulnerable activities in above-average risk countries because of social, economic, and political factors. It is also presumed that the firm has already chosen an appropriate activity for international expansion and that it now faces the "where" problem.

For illustrative purposes, the problem is confined to a situation in which there are three countries, K, L, and M, remaining after preselection on obvious characteristics. At first sight, there do not seem to be enough differences in attractiveness to make a clear-cut decision between the three countries. Thus specification according to the twelve geographic attributes is needed to make the choice. For the three remaining countries, the information contained in Table 4 is available.

Aided by the geographic specification, the structured evaluation of the "where" decision is made significantly easier. The prevailing criterion is the reduction of the firm's total risk by additional internationalization, and so country M is least suitable of the three. In evaluating the pros and cons of the other two countries, the firm's scores in the followup analysis should be kept in mind. The economic circumstances in the present geographic areas covered by the firm are rather unfavorable, and so country K, which may improve the company's score on this important characteristic, is a prime candidate.

Having considered the direct impact of additional foreign operations on the risk position of the firm—the strategic element that is primarily applicable— attention should also be paid to the indirect impacts of international expansion on the other strategic elements. In this respect, country L, with a better operating profitability than country K, is slightly superior, but both countries are suitable from the point of view of the impact on opportunities, action range, and endurance. Since country K has the superior risk position, the slight return sacrifice is considered acceptable.

The supplemental specification justifies the choice of country K on both a relevant and a comprehensive basis. This is one of the achievements of the methodology presented in this paper. Therefore, since in the example case it is clear that choosing country K for internationalization will improve the risk position and will not harm the other strategic elements, it is recommended that the firm extend the core business (or an activity closely related to it) into country K.

Note that country K is not the "best" of the three countries from the perspective of opportunities. Country M is clearly the better choice from this point of view, but it also has the highest risk. If the Resilience position of the example firm had been strong, perhaps country M would have been the choice to exploit the highly attractive investment climate and good operating profitability.[9] This shows that the methodology presented is able to discriminate

Table 4. Geographic Specification

	K	L	M
Economic circumstances	Good	Medium	Good
Environmental change	No appreciable	Small favorable	Small favorable
Investment climate	Similarly attractive	Similarly attractive	Highly attractive
Inflation impact	Low favorable	No appreciable	No appreciable
Geographic risk	Low	Low	High
Cash-flow transferability	No problems	Relatively lower	No problems
Geographic cash-flow variability	Average	Average	More than average
Geographic cash-flow growth rate	Moderate	Good	Good
Geographic market growth rate	Moderate	Good	Good
Accessibility for cash-flow anticipation geographically	Good	Average	Average
Operating profitability/operating risk geographically	Moderate/low	Good/moderate	Good/high
Capital requirements	Medium	Medium	High

between alternatives when the situation is evaluated in its proper environmental context.[10]

CONCLUSIONS

When the issue of internationalization is mentioned, one often focuses attention on the increase in opportunities available with such policies. Another usual notion is that moving into new geographic areas will expose the firm to greater risk. The previous discussion has shown that these conceptions are at least in part based on unjustified generalizations.

If the current strategic posture of the firm is used as the basis on which future actions will be predicated, and if reasons for taking these actions are derived from a typological assessment of the strengths and weaknesses in the departure situation, more appropriate guidance is possible. In the example, the applicable typification specifically included various facets from the perspective of risk. It was shown that the internationalization actions resulting from this comprehensive analysis actually permitted the firm to reduce its overall risk. Thus it was able to improve its strategic posture.

Note that this occurred partially because the "what" problem—which activity to expand internationally—was also addressed by referring to the departure situation. Selection of other, more risky activities than the core business would not have resulted in a reduction of the firm's risk—indeed, risk may have increased. But, resolving both questions—what and where—according to the strategic requirements of the departure situation results in a balanced set of recommendations.

Thus the procedures derived in this paper have been shown to be widely applicable and valid. In the final analysis, the previous illustrations of strategic relevance of "quite divergent country selections for different problem situations" confirm the discriminating power of the methodology developed.

GLOSSARY

1. Accessibility for Cash-Flow Anticipation (Geographically). This refers to the degree to which management has confidence in its ability to forecast accurately the expected future cash flow(s) anticipated to originate from the project(s) in the geographic area under analysis.

Reference point: management's perception of the accessibility for cash-flow anticipation of what they believe to be a "normal" or reasonably representative current project in the geographic area under consideration, as regards the associated reliability from the business sector(s) in analogous geographic areas in which the company or its reference firm is active

Classification: very reliable anticipatory; good anticipatory; reasonable anticipatory; poor anticipatory; very poor anticipatory

2. Cash-Flow Transferability of Generated Profits. Cash-flow transferability of generated profits from the firm's projects within a geographic area under study refers to the extent to which the host governments place restrictions on the movement of generated profits to other elements of the firm outside the host country.

Reference point: the median country of all countries in which the company or its reference firm is active arrayed according to management's perception of the transferability of generated profits

Classification: very high; relatively higher; similar; relatively lower; very low

3. Economic Circumstances (General) Geographically. General economic circumstances refers to the assessment by management of the overall economic climate in the geographic area under study.

Reference point: the economic climate in the median country, arrayed by management's perception of the attractiveness of general economic circumstances, from the point of view of the company's home base, of all countries in which the company or its reference firm is active

Classification: highly favorable; favorable; similar; unfavorable; highly unfavorable

4. Environmental Change regarding Project's Return. Environmental change regarding project's return is concerned with the assessment by management of the impact of environmental change on the profitability of the project(s) under study. In this respect, the expected change in the project's return from the main geographic area of the core SBU and the main geographic areas of the noncore activities deserve special consideration.

Reference point: no specific reference point for this relationship since it simply represents a relative categorization of characteristics according to management's perception of the impact of environmental change on the project's return on investment

Classification: substantial favorable change; small favorable change; no appreciable change; small unfavorable change; substantial unfavorable change

5. *Growth Rate of Cash Flow (Geographically)*. The geographic cash-flow growth rate refers to the annual compound rate of increase in net cash flow available to the firm from the intended geographic area for the project(s) under study.

> *Reference point:* the median cash-flow growth rate from an array generated by management's perception of the cash-flow growth rates for all industrial sectors in analogous geographic areas in which the company or the reference firm is active
>
> *Classification:* very high; relatively higher; similar; relatively lower; very low

6. *Growth Rate of the Market (Geographically)*. This growth rate refers to the annual compound rate of increase in total demand for the products or services in the intended geographic area supplied by the project(s) under study.

> *Reference point:* the median market growth rate from an array generated by management's perception of the market growth rate for all industrial sectors in analogous geographic areas served by the company or its reference firm
>
> *Classification:* very high; relatively higher; similar; relatively lower; very low

7. *Inflation Sensitivity of Project's Business Cost*. Inflation sensitivity of business cost refers to management's assessment of the speed and relative magnitude of changes in business costs of the relevant project(s) in response to a change in the rate of inflation in the geographic area under study.

> *Reference point:* the inflation sensitivity of business costs of the median of all activities in analogous areas in which the company or its reference firm is active, ranked by management's perception of the inflation sensitivity of project's business costs
>
> *Classification:* very low; relatively lower; similar; relatively higher; very high

8. *Inflation Sensitivity of Project's Revenue*. Inflation sensitivity of project's revenue refers to the assessment by management of the speed and relative magnitude of changes in the revenue of the project(s) in question in response to a change in the rate of inflation in the geographic area under analysis.

> *Reference point:* the inflation sensitivity of the revenue of the median of all activities in analogous areas in which the company or its reference firm is active, ranked by management's perception of the inflation sensitivity of the project's revenue
>
> *Classification:* very high; relatively higher; similar; relatively lower; very low

9. Investment Climate for Project(s) by Geographic Area. The project's investment climate in the geographic area in question is a judgmental feature that converts into an ordinal ranking by management's evaluation of the attitude toward business in general and the specific project in particular in the geographic area under consideration.

> *Reference point:* the assessment of the attractiveness of the investment climate in the median country of all countries in which the company or its reference firm is active arrayed with respect to management's perception of the investment climate from the point of view of the company's home base
>
> *Classification:* highly attractive; more attractive; similarly attractive; less attractive; substantially less attractive

10. Profitability Index (Operating) by Project(s) Geographically. The operation profitability index for project(s) in the geographic area under analysis is an approximate after-tax but before-interest concept calculated as the present value of the project's net cash inflows (adjusted for any economic interdependencies with the firm's current activities) divided by the present value of the project's net cash outflows, where the cash flows are geographically determined.

The classification "similar" is applicable when the ratio for the project(s) in the area in question is within ±10 percent of the reference ratio of the firm.

> *Reference point:* the operating profitability index of the firm's current activities in analogous geographic areas
>
> *Classification:* very high; higher; similar; lower; very low

11. Risk (Geographically) of the Project's Cash Flow. Risk (geographically) regarding the project's cash flow refers to the unfavorable consequences of the uncertainty that is associated with both project-specific and geographic area-specific considerations; it is defined as management's perception, for the project(s) under study, of the total risk (political, economic, sociological, etc., if feasible, taking into account interdependencies between the project[s] under review and the firm's current activities) as far as it affects that project's business within the geographic area in question.

> *Reference point:* the risk of the relevant project(s) associated with the median of the geographic areas in which the company or its reference firm is active, arrayed by management's perception of the total (political, economical, sociological, etc.) risk of engaging in business activity in those geographic areas
>
> *Classification:* very low; relatively lower; similar; relatively higher; very high

12. Risk (Operating) of Project(s) Geographically. Operating risk refers to management's perception of the unfavorable consequences of the uncertainty that is associated with operating attributes of the project(s) under study, taking interdependencies into account as far as they relate the project(s) under study to the firm's current activities, but it is considered in a geographic context; thus, it is associated with project(s) in the geographic area under analysis.

> *Reference point:* management's perception of that activity of the firm in analogous geographic areas which is associated with average or normal operating risk
> *Classification:* very low; relatively lower; similar; relatively higher; very high

13. Variability of Cash Flow of Project(s) Geographically. Variability of cash flow of project(s) refers to the extent to which the net cash flow of the project(s) in question tends to fluctuate from year to year and is measured by the coefficient of variation of the net cash flow of the project(s) in the geographic area under review.

> *Reference point:* the coefficient of variation of the monthly net cash flow of the project(s) in the area in question, calculated over a four-year period one year removed from the present. The valid comparison is the relevant coefficient of variation of the monthly cash flow of the project(s) in the area in question for the most recent year versus the same number computed from past data.
> *Classification:* very low; relatively lower; similar; relatively higher; very high

NOTES

1. Preplanning was introduced in [4]. Further development and extension appeared in [6] and [8].

2. For more information on strategic management, see [1].

3. The concept of the reference firm was developed in [5].

4. For more on PARE, see [5] and [7].

5. The valuation models are expounded by [12] and [11]. A concise summary of the contrasting positions appears in [10]. An extended discussion of the implications of the valuation theories in the PARE context is given in [6] and [8].

6. The strategic element labeled corporate risk, as distinguished from capital market or beta risk, is defined for the purpose on hand as management's perception of the variability of the company's cash flow relative to that of the reference firm. This approach to total risk departs from the pragmatic insight that risk, *in terms of the variables over which management has control to promote good performance of the company,* can meaningfully be assessed through this comparison anchored to a capital market-validated benchmark or reference firm. In this respect, measurement or estimation problems regarding covariance issues play only a minor role since mostly it can be reasonably assumed that the correlation

between the cash flow for the company in question and "the market" is roughly similar as between the reference firm and "the market": The relative comparison in corporate perspective simplifies then to one of variability perception alone.

For the present purpose, notwithstanding the significance of CAPM for financial decisions in other problem situations, beta as a risk measure for corporate project set preplanning is of little utility for two reasons. First, it is primarily intended for other purposes and is not defined in terms of the variables over which management has control to promote good performance of the firm. Second, the shareholders are not the only group to whom the firm has a moral obligation.

Corporate risk, as distinguished from capital market or beta risk, is important to the other groups, and a reflection upon it from the perspective of the significant stakeholder groups should also enter the project set selection process. If ignored, corporate risk can result in psychological and sociological aberrations that in the aggregation can have adverse capital market impacts. Systematic risk of the CAPM focuses attention on market reaction to managerial actions, while what is needed from the manager's standpoint is concentration on the actions themselves. This requirement can be fulfilled more satisfactorily through an analysis of the movement of project cash flow with that of the other activities under review. In making resource allocation decisions, it is necessary to focus attention at the microfirm level on managerial actions and their implications mainly in the capital and product markets, as well as within the organization and the societal environment.

7. The expanded PARE chart and analysis was developed in [7].

8. For more information on geographic specifications, see [2, 7, 9].

9. For more information on internationalization to boost opportunities, see [7, Chapter 8].

10. It was clear from the data given in the examples that a single country was preferred over the other alternatives. At times, however, because of either a greater number of factors to be considered or many more alternatives, or both, the choice will not be so obvious. In this case, a more formal method of mathematical programming deserves consideration as an aid for determining efficient solutions. Multiple Objective Discrete programming, or MOD programming, is particularly well suited for this application. For more information on MOD programming, see [3].

REFERENCES

[1] Ansoff, H. Igor; Declerck, Roger P.; and Hayes, Robert L., eds. *From Strategic Planning to Strategic Management.* London: John Wiley & Sons, 1976.

[2] Ansoff, H. Igor, and Leontiades, James C. "Strategic Portfolio Management," *Journal of General Management* 4, No. 1 (1976), pp. 13–29.

[3] Crum, Roy L., and Derkinderen, Frans G.J. "Multicriteria Approaches to Decision Modeling," in Roy L. Crum and Frans G.J. Derkinderen, eds., *Capital Budgeting under Conditions of Uncertainty.* Boston: Martinus Nijhoff Publishing, 1981.

[4] Derkinderen, F.G.J. "Financially-Oriented Categories of SBUs for Enhancing Strategic Analysis," Nijenrode Report 73-2, The Netherlands School of Business, 1973.

[5]   Derkinderen, Frans G.J. "Pre-Investment Planning," *Long Range Planning* 10 (February 1977), pp. 1–8.

[6]   Derkinderen, Frans G.J., and Crum, Roy L. "Strategic Management of the Financial Resource Allocation Process," eighth annual meeting of the Financial Management Association, Minneapolis, Minnesota, October 1978.

[7]   Derkinderen, Frans G.J., and Crum, Roy L. *Project Set Strategies.* Boston: Martinus Nijhoff Publishing, 1979.

[8]   Derkinderen, Frans G.J., and Crum, Roy L. "Capital Budgeting as an Open System Process," in Frans G.J. Derkinderen and Roy L. Crum, eds., *Readings in Strategies for Corporate Investment.* Boston: Pitman Publishing, 1981.

[9]   Derkinderen, F.G.J., and Hoof, A.J.C.M. van. "International Expansion of Business Activities: Typological Aid for Decision Preparation," Nijenrode Paper 78–7, The Netherlands School of Business, 1978.

[10] Durand, David. "Cost of Debt and Equity Funds for Business: Trends and Problems of Measurement," Conference on Research on Business Finance, National Bureau of Economic Research, New York, 1952, pp. 215–247.

[11] Gordon, M.J. "Optimal Investment and Financial Policy," *Journal of Finance* 18, No. 2 (May 1963), pp. 264–272.

[12] Modigliani, Franco, and Miller, Merton H. "The Cost of Capital, Corporate Finance, and the Theory of Investment," *American Economic Review* 48 (June 1958), pp. 261–297.

II ESTIMATING THE COST OF CAPITAL

5 ESTIMATING THE MARKET RISK PREMIUM

Eugene F. Brigham and Dilip K. Shome
University of Florida

One of the basic approaches to estimating the cost of common equity capital is the risk premium method, sometimes called the yield spread method. Analysts recognize that because investors are risk averters, the required rate of return increases as the riskiness of financial assets increases. Therefore, if investors have the opportunity to buy default-free U.S. Treasury bonds with a yield of 8 1/2 percent, they would require higher rates of return on corporate bonds and still higher returns on common stocks.[1] The question is: How much higher? If we knew the answer to that question, we could, at any given time, determine the cost of common equity simply by adding the risk premium to the current yield on Treasury bonds.

The basic idea behind the risk premium approach is indicated in Figure 1. The horizontal axis reflects risk—the further to the right a particular security lies, the greater its investment risk. Since U.S. Treasury bonds are free of default risk, they are shown at the origin. The vertical axis gives required rates of return, while the lines labeled SML_{1964} and SML_{1978} are "security market lines," which show, at two points in time, the assumed relationship between a security's risk and its required rate of return.

79

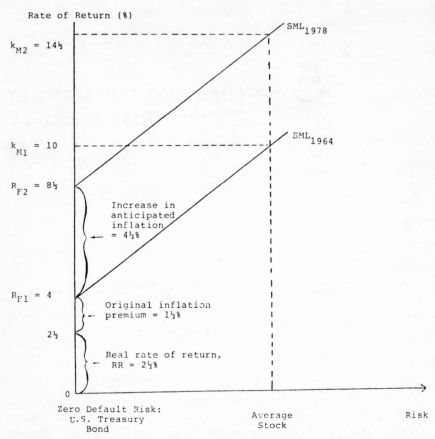

Figure 1. Relationship between Inflation, Risk, and Required Rates of Return

The term R_F designates the risk-free rate, or the rate of interest on U.S. Treasury bonds. It consists of a "real rate," or inflation-free rate (RR), which is assumed in Figure 1 to be 2 1/2 percent, plus a premium for expected inflation:

$$R_F = RR + \text{inflation premium}$$

$$= 2\ 1/2\ \% + \text{expected rate of inflation.}$$

In the early 1960s, the annual rate of inflation was about 1 1/2 percent, so the riskless rate, R_{F1} in Figure 1, was about 4 percent. In 1978, the expected long-term inflation rate was about 6 percent, which resulted in an 8 1/2 percent rate on long-term governments.

Corporate bonds are riskier than U.S. government bonds, and so their yields are higher. Recently, AAA bonds have yielded about half a percentage point more than governments, and the risk premiums rise for lower-rated corporate bonds. (See the appendix.) Therefore, if corporate bonds were shown in Figure 1, their risks would lie between the zero risk of U.S. Treasury bonds and the risks inherent in common stocks. Common stocks in general are, of course, much riskier than bonds; therefore, their risk premiums are also much higher. In the graph, we assume that the risk premium on an average share of common stock is 6 percent. Therefore, when the yield on government bonds is about 4 percent, as it was in 1965, the required rate of return on an average share of common stock would be about 10 percent. In 1978, when inflation had pushed the riskless rate up to 8 1/2 percent, the required rate of return on an average share of stock would have been 14 1/2 percent.

Although the concept of risk premiums is widely accepted, there is no consensus regarding how to measure either these premiums or their general level. The 6 percent figure assumed above is often cited in utility rate cases, textbooks, and the like, but generally without much support.

The primary purpose of this study is to investigate the risk premium on an average share of common stock. Secondary considerations in the study include the following: (1) To what extent does the risk premium on common stock vary over time? (2) How do risk premiums vary among common stocks? (3) What factors cause risk premium variations among stocks?

THE RISKLESS RATE

One question that arises immediately in a study of risk premiums is the best choice for the riskless rate. The principal alternatives are (1) the rate on short-term U.S. Treasury securities (Treasury bills) and (2) the rate on long-term Treasury bonds. Both types of securities are free of default risk, but neither is completely riskless because both are exposed to *interest-rate risk* (the risk of a decline in the value of the outstanding bonds as a result of an increase in interest rates) and to *purchasing-power risk* (the risk of a decline in the real value of interest and principal due to an increase in inflation). Long-term bonds are more exposed to both interest-rate and purchasing-power risk than are Treasury bills and other short-term government debt. Therefore, bills are closer to being truly riskless than are bonds, and for this reason a number of people have argued that risk premiums on common stocks should be based on bills rather than on Treasury bonds.[2]

However, there is a fundamental problem with basing common stock risk premiums on short-term Treasury bills—namely, the fact that bill rates are subject to short-term phenomena that do not affect long-term rates, or at least affect long-term rates differently. First, consider inflation. Nominal security returns are equal to a pure rate of return (RR), plus a premium for expected inflation (IP), plus a risk premium (RP), plus an error term (e) that reflects random market factors that cause temporary disequilibrium:

$$\text{Nominal expected return} = RR + IP + RP + e. \tag{1}$$

There is no reason to think that RR will be different for Treasury bonds or bills, but there is a very good reason to think that IP, RP, and e will be different for bonds versus bills. First, IP reflects expected inflation *over the life of the security*. Therefore, a thirty-day Treasury bill reflects expected inflation during the next thirty days, while a thirty-year bond reflects the average rate of expected inflation over the next thirty years. These two rates could certainly differ, and this fact is, indeed, one reason why short-term rates are so much more volatile than long-term rates. Second, the risk premium, RP, could differ between bills and bonds: Bonds should, because of their much greater exposure to interest-rate and purchasing-power risk, have a larger risk premium. Finally, consider the error term. Random movements in interest rates are caused by such factors as the current level of corporate liquidity, Federal Reserve monetary policy, U.S. Treasury surpluses or deficits, and the activity of foreign and domestic currency dealers and speculators. These random movements are probably larger (in either a positive or a negative direction) for bills than for bonds because bills are the securities that the Treasury, the Federal Reserve, corporate treasurers, and currency dealers and speculators all use in their normal operations. The larger error term for bills also helps explain why bill rates are so much more volatile than bond rates.

Now consider the implications of all this for the choice of short-term or long-term government debt instruments as the basing point in our study of common stock risk premiums. We are seeking a risk premium that can be added to the current observed and quoted market rate on debt securities, which we can then use to obtain an estimate of the current cost of equity capital. Both bonds and common stocks are long-term securities, and so their returns should reflect long-term inflation. Further, neither type of security is used as an instrument of monetary policy, or by currency speculators, or as a buffer for temporary changes in corporate liquidity, or by international currency speculators. Treasury bills are, of course, used for all these purposes. Therefore it is far more logical to think that the cost of common equity is correlated with interest rates on long-term bonds rather than with those on bills, and for this reason we based our common stock risk premiums on long-term bonds rather than on short-term bills.

The Government Bond Rate

There are a number of different issues of long-term Treasury securities, and they sell at different premiums or discounts depending on their coupon interest rates.

Table 1. Long-Term Treasury Bond Yields

	As Reported in the FRB during the Year in Question	As Taken from the Treasury Constant Maturity Series	Difference
1973	6.30%	7.12%	0.82%
1974	6.99	8.05	1.06
1975	6.98	8.19	1.21
		Average	1.03%

Further, certain deep discount, or "flower," bonds sell on a lower-yield basis because they may be surrendered at par value to pay estate taxes. (These bonds are called "flower bonds" because they are associated with funerals.) In other words, a $1000 par value, 3 percent coupon, twenty-year bond would have a theoretical value of $505 if the going rate of interest on twenty-year government bonds were 8 percent, but to a wealthy individual with terminal cancer and a one-month expected life, the bonds would be worth approximately $1000 because they could be used to pay $1000 of estate taxes. Therefore these bonds sell at high prices, and their yields are far below the yields on new bonds that sell at close to their par value.

Because of the flower bond phenomenon, indices of U.S. Treasury bond yields may be distorted, and so one must exercise care in selecting the best index. Our choice was the U.S. Treasury "Constant Maturity Series," which gives relatively little weight to flower bonds.[3] This particular series has been published in the *Federal Reserve Bulletin* since 1977; earlier editions of the *FRB* used a series that was heavily weighted with flower bonds. To get some idea of the effects of including flower bonds, consider the set of data for the period 1973-1975 shown in Table 1. Using the yield data as reported in the *Federal Reserve Bulletin* would have resulted in an overstatement of the risk premium of approximately one full percentage point.

ALTERNATIVE METHODS OF ESTIMATING RISK PREMIUMS

Three basic procedures can be used to estimate risk premiums: (1) historical studies of the returns actually earned on stocks and bonds, (2) surveys of institutional portfolio managers, and (3) premiums obtained by subtracting the yield on Treasury bonds from the average expected rate of return on a group of "representative" common stocks. These three methods are discussed in the following sections.

HISTORICAL RETURN PATTERNS

There have been a number of historical studies of the actual rates of return one would have earned on stock and bond portfolios over various past holding periods. In these studies, researchers assume that a portfolio of stocks is formed, held for a period of time, and then liquidated. Similarly, a bond portfolio is formed, and its historical rate of return is estimated. The difference between returns on the stock and bond portfolios is then determined, and the difference is the *historical risk premium.*

There are a number of problems with historical risk premiums; some of them are listed and discussed briefly below.

Methods of Calculating Returns

There are many alternative ways to calculate past realized rates of return. First, what stocks should be included in the stock portfolio, and what bonds in the bond portfolio? Should each security be given equal weight, or should larger companies be given greater weight? If market value (or total capitalization, as it is called) is to be used to weight securities, should the weights be set on the basis of beginning values or ending values, or should the portfolio be adjusted over time so as to maintain a constant weighting system? How should taxes on interest, dividends, and capital gains be handled? Should we assume that dividends (either before-tax or after-tax) are reinvested in or are withdrawn from the portfolio? What assumption should be made about brokerage commissions if dividends are assumed to be reinvested or if the portfolio is periodically balanced so as to maintain constant weights? If the holding period is more than one year, should the rate of return for the entire period be stated as an arithmetic average of the annual rates of return, as the geometric average return, or as the "internal rate of return?"

Substantial differences in reported rates of return on both the stock and bond portfolios can result from the choice of calculating procedures; thus the choices made here can exert a substantial influence on the reported risk premiums.[4]

Holding Period Used

The particular holding period used can make a huge difference in the final outcome. If short holding periods are used, returns will be highly volatile, but

even assuming holding periods of twenty years or more, realized rates of return—
and consequently risk premiums—can vary by as much as 15 percentage points.
Even with holding periods in the twenty-five- to fifty-year range, and ending
in 1976, the calculated rate of return on common stocks (before personal taxes)
ranged from 8.1 percent to 13.4 percent. Returns on long-term U.S. government bonds ranged from 2.9 percent to 3.5 percent (capital losses on bonds
held down their realized returns) over the same period, and so the risk premium
on an average stock as determined by historic data could range from 4.6 percent
to 10.5 percent with 1976 as the ending year.[5] If shorter periods were used,
wider ranges of risk premiums could be obtained. Also, choosing as an ending
point a year when the stock market closed very strong (such as 1968) or very
weak (such as 1974) would have a tremendous effect on the calculated risk
premiums.

Conceptual Weakness

In addition to these data problems, there is also a conceptual weakness in the
use of past data to estimate risk premiums. The risk premium built into the cost
of common equity at any point in time reflects the differences between expected future returns on stocks and expected future returns on bonds. *Ex ante,*
or expected, returns may, on rare occasions, equal the actual *ex post* returns that
were realized in some past period, but this would be the exception, not the rule.
For example, the consensus view of investors may be that if they buy a portfolio
of common stocks on January 1, 1979, and hold them until December 31, 1984,
they will earn a before-tax rate of return (dividends plus capital gains) of 14
percent. This is the *ex ante* expected return. However, on December 31, 1984,
if one looks back and determines the actual *ex post* realized rate of return from
January 1, 1979, to December 31, 1984, it will almost certainly be higher or
lower than the 14 percent expected return. The actual realized return might
even be less than the realized return on bonds. If so, this would indicate a *negative* risk premium, which is nonsense.

The argument is sometimes made that investors, over long holding periods, do
actually earn returns that are equal to their required returns. Supposedly,
"investor rationality" brings about this equality. In other words, if investors are
disappointed by low returns over some period, then security prices will decline
to the point where returns in subsequent periods will pull the average realized
return back up to the expected level. We find this argument unappealing.

Another argument for thinking that past returns equal expected returns
goes as follows: (1) Businesses, when making real asset investments (capital
budgeting), have a good idea of investors' expected and required returns and
use this knowledge when setting project hurdle rates. (2) Assuming a reasonable

degree of proficiency in the capital budgeting process, then *ex post* realized returns will turn out to be fairly close to *ex ante* expected returns. Notice, however, that this proposition assumes that corporations already know with a fair degree of precision what many people find very hard to measure—the cost of equity capital. This is a tenuous assumption at best.

Because of these problems, risk premiums based on historic returns data are highly questionable. At best, historic risk premiums can be used as a guide in the development of usable risk premiums. However, for purposes of estimating the cost of capital, it seems more logical to base risk premiums on forward-looking, rather than backward-looking, data.

SURVEYS OF PORTFOLIO MANAGERS

A second approach to the development of risk premiums is to survey institutional portfolio managers. To see how this approach operates, one must understand how the portfolio managers of large institutional investors generally operate when they decide to invest or not to invest in a given stock:

1. A DCF rate of return (dividend yield plus capital gains yield) is estimated for each stock under consideration. This gives an expected rate of return for each stock. To illustrate, a bank trust department portfolio manager might obtain from the bank's security analysts a projection that American Telephone's dividends, which were $4.60 during 1978, will grow at a rate in the range of 5 to 6 percent per year for the next five years and that the price of the stock will also grow at this same rate. If the stock is purchased at a price of $60 per share, held for five years, and then sold, it will have provided an annual market value rate of return in the range of 13.0 to 14.1 percent.

2. Obviously, common stocks are not riskless. For example, AT&T's stock price declined from a high of about $75 in the mid-1960s to about $39 in 1974. Because different stocks are regarded as facing different amounts of risk exposure, institutional investors find it useful to group each stock into one of several "risk classes." Five risk classes are often used. Group 1 might be composed of the 20 percent of the stocks judged least risky, group 2 would consist of the next least risky stocks, and so on. (These risk groupings are based partly on quantitative data, but the actual placements are largely judgmental.)

3. The next step is to establish a required rate of return for each stock. This could be done by adding a premium to the U.S. Treasury bond rate or to a corporate bond rate such as the AA rate. For the S&P 400 stocks, these premiums are typically established at rates close to those shown in

Table 2. Equity Risk Premiums

Stock Risk Group	Risk Premiums	
	Over U.S. Treasury Bonds	Over AA Corporate Bonds
1. Lowest risk	4.5–5.0%	3.5–4.0%
2. Second lowest risk	5.0–5.5	4.0–4.5
3. Average	5.5–6.0	4.5–5.0
4. Second highest risk	6.0–6.5	5.0–5.5
5. Highest risk	6.5–9.0	5.5–8.0

Table 2. These premiums are based partly on what investors think is reasonable, given their perceptions of current conditions and their aversion to risk, and this, in turn, is influenced by historic risk/return relationships.
4. The expected and required returns are next compared. If expected returns on stocks exceed required returns, investors tend to buy equities rather ⁓than debt, and vice versa. Any company or industry whose expected return exceeds its required return by a relatively large amount is favored, and conversely. When the consensus view of investors is that the expected returns of most stocks are above or below their required returns, the collective actions of investors will cause stock prices to rise or to fall. Such price changes, in turn, will restore equilibrium to the market, with expected returns equal to required returns.

A study was recently conducted by Charles Benore of Paine Webber Mitchell Hutchins, a leading institutional-oriented investment banking concern, in an attempt to quantify the ideas in the preceding paragraphs [1]. A summary of Benore's study is given in Table 3. Of the portfolio managers surveyed, 89 percent assigned a risk premium of from 4 to 6 percentage points, with an average of 4.91 percentage points, to utility stocks over AA bonds. Since AA bonds typically yield about one percentage point more than long-term government bonds (see appendix), this suggests a premium over governments of about 6 percentage points. Of course, the Mitchell Hutchins study is restricted to electric utilities, but it is suggestive of the risk premiums for stocks in general.

GORDON MODEL (DCF) RISK PREMIUMS

This survey approach is conceptually superior to the historical return approach in that it attempts to estimate risk premiums based on *expected* returns rather

Table 3. Survey of Portfolio Managers

I. Question put to portfolio managers:

Assuming that an AA, long-term utility bond currently yields about 8½ percent, the utility common stock for the same company would be attractive to you relative to the bond if its expected total return was at least:

Total Return	Indicated Risk Premium (basis points)
over 18%	over 900
17–18	900
16–17	800
15–16	700
14–15	600
13–14	500
12–13	400
11–12	300
10–11	200
under 10	under 200

II. Distribution of responses:

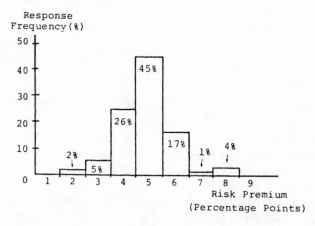

Weighted average (expected value) risk premium: 4.91 percent.

Source: Benore [1].

than *realized* returns. However, survey data may be biased or otherwise unreliable. Therefore, as an alternative to asking investors for the risk premiums they use, we have reversed the process and inferred from the stock prices and bond yields that exist in the market the risk premiums that apparently exist.

We know that the financial markets are dominated by the large institutional investors—they own one-third of the outstanding common stock, and they are responsible for between 70 and 75 percent of the volume of trading on the major stock exchanges. The institutions also effectively control the prices of most publicly traded stocks—such stocks tend to sell, in essence, at whatever price the institutional investors as a group feel they are worth.

Different institutions use different data bases and methodologies for valuing stocks, and each analyst tries to do something unique to get an edge on the other 50,000 or so professional analysts who are seeking to forecast stock prices and to pick the best buys from among the thousands of available stocks. Discussions with analysts and portfolio managers, a review of investments textbooks and of such professional journals as the *Institutional Investor* and the *Analysts' Journal,* and a study of materials prepared by the Financial Analysts' Federation and the Institute of Chartered Financial Analysts suggest that we can form a reasonably accurate estimate of the consensus expected rate of return by use of the standard constant growth Gordon model:

$$k = D_1/P_0 + g.$$

Here k is the expected rate of return, D_1 represents the dividends expected during the next twelve months, P_0 is the current price of the stock, and g is the long-run expected growth rate in dividends.

If we develop an expected return, k, for the market index and then subtract from this return the yield on a risk-free security, we will have estimated a forward-looking expected risk premium for the market. Under conditions of market equilibrium, this expected risk premium would also equal the required premium. Thus

$$RP_M = [(D_1/P_0)_M + g_M] - R_F.$$

The accuracy of this method depends on the proper measurement of the riskless rate and on the validity of the application of the constant growth Gordon model to the market index.

Measurement of Expected Return on Market Index

As applied to a market portfolio, the DCF equation is of this form:

$$k_M = E(R)_M = (\text{dividend yield})_M + (\text{growth rate in dividends})_M,$$

where

$$(\text{dividend yield})_M = \frac{\text{total dividends expected to be paid on all stocks in next period}}{\text{total current market value of all stocks}},$$

$$(\text{growth rate in dividends})_M = \text{constant long-term rate at which dividends are expected to grow.}$$

There are problems with this procedure, including the following:

1. The model applies only to companies whose future growth rates are expected to be relatively constant. This means that it is most applicable to the larger, more mature companies, while it is not applicable at all (without a major reformulation) to smaller, rapidly developing companies.
2. Major difficulties may be encountered in estimating the expected long-run dividend growth rate. Indeed, this is by far the most difficult aspect of the project.

Even though problems exist, they are not insurmountable, and security analysts must deal with them on a daily basis. Also, it may be reasonable to assume that errors associated with estimates of individual companies will, to a large extent, cancel one another out when we average across all companies to develop the risk premium on the market portfolio.[6]

The S&P 400 and Other Large Companies

Our solution to the first problem—the fact that the constant growth model is not applicable to smaller companies—can be handled by restricting our analysis to larger, more mature companies, such as those included in the S&P 400 Industrial Index. Most of these companies have been in business for many years, they are well-established in their lines of business, and their sales and profits tend to move with the level of general economic activity. Certainly, none of the companies is expected to grow at an identical rate from year to year, but, for most of them, the expected long-run future growth rate is constant in the sense that the best estimate of the growth rate g for, say, 1985 is identical to the best estimate for 1986.

Of course, limiting our analysis to larger companies means that we cannot draw from the study any inferences about risk premiums and the cost of capital for smaller companies. On the other hand, limiting the analysis does permit us to make better estimates of these values for larger firms.

Estimating Growth Rates

The most difficult problem in implementing the DCF model is to obtain a good estimate of the expected future growth rate. If a company has experienced a relatively steady, stable growth in earnings and dividends, and if this past rate of growth is expected to continue into the future, then past growth rates might afford some basis for projecting future growth. However, because of inflation and other factors, the steady growth situation has not held for most companies in recent years.

Since simply projecting past trends is not generally a satisfactory procedure, analysts have developed other methods for making growth forecasts. One well-recognized and widely used procedure for forecasting long-term future growth rates (g) involves multiplying the fraction of a company's earnings that investors expect it to retain (b) by the expected rate of return on book equity (ROE):

$$g = b \times \text{ROE}.$$

This procedure produces exactly correct estimates of future growth if, and only if, the following conditions hold:

1. The percentage of earnings retained can be measured accurately and is constant over time.
2. The company sells no new common stock or sells it at book value.
3. The expected future rate of return on book equity can be measured accurately and is constant over time.

If these three conditions are expected to hold true into the indefinite future, then a precise estimate of the future growth rate can be obtained with the equation. If these conditions are not met exactly, then the equation will not produce an exactly accurate growth estimate. Since the three conditions have not held exactly in the past and will not hold exactly in the future, the formula has limitations. However, the formula does give a reasonably accurate estimate of long-term growth, and it is, in any event, more accurate than an estimate based only on past data.

To estimate g_M, the expected market growth rate, we need estimates of b_M and ROE_M. Most companies have target payout ratios that are reasonably stable over time; so their target retention rates (b) are also reasonably stable.

Earnings vary from year to year, and so the actual (as opposed to the target) payout and retention rates will vary, but these variations will be around the target values. Therefore, to estimate the target retention rate (which is the value we need for the growth rate formula), we may take an average of retention rates in the recent past. The period used to develop the average should be long enough to cover both peaks and troughs of business cycles, but not so long as to include data that are "ancient history" and that no longer reflect the firm's operating conditions.

There is no one correct method for developing expected future growth rates from past data. Different investors surely process and interpret existing data differently and thus reach different conclusions as to the best estimate of a firm's future growth.[7] Therefore, depending on our assumptions as to how most investors derive growth estimates, we can obtain different projected growth rates and hence different estimates of expected market returns and risk premiums. An econometric framework would be useful to help determine whether one growth estimation procedure was superior to another. However, econometric problems are simply overwhelming with a sample as heterogeneous as the S&P Industrials. Therefore, in our study we examined two alternative methods for estimating growth rates:

1. Method 1: Weighted Average Data. Investors may give more weight to more recent data than to earlier data. On this assumption, we estimated the value in year t of the expected retention rate for year $t + 1$ and future years as

$$(b_M)_{t+1} = 0.4(b_M)_t + 0.3(b_M)_{t-1} + 0.2(b_M)_{t-2} + 0.1(b_M)_{t-3},$$

where

$$(b_M)_t = 1.0 - \frac{\text{all common dividends paid by all S\&P 400 firms in year } t}{\text{total earnings available to common stockholders in year } t}$$

$$= 1.0 - \frac{(DIV_M)_t}{(\text{earnings}_M)_t}.$$

The expected rate of return on common equity (ROE) was calculated similarly:

$$(ROE_M)_{t+1} = 0.4(ROE_M)_t + 0.3(ROE_M)_{t-1} + 0.2(ROE_M)_{t-2} + 0.1(ROE_M)_{t-3},$$

where $(ROE_M)_t$ is the market value weighted average return on book equity,[8]

$$(\text{ROE}_M)_t = \left[\sum_{i=1}^{400} (\text{MVF}_i)\,(\text{ROE}_i) \right]_t$$

Here MVF_i is the market value fraction of each company i, (market value firm i)/total market value. ROE_i is the return on average common equity.

Given these estimates of the market retention rate and the market ROE, we obtain an estimate of the expected future market growth rate as follows:

$$(g_M)_{t+1} = (b_M)_{t+1} \times (\text{ROE}_M)_{t+1}.$$

2. Method 2: Normalized Data. In our second growth-estimating procedure, we first assume that investors expect payout and retention rates, as a matter of corporate policy, either to be stable or to fluctuate around a target level. Accordingly, we calculated the expected retention rate for the market for year $t + 1$ as the ratio of total earnings retained to total earnings available over the preceding five years:

$$(b_M)_{t+1} = 1.0 - \frac{\substack{\text{total dividends paid by}\\ \text{all S\&P 400 firms during the last five years}}}{\substack{\text{total earnings for all S\&P 400 firms during}\\ \text{the last five years}}}.$$

Thus, at the end of 1977, we would estimate the expected retention rate for 1978 and thereafter as

$$(b_M)_{1978} = 1.0 - \frac{\substack{\text{total dividends paid by}\\ \text{S\&P 400 firms in years 1973–1977}}}{\substack{\text{total earnings for all S\&P 400}\\ \text{firms in years 1973–1977}}}.$$

Our estimate of the market ROE uses the notion that dividends are paid out of "normalized" earnings; hence dividends paid can be used to estimate normalized ROE. We go through these steps:

1. Determine the normalized rate of return on average book equity for each company:

$$\text{normalized ROE}_i = \frac{\text{expected earnings}}{\text{expected book value}}$$

$$= \frac{\text{expected dividends}}{\text{expected payout rate}} \times \frac{1}{\text{expected book value}}$$

$$= \frac{\text{current dividends } (1 + g)}{(\text{expected payout})\,(\text{current book value})\,(1 + g)}.$$

The $(1 + g)$ terms cancel, leaving

$$\text{expected ROE}_i = \frac{\text{current dividends}}{(1 - \text{expected retention rate})(\text{current book value})}.$$

The expected retention rate is again defined as the five-year simple average, and the estimation process assumes that in the long run, earnings, dividends, and book values are all expected to grow at the same rate.

2. Having determined the expected ROE for each company, we next aggregate to determine the value weighted ROE for the S&P 400 as

$$\text{VWROE} = \sum_{i=1}^{400} (\text{MVF}_i)(\text{ROE}_i).$$

The calculated value of VWROE_t is used as the estimated ROE_M for future years.

3. With b_M and ROE_M thus determined, we estimate the expected future market growth rate as follows:

$$(g_M)_{t+1} = (b_M)_{t+1} \times (\text{ROE}_M)_{t+1}.$$

Estimating Dividend Yields

Once we have estimated the expected growth rate, the next element needed to implement the constant growth Gordon model is the dividend yield on the market:

$$\begin{aligned}\text{expected market dividend yield}_{t+1} &= \frac{(\text{total dividend on S\&P400}_t)(1 + g_M)}{\text{total market value of S\&P 400}} \\ &= \frac{(D_M)_t (1 + g_M)_{t+1}}{\text{MV}_t}.\end{aligned}$$

In our own analysis, we found the market value of the S&P 400 based on December 31 closing prices. We considered using various types of average stock prices, but we ultimately concentrated on spot prices because they are conceptually better. Since the stock market is relatively efficient, especially for large companies such as those in the S&P 400, the year-end closing price should reflect all currently available information on that date, and any average price based on earlier data would probably be misleading in the sense that earlier prices would not reflect information and market conditions as of December 31. Of course, using a spot price does mean that this price can reflect some random movement away from the equilibrium price, but in an efficient market such random fluctuations are not likely to be large.[9]

The Market Risk Premium

Having determined the expected growth rate and dividend yield on the market, we can sum these two components to obtain the expected rate of return on the market:

$$(k_M)_{t+1} = \frac{(D_M)_t \, (1 + g_M)_{t+1}}{(MV)_t} + (g_M)_{t+1} .$$

Subtracting the yield to maturity on U.S. treasury bonds (R_F) from k_M produces an estimate of the risk premium that investors require on the market:

$$RP_M = k_M - R_F .$$

Here R_F is the December yield for the twenty-year Constant Maturity Series.

In effect, we have estimated market returns looking forward from December of a particular year. The bond yields used are returns that will be earned (with certainty) if the bonds are purchased and held to their twenty-year maturity. The difference between these two yields is an estimation of the risk premium on the market.

Table 4 shows the estimated market risk premium using method 1, the 4-3-2-1 weighting procedure, to estimate the growth rate, while Table 5 shows the premiums estimated using method 2. Figure 2 gives a plot of the annual risk premiums, together with the price/earnings ratio for the S&P 400 Index. The key points of interest in the tables and graph are these:

1. Risk premiums seem to vary from year to year. Some of this year-to-year variation probably reflects random errors in our estimating procedures, although some undoubtedly reflects changes in investors' outlooks and degrees of risk aversion.
2. Two clear trends in risk premiums are evident in the graph—risk premiums drifted downward rather steadily from the mid-1960s until 1974, but they have climbed sharply in recent years.
3. The risk premium and P/E graphs are almost mirror images of one another —strong stock markets with high P/E ratios are associated with and are caused in part by low risk premiums. Low risk premiums, in turn, are probably caused in part by a high degree of investor confidence and a general reduction in risk aversion, or a feeling that the riskiness of stocks relative to that of bonds has declined.

Table 4. Value Weighted Risk Premiums Using Aggregate Market Data (Growth Rate Measure $[g_1]_M$) Based on Four-Year Weighted Average Data)

Year	Dividend Yield $(Y)_M$	Growth Rate $(g_1)_M$	Expected DCF Return on Equity $(k = Y + g)_M$	Twenty-Year Government Bond Yield (R_f)	Risk Premium $(RP = k - R_f)_M$	Five-Year Moving Average (RP) av.
1963	3.74%	6.35%	10.09%	3.92%	6.17%	
1964	3.30	5.99	9.29	4.19	5.10	
1965	3.18	6.05	9.23	4.18	5.05	
1966	2.96	6.69	9.65	4.50	5.15	
1967	3.60	7.46	11.06	4.76	6.30	5.55%
1968	2.88	8.15	11.03	5.59	5.44	5.41
1969	2.85	8.66	11.51	5.88	5.63	5.51
1970	3.18	8.48	11.66	6.91	4.75	5.45
1971	3.16	8.00	11.16	6.28	4.88	5.40
1972	2.75	7.95	10.70	6.00	4.70	5.08
1973	2.39	7.78	10.17	5.96	4.21	4.83
1974	3.16	8.01	11.17	7.29	3.88	4.48
1975	5.02	9.40	14.42	7.91	6.51	4.84
1976	3.84	10.39	14.23	8.23	6.00	5.06
1977	3.73	11.08	14.81	7.30	7.51	5.62
1978	5.06	10.71	15.77	7.87	7.90	6.36
Average	3.42%	8.20%	11.62%	6.05%	5.57%	

Note: The values shown for each year are expected values for that year as of December 31 of the preceding year. Thus the 1978 figures show the projected dividend yield, growth rate, and DCF rate of return for 1978; the yield on U.S. Treasury bonds as of December 1977, which is the expected return for 1978 and thereafter; and the risk premium projected for 1978.

Table 5. Value Weighted Risk Premiums Using Aggregate Market Data (Growth Rate Measure $[g_2]_M$ Based on Five-Year Simple Average Data)

Year	Dividend Yield $(Y)_M$	Growth Rate $(g_2)_M$	Expected DCF Return on Equity $(k = Y + g)_M$	Twenty-Year Government Bond Yield (R_f)	Risk Premium $(RP = k - R_f)_M$	Five-Year Moving Average (RP) av.
1963	3.80%	6.46%	10.26%	3.92%	6.34%	
1964	3.37	6.77	10.14	4.19	5.95	
1965	3.25	6.92	10.17	4.18	5.99	
1966	3.02	7.37	10.39	4.50	5.89	
1967	3.68	7.82	11.50	4.76	6.74	6.18%
1968	2.94	7.88	10.82	5.59	5.23	5.96
1969	2.90	7.99	10.89	5.88	5.01	5.77
1970	3.25	8.37	11.62	6.91	4.71	5.52
1971	3.21	7.67	10.88	6.28	4.60	5.26
1972	2.81	7.51	10.32	6.00	4.32	4.77
1973	2.45	7.55	10.00	5.96	4.04	4.54
1974	3.24	8.03	11.27	7.29	3.98	4.33
1975	5.10	9.12	14.22	7.91	6.31	4.65
1976	3.90	9.33	13.23	8.23	5.00	4.73
1977	3.71	10.21	13.92	7.30	6.62	5.19
1978	5.19	11.37	16.56	7.87	8.69	6.12
Average	3.49%	8.15%	11.64%	6.05%	5.59%	

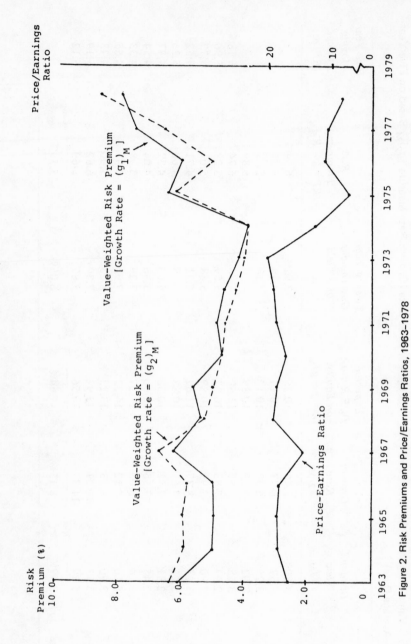

Figure 2. Risk Premiums and Price/Earnings Ratios, 1963–1978

4. Because some of the year-to-year variations are undoubtedly caused by random errors, the five-year moving averages may be more reflective of the true market risk premiums than are the actual annual numbers. The moving averages are, of course, very much more stable than the annual risk premiums.

5. Although the annual risk premiums are somewhat sensitive to the choice of method used to calculate the expected growth rate, on the whole the two procedures produce results that are quite consistent. This is especially true of the moving average data and the average risk premiums over the sixteen-year period.

INDIVIDUAL COMPANY RISK PREMIUMS

All the calculations and results discussed thus far were obtained from aggregated data; in effect, we aggregated data for the S&P 400 and then treated the 400 as if it were a single firm. In an earlier study, we estimated individual risk premiums on each of the 400 companies and then aggregated these data to develop a market risk premium [2]. One problem that surfaced almost immediately was that the risk premium estimates for a few companies in a few years were clearly unreasonable. Based on historical data, on interviews with portfolio managers, and on a review of the literature, we concluded that it is most unlikely that the true risk premium for an S&P 400 stock could ever exceed 10 percentage points, nor is it likely that a risk premium for any stock could be less than about 3 percentage points.

An examination of the raw data showed that while the majority of the companies had risk premiums that were not obviously unreasonable, in a few of the years some of the smaller members of the S&P 400 had calculated risk premiums that were negative, while others had premiums of 20 percent or more.[10] Because of these problems, we abandoned the idea of developing market risk premiums by averaging the premiums for individual companies.[11]

Based on our experience in the previous study, we have concluded that more reliable company risk premiums can be obtained by using the aggregate market risk premium as a base and then adjusting up or down for companies thought to be more or less risky than average. Relative corporate riskiness could be based on beta coefficients (historic or fundamental), on other quantitative measures of risk, or even on qualitative judgment.

In our own work, using risk premiums to help estimate the cost of equity, we have proceeded as follows: (1) We group the S&P 400 into five risk classes on the basis of Merrill Lynch adjusted betas. (2) We apply the average beta for each group to the 1978 moving average risk premium to obtain an estimated average risk premium for the group. The group averages are shown in Table 6.

Table 6. Risk Premiums by Risk Groups

Risk Group	Average Beta[a]	$\beta_G \times RP_M$[b]
Lowest	0.80	4.9%
Second lowest	0.90	5.5
Average	1.00	6.1
Second highest	1.10	6.7
Highest	1.20	7.3

[a]The group average beta is the unweighted average of Merrill Lynch adjusted betas for the firms in the group. There are eighty firms in each risk class. The average betas are rounded to the closest 0.05.

[b]We use here the five-year moving average market risk premium as calculated by method 2, which is 6.12 percent. See Table 5.

(3) We add the current yield (e.g., the July 1979 yield) on U.S. Treasury bonds to the group risk premiums to obtain an estimate of the current cost of equity for the group. (4) We decide where a particular company lies with regard to the risk spectrum, and then we use the appropriate group average cost of capital as an estimate of that firm's cost of equity.

OTHER STUDIES OF RISK PREMIUMS

Ibbotson and Sinquefield [6] have studied the historic relationship between returns on stocks and bonds, and Benore has studied forward-looking risk premiums on a survey basis. In a recent study, Malkiel examined risk premiums using a methodology very similar to ours [7]. Malkiel used the Gordon model to estimate the expected rate of return on the thirty Dow Jones industrial stocks in each year from 1960 to 1977. He based his growth rate forecast on *Value Line* earnings growth forecasts, and he used ten-year maturity government bonds as a proxy for the riskless rate. Further, he assumed that each company's *Value Line* growth rate would, after the initial five-year period, move toward the long-run national growth rate (currently 3.6 percent). Malkiel reported that he tested the sensitivity of his results against a number of different types of changes, but, in his words, "The results are remarkably robust and the estimated risk premiums are all very similar to those displayed on the chart" [7, p. 300].

Figure 3 shows a plot of Malkiel's risk premiums together with the ones we obtained by method 1 (Table 4). Our years have been shifted back one to make our data comparable to Malkiel's. The significant differences are these:

1. Our risk premiums are much higher than Malkiel's in the earlier years. This probably results from the fact that his sample consisted of the thirty Dow Jones stocks while we used the S&P 400. During the decade of the 1960s, institutional investors tended to favor the larger companies (this was the era of the famous two-tier market), and so it is quite possible that a wide gap in risk premiums existed between the samples during those years.

2. Our annual data tracked those of Malkiel quite closely from about 1968 through 1975. However, our measured risk premiums became much higher than his in 1976 and 1977. This later difference could reflect the different samples, with investors favoring blue chips such as those in the Dow after the crash of 1974-1975, or it could reflect Malkiel's assumption that all growth rates are expected to decline to 3.6 percent in the future.[12]

3. Our moving average risk premium, which is the one in which we have the most confidence, tracks Malkiel's data relatively well in recent years, the exception being 1974 when the annual data show a sharp peak.

4. During the 1960s and continuing to 1974, our data show a rather steady decline in risk premiums, while Malkiel's show, if anything, a slight upward trend. Again, this difference could be caused by the difference between our sample and his, or by our different bond maturities.

Malkiel's risk premium analysis was not the central focus of his study—his focus was on reasons why the United States has lagged behind certain other

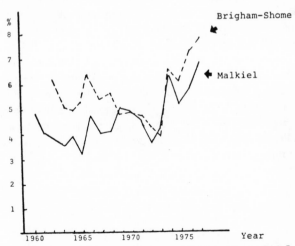

Figure 3. Comparison of Malkiel's and Brigham-Shome Risk Premiums

nations in expanding and improving its stock of physical capital. He discussed the increase in risk premiums and the accompanying rise in the cost of equity capital as one cause of the capital expansion lag. His data (and ours) certainly support his major contention. At the same time, Malkiel's data tend to support our estimates, especially in the more recent years.

CONCLUSIONS

The purpose of this paper was to estimate a market risk premium for use as a basing point in the determination of the cost of equity for a firm. In the past, most analysts requiring a risk premium for their work have used historical holding period return spreads, such as those provided by Ibbotson and Sinquefield, or else risk premiums based on survey data, such as those of Benore. Malkiel is the major exception—he used forward-looking risk premiums designed to capture expectations about future returns, and his methodology and results are similar to ours.

We used the DCF constant growth model (the Gordon model) to determine the expected rate of return on the S&P 400 stock index over the period 1963–1978. From these expected annual returns, we subtracted the yield to maturity on twenty-year U.S. Treasury bonds to obtain the market risk premium on the S&P 400. Our calculated risk premiums were generally in the 4 to 6 percent range from the early 1960s through 1973, and the trend over time was toward slightly lower premiums. However, since 1974 the trend has been sharply upward, and in 1978 risk premiums were at record levels for the years examined. (Our data in the more recent years were consistent with those of Malkiel, but there were some differences in earlier years.)

The most critical assumptions of our procedure are that the constant growth Gordon model applies and that investors estimate future growth rates as the product of the average retention rate over the last four or five years times the average ROE during this same period. For large, mature companies, such as those in the S&P 400, these assumptions seem reasonable, but there is no way of ascertaining the "true" aggregate expected growth rate and hence no way to test the validity of our results.[13] They seem reasonable to us, but others will have to judge for themselves.

Appendix Table 1. Yield Differentials on Various Types of Bonds, 1960–1978 (Average of Monthly Values)

| | Government Bonds | | Utility Bonds | | | | Yield Spreads | | | | | | |
Year	Short-Term	Long-Term	AAA	AA	A	BBB	AAA-L.T. Government	AA-AAA	A-AAA	BBB-AAA	A-AA	BBB-AA	BBB-A
1960	3.85	3.99	4.51	4.54	4.66	4.82	0.52	0.03	0.15	0.31	0.12	0.28	0.16
1961	3.51	3.90	4.47	4.52	4.61	4.70	0.57	0.05	0.14	0.23	0.09	0.18	0.09
1962	3.32	3.95	4.29	4.37	4.42	4.53	0.34	0.08	0.13	0.24	0.05	0.16	0.11
1963	3.56	4.02	4.29	4.32	4.37	4.45	0.27	0.03	0.08	0.16	0.05	0.13	0.08
1964	3.84	4.17	4.41	4.44	4.50	4.60	0.24	0.03	0.09	0.19	0.06	0.16	0.10
1965	4.07	4.23	4.52	4.55	4.63	4.77	0.29	0.03	0.11	0.25	0.08	0.22	0.14
1966	4.95	4.68	5.19	5.23	5.37	5.64	0.51	0.04	0.18	0.45	0.14	0.41	0.27
1967	4.69	4.90	5.61	5.67	5.80	6.07	0.71	0.06	0.19	0.46	0.13	0.40	0.27
1968	5.41	5.33	6.24	6.36	6.56	6.88	0.91	0.12	0.32	0.64	0.20	0.52	0.32
1969	6.42	6.22	7.22	7.39	7.57	7.90	1.00	0.17	0.35	0.68	0.18	0.51	0.33
1970	7.19	6.75	8.11	8.35	8.70	9.12	1.36	0.24	0.59	1.01	0.35	0.77	0.42
1971	5.32	5.94	7.54	7.71	8.24	8.62	1.60	0.17	0.70	1.08	0.53	0.91	0.38
1972	5.83	5.67	7.41	7.53	7.80	8.05	1.74	0.12	0.39	0.64	0.27	0.52	0.25
1973	6.88	6.12	7.72	7.83	8.03	8.17	1.60	0.11	0.31	0.45	0.20	0.34	0.14
1974	7.75	6.59	8.45	8.63	8.75	9.08	1.86	0.18	0.30	0.63	0.12	0.45	0.33
1975	7.37	8.21	8.84	9.17	9.50	10.21	0.63	0.33	0.66	1.37	0.33	1.04	0.71
1976	6.50	7.87	8.50	8.82	9.05	9.64	0.63	0.32	0.55	1.14	0.23	0.82	0.59
1977	6.21	7.69	8.14	8.44	8.60	8.86	0.45	0.30	0.46	0.72	0.16	0.42	0.26
1978													
Average	5.37	5.57	6.41	6.55	6.73	7.01	0.85	0.13	0.32	0.59	0.18	0.46	0.28
Standard Deviation							0.55	0.10	0.20	0.36	0.12	0.27	0.17

Source: Standard & Poor, Security Price Index, 1978.

103

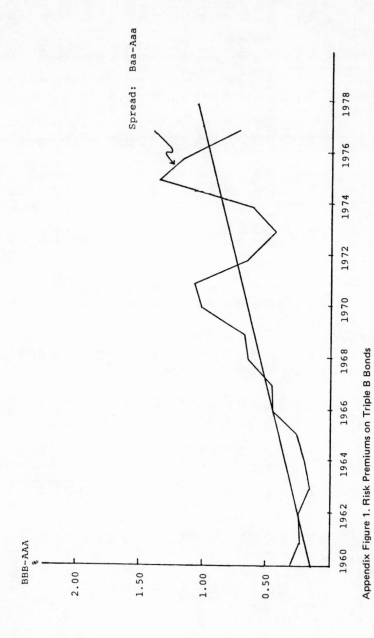

Appendix Figure 1. Risk Premiums on Triple B Bonds

NOTES

1. U.S. Treasury bonds are riskless in the sense that they are free of default risk. However, they are not completely riskless because their holders still face the dangers of purchasing-power loss (inflation risk) and the loss of capital values if interest rates rise (interest-rate risk). The risk premiums developed herein include differential yields caused by these two factors, as well as by default premiums.

2. This is particularly true of advocates of the CAPM. See Carleton [4] for a more complete development of this point. Carleton noted the points we express and strongly opposed using bills in common stock risk premium studies.

3. If flower bonds were used in the series, the effect would be to lower the reported yield on long-term governments and, therefore, to increase the reported risk premiums. Since we have chosen a series that excludes these bonds, our calculated risk premiums are smaller than would otherwise be the case.

4. For an extended discussion of these problems, see [5].

5. 1976 is the last year for which data were available in most of the major studies.

6. The situation here is similar to that encountered in portfolio analysis. Betas of individual securities tend to be unstable and to reflect a great deal of measurement error. However, when companies are grouped into portfolios, the portfolio betas tend to be highly stable. The same type of situation may also exist here.

7. Indeed, as Brown and Rozeff [3] have shown, analysts use subjective information that would be hard, if not impossible, to extract from historic data.

8. One could develop aggregate data on the basis of either book value or market value weights. Market value weights are more consistent both with financial theory and with the fact that industrial companies with higher market/book ratios are growing faster and, hence, making larger incremental investments than firms with low M/B ratios.

We should also note that the choice of a four-year period and the 0.4, 0.3, 0.2, and 0.1 weights is arbitrary, but that we did some tests using longer and shorter periods and with weights set by exponential smoothing techniques. The results were not materially influenced by the use of exponential smoothing, and the choice of periods did not matter within the range of three to six years.

9. We experimented a bit with stock prices, within the limits imposed by use of the Compustat Data Tapes. We used (1) the average of the beginning price and the ending price and (2) the average of the high and the low for the year, as well as the ending spot price. Again, the choice of stock price definition did not materially affect the calculated risk premiums.

10. The negative premiums arise if a firm has (1) low dividends, and hence a low dividend yield, and (2) an abnormally low rate of return on equity, which produces a low or even negative growth rate. If this condition holds for several years, especially during the last two years to which our formula gives special weight, then the combination of dividend yield plus growth rate can be less than the yield on Treasury bonds, producing a negative risk premium. This situation is *always* regarded as being temporary — investors expect the ROE to return to normal levels, pulling up earnings, dividends, and the growth rate.

Large risk premiums can arise in two ways. First, a company may have a very high ROE, say 30 percent, and may retain most of its earnings, which would give it a k value of close to 30 percent. Subtracting R_F would produce a risk premium of over 20 percent. If the high ROE is a temporary cyclical phenomenon, then our smoothing process would reduce the risk premium, but if it persists for four years, we would report the high premium. While companies can and do earn very high ROEs in the short run, it is unrealistic to project a continuation of an ROE of over 20 percent, combined with a low payout ratio, over the long run. The second factor that can cause high risk premiums is that, on rare occasions, some of the S&P 400 companies have had large write-offs, which have reduced reported equity to low levels. Later, "normal" profits are divided by the very low reported equity values, and this results in very high reported ROEs and risk premiums.

11. We should note, however, that the premiums based on average data for individual companies were actually quite similar to those based on aggregated data. The highs and the lows tended to offset one another. Nevertheless, we feel much more comfortable with the aggregated data premiums as reported in the present study.

12. We chose not to use a growth decay function because it seems unrealistic to assume a low terminal growth rate given likely inflation rates, earnings retention rates, and ROEs. The earnings and dividend growth rates for a firm that earns a normal return on equity and that retains about half of its earnings ought to be substantially in excess of the inflation rate, which seems likely to exceed 6 percent on into the future.

13. One possible test is based on the market value/book value ratio of the S&P 400. In periods when our calculated required rate of return on stocks is less than the expected ROE on book equity, the market/book ratio should exceed 1.0, and conversely if the expected ROE is less than the required rate of return.

REFERENCES

[1]   Benore, Charles. "A Survey of Investor Attitudes toward the Electric Power Industry," Paine Webber Mitchell Hutchins, June 13, 1978.

[2]   Brigham, E. F., and Shome, D. K. "A Study of Risk Premiums on Common Stocks," Public Utility Research Center, University of Florida, January 1979.

[3]   Brown, L. D., and Rozeff, M. S. "The Superiority of Analyst Forecasts as Measures of Expectations: Evidence from Earnings," *Journal of Finance* (March 1978).

[4]   Carleton, Willard T. "Comment on the Use of the CAPM in Public Utility Rate Cases," *Financial Management* (Autumn 1978), pp. 57–59.

[5]   Fisher, Lawrence, and Lorie, James H. *A Half Century of Returns on Stocks and Bonds.* Chicago: University of Chicago Graduate School of Business, 1977.

[6]   Ibbotson, R. G., and Sinquefield, R. A. *Stocks, Bonds, Bills, and Inflation: Historical Returns (1926–1978).* Charlottesville, Va.: Financial Analysts Research Foundation, 1979.

[7]   Malkiel, B. G. "The Capital Formation Problem in the United States," Journal of Finance (May 1979), pp. 291–306.

6 GROWTH OPPORTUNITIES AND REAL INVESTMENT DECISIONS

J. E. Broyles and I. A. Cooper
London Business School, Great Britain

Several authors, especially Myers [4], have noted that part of the value of any company is attributable to its opportunities to make investments, at future dates, that have positive net present values. A generic term for such opportunities is *growth opportunities*.

In his paper, Myers investigates the impact of such growth opportunities on the optimal capital structure of a firm. Growth opportunities will affect real investment decisions, as well as financing decisions, of firms. This paper shows two ways in which capital budgeting procedures must be adjusted to take account of the options implicit in future opportunities for growth.

The first adjustment concerns the choice of discount rate for risky capital projects. Franks and Broyles [2] have suggested a procedure for employing the Capital Asset Pricing Model (CAPM) in the choice of discount rates for investments in real assets. The procedure involves determining the systematic risk (beta) for the average project in a company (or division) by measuring the beta of the firm (or a collection of similar firms in the same market) adjusted for financial leverage. A further adjustment for an individual project's operational

107

leverage establishes the beta for the project. The project's beta is then used in the CAPM to determine an appropriate discount rate for the project. However, we will show that a further adjustment to estimates of beta based on market prices is required, since market values of a company reflect the value of growth opportunities, as well as the value of existing assets already in place. The appropriate beta for capital budgeting is that of the asset once it has been created (since it is the cash-flow stream of the asset in place that is being discounted). This can be derived by adjusting the beta estimated from market value by a factor that reflects the extent of the growth opportunities facing the firm.

The second adjustment that must be made affects the acceptance criterion. Normally, it is advocated that companies accept projects with net present values greater than zero. However, net present values, as conventionally computed, do not reflect the value of the investment as a growth opportunity even if investment is postponed. The opportunity cost of postponement can substantially affect optimal real investment decisions by companies.

The topics covered in this paper are: assumptions and growth opportunity valuation, adjusting betas for growth opportunities, the timing of investment decisions, and the impact of competition in product markets.

The valuation model used is the Black-Scholes option valuation model. To achieve the arbitrage underlying this model requires the existence of assets that can hedge the option. The conditions necessary for this are set out fully in the next section.

ASSUMPTIONS AND GROWTH OPPORTUNITY VALUATION

A growth opportunity is the ability to make a real investment, at some future date, that may turn out to have a positive net present value at that time. There are three crucial elements in this opportunity: the time at which the investment should be made, the investment required to create the new asset at that date, and the value of the asset, once created.

Assumption A1: A growth opportunity consists of the option to invest, at time T, an amount $I(T)$ that will create an asset of value $A(T)$.

The impact of this opportunity (at some time prior to T) on the value of the company concerned will be determined by expectations about asset value $(A(T))$ and the investment required $(I(T))$, both of which may be random when viewed from time t ($<T$). To value growth opportunities as individual entities, we need the condition that gives value additivity. This condition will also prove useful in setting up a Black-Scholes hedge.

Assumption A2: The payoff contingent state space of $(A(T) - I(T))$ at time T is spanned by securities in the market.

This condition implies that the company can value its growth opportunity independently of other assets that it possesses. It also means that there are securities in the market that can be combined to give a portfolio at time t $(<T)$ that will have the same value $A(t)$ as the underlying real asset.

The value of this portfolio plays the same role as the underlying stock in the Black-Scholes call option valuation formula. A riskless hedge can be set up between this portfolio and the growth opportunity and, by varying the amount of the portfolio sold against the growth opportunity, the riskless hedge may be maintained. Another condition necessary to the Black-Scholes valuation formula is that the exercise price of the option be fixed. The equivalent of the exercise price here is the investment required to create the new asset $(I(T))$. This is likely to vary with the value of the growth opportunity, and we make a simple linear assumption:

Assumption A3:

$$I(T) = \bar{I}(T) + (1 - \alpha) A(T) \qquad 1 > \alpha > 0.$$

This implies that there is a fixed component of the investment required to create the new asset, as well as a variable component that increases with the value of the asset, but not as quickly.[1]

The final assumption necessary concerns the return dynamics of the value of the underlying asset, $A(t)$. There is ample evidence that returns on equity securities are approximately lognormally distributed. This should be true *a fortiori* here since we are eliminating the option element, which would induce nonlognormality in the value of the growth opportunity, and just looking at the value of the underlying asset, $A(t)$.

Assumption A4: $A(t)$ follows an Itô process.

The optimal decision at time T will be to undertake the investment if it has a positive net present value:

$$\text{Accept at } T \text{ if} \quad A(T) > I(T)$$

$$A(T) > \bar{I}(T) + (1 - \alpha) A(T)$$

$$\alpha A(T) > \bar{I}(T).$$

This growth opportunity is thus a call option on the asset $\alpha A(t)$, with an exercise price of $\bar{I}(T)$. Given assumptions A1-A4, we may price the growth opportunity by using the Black-Scholes formula:

$$G(t) = \alpha A(t) N(d_1) - \bar{I}(T)e^{-r\tau}N(d_2), \tag{1}$$

where

$G(t)$ is the value at time t of the growth opportunity;
$N(\cdot)$ is the normal distribution function;
r is the continuous risk-free rate;
σ^2 is the variance rate of the return of $A(t)$;

and

$$\tau = T - t$$

$$d_1 = \frac{\log \alpha A(t) / \bar{I}(T) + (r + \tfrac{1}{2}\sigma^2)\tau}{\sigma\sqrt{\tau}}$$

$$d_2 = d_1 - \sigma\sqrt{\tau}.$$

The response of this value to the various parameters has been adequately discussed in Black and Scholes [1] and Galai and Masulis [3].

THE VALUE OF THE COMPANY AND BETAS FOR USE IN CAPITAL BUDGETING

So far we have discussed the valuation of a single growth opportunity. A company consists of many assets in place and many growth opportunities. Given our value additivity assumption, the total value of the company will be

$$V(t) = \sum_{i=1}^{n} E(t, i) + \sum_{T=t+1}^{\infty} \sum_{j=i}^{M(T)} G(t, T, j), \qquad (2)$$

where

$V(t)$ is the value of the company at time t;
n is the number of assets in place at time t;
$M(T)$ is the number of growth opportunities for time T;
$E(t, i)$ is the value at time t of the ith existing asset;
$G(t, T, j)$ is the value at time t of the jth growth opportunity for time T.

The usually advocated method of computing a discount rate for capital budgeting involves estimating a beta for the new asset based upon market returns for assets of similar systematic risk. This is done by estimating the betas of companies in the industry of the new project.

From (2) the beta of a company is given by

$$\beta(V)V(t) = \sum_{i=1}^{n} \beta(E, t, i)E(t, i) + \sum_{T=t+1}^{\infty} \sum_{j=1}^{M(T)} \beta(G, t, T, j)\, G(t, T, j), \qquad (3)$$

where

$\beta(E, t, i)$ is the beta of the ith existing asset;
$\beta(G, t, T, j)$ is the beta at time t of the (Tj)th growth opportunity.

From (1) it is possible to show that[2]

$$\beta(G)G(t) = \alpha A(t)\, N(d_1)\, \beta(A). \qquad (4)$$

Here the subscripts have been dropped for simplicity of presentation, but this expression applies to each growth opportunity separately. Using (1), we can eliminate the value of the underlying asset from (4):

$$\beta(G)G(t) = \{G(t) + \bar{I}(T)e^{-r(\tau)}\, N(d_2)\}\, \beta(A). \qquad (5)$$

It is well known that the beta of a company is only suitable for use in capital budgeting if the risk of the project can be related to the risk of the company. Clearly, this does not imply that the beta of all growth opportunities is the same as the mean beta of existing assets, since the former vary over time as the growth option matures.

Even if there are no actual companies with all assets of the same risk, the use of such a company as an example will give an expression for the bias induced by growth opportunities.

Assumption A5:

$$\bar{\beta} = \beta(E, t, i) = \beta(E, t, j) = \beta(A, t, T, i) = \beta(A, t, T, j) \qquad \text{all } i, j, \qquad (6)$$

where

$$\beta(A, t, T, j) = \beta(A(t)) \text{ for growth opportunity } Tj.$$

Using (3), (5), and (6) gives

$$\beta(V)V(t) = \sum_{i=1}^{n} \bar{\beta}E(t, i) + \sum_{T=t+1}^{\infty} \sum_{j=1}^{M(T)} \bar{\beta}G(t, T, j)$$

$$+ \sum_{T=t+1}^{\infty} \sum_{j=1}^{M(T)} \bar{\beta}PV_t(\bar{I}, T, j), \qquad (7)$$

where

$$PV_t(\bar{I}, T, j) = \bar{I}(T, j)e^{-r(T-t)}N(d_2(T, j)).$$

Using (2) gives

$$\beta(V)V(t) = \bar{\beta}V(t) + \bar{\beta}PV_t(\bar{I}), \qquad (8)$$

where

$$PV_t(\bar{I}) = \sum_{T=t+1}^{\infty} \sum_{j=1}^{M(T)} PV_t(\bar{I}, T, j).$$

Suppose that $\beta(V)$ is estimated from market returns. The correct beta to use in capital budgeting for this company is $\bar{\beta}$, since this reflects the risk of the cash flows generated by an asset once in place; it is these cash flows that are being discounted to give a present value. Equation (8) gives the adjustment that must be applied to the market estimate of beta for use in capital budgeting.

$$\bar{\beta} = \beta(V) \left\{ \frac{V(t)}{V(t) + PV_t(\bar{I})} \right\}. \qquad (9)$$

This adjustment clearly reduces the beta. The reason is simple: Market-based betas contain the extra volatility of growth opportunities. If the decision being made concerns the creation of a new asset, this extra volatility will not be present in the cash-flow stream from the asset, once created.

Although the adjustment given in (9) is simple, it contains one term, $PV_t(\bar{I})$, that has not yet been given an intuitive interpretation. The easiest case is where there is no variable element in the investment required to undertake the growth opportunity. In this case, alpha is unity and $PV_t(\bar{I})$ is the present value at time t of all future investment in growth opportunities. The magnitude of this adjustment can be seen by considering two extreme cases:

1. No growth opportunities
2. No existing assets

In case 1, there is no adjustment necessary, and the market beta is equal to the capital budgeting beta. In case 2, the adjustment factor necessary to convert the market beta into a capital budgeting beta falls as the value of the growth opportunities falls relative to the investment required. This adjustment factor can never fall to zero as long as the company has any value.

A typical growth company might spend 5 percent of its current value on growth each year, over and above the investment required to maintain its existing assets.[3] If this investment in growth is expected to continue at the same level in perpetuity, and we discount it at a rate of, say, 10 percent, we get

$$PV_t(\bar{I}) = 0.50V(t) \tag{10}$$

and

$$\bar{\beta} = 0.33\beta(V).$$

Thus, even with these conservative assumptions about growth, we get a sizable adjustment to the market beta to give a beta for use in capital budgeting.

Where the investment in the growth opportunities varies with the value of those opportunities ($\alpha < 1$), the adjustment factor depends only on the present value of the fixed element in the investment. In this case, the minimal level of expenditure on a particular growth opportunity occurs when

$$\bar{I} + (1 - \alpha)A = A \tag{11}$$

so that

$$\bar{I} + (1 - \alpha)A = I_m = A, \tag{12}$$

where I_m is the minimum amount that would be spent on this opportunity if it proved to be profitable. Rearranging (12) gives

$$\bar{I} = \alpha I_m. \tag{13}$$

Thus $PV_t(\bar{I})$ may be reinterpreted as the present value of the minimal profitable levels of investment on growth opportunities adjusted downward to the extent that the amounts of these investments are variable.

For example, consider an all-equity financed company that is generating a perpetual income stream from current assets of $10 million p.a. The beta of this income stream is 0.5, and the market value of existing assets is $100 million. The company will, one year from now, double its capacity at a cost of $80 million if the investment proves profitable at that time. The revenue stream from the new capacity will be identical to that from the old. The variance rate of returns on existing capacity is .1 per year on a continuous basis. The risk-free rate is 5 percent.

The value of the growth opportunity is

$$G = 100N(d_1) = 80e^{-.05}N(d_2)$$

$$d_1 = \frac{\log(100/80) + (.05 + .5 \times .1)}{\sqrt{.1}} = 1.022$$

$$d_2 = d_1 - \sqrt{.1} = .706$$

$$G = 100 \times .847 - 80 \times .951 \times .760 = 26.9$$

$$V = 126.9$$

$$PV(I) = 57.8$$

$$\beta(V) = .5 \left(\frac{126.9 + 57.8}{126.9} \right) = .73.$$

If the company employed a market beta for capital budgeting, its cutoff rate would be

$$R = R_f + (\bar{R}_m - R_f)\beta(V) = .5 + .10 \times .73 = 12.3 \text{ percent.}$$

But it should employ the beta of the asset in place, giving a cutoff rate of

$$R = .5 + .10 \times .5 = 10 \text{ percent.}$$

The upward bias in the required rate of return is in this case quite large.

THE TIMING OF INVESTMENTS

Up to this point we have assumed that the time (T) at which the investment in the growth opportunity will be made is fixed and given. Out of all possible fixed exercise dates, there will be one that gives the maximum value for the particular growth opportunity under consideration. This value will not necessarily be the actual value of the growth opportunity that would result from a policy where the investment date varies with the history of the growth opportunity up to that point.

The purpose of this section is to consider the impact of the timing of investment in growth opportunities upon optimal capital budgeting rules. For an individual growth opportunity to be exercised at a fixed date, its value is

$$G(t, T) = A(t, T)N(d_1^T) - I(T)e^{-rt}N(d_2^T), \tag{14}$$

where

$G(t, T)$ is the value of the growth opportunity if exercised at T;
$A(t, T)$ is the value at t of the variable payoff at $T(A(T))$;
$I(T)$ is the fixed part of the investment at $T (\bar{I}(T))$;
d_1^T, d_2^T are defined as before for $A(t, T), I(T)$.

Changing the exercise date changes the value of the growth opportunity:[4]

$$\frac{\delta G(t,\,T)}{\delta T} = \frac{\delta A(t,\,T)}{\delta T}\,N(d_1^T) - \frac{\delta I(T)}{\delta T}\,e^{-rt}N(d_2^T)$$

$$+ I(T)e^{-rt}\,[f(d_2^T)\sigma/2\sqrt{\tau} + rN(d_2^T)]. \tag{15}$$

An optimal fixed exercise date is given by setting (15) equal to zero, but this may not be an optimal overall policy since a variable exercise date must have at least as great a value.

If the investment is currently profitable, then $A(t,\,t)$ is greater than $I(t)$, and the investment will have more value as a growth opportunity. However,

$$\left.\frac{\delta G(t,\,T)}{\delta T}\right|_{T=t} > 0; \tag{16}$$

then substituting (for a currently profitable investment) the values

$$d_1^t = d_2^t = \infty$$

so that

$$f(d_1^t) = 0$$

$$N(d_1^t) = N(d_2^t) = 1,$$

the condition (16) gives

$$\left\{\frac{\delta A(t,\,T)}{\delta T} - \frac{\delta I(T)}{\delta T} + I(T)r\right\}_{T=t} > 0 \tag{17}$$

$$-\left.\frac{\delta \mathrm{NPV}(t,\,T)}{\delta T}\right|_{T=t} < I(t)r, \tag{18}$$

where NPV$(t,\,T)$ is the net present value at time t of the unconditional payoffs at time T.

The speed at which the net present value of the project is eroded depends upon the reactions of competitors. Equation (18) states that a sufficient condition for postponing a profitable investment is that the rate of erosion of net present value should be less than the interest that can be earned on the amount of the investment. Since (18) is based on a fixed investment date and considers only an incremental postponement of the project, it is not a necessary condition for postponement. The necessary condition is that the value of the investment as a growth opportunity be greater than its value as an asset in place.

The conditions for the asset to have more value as a growth opportunity are:

1. The rate of erosion of competitive advantage is low.
2. The investment required is high.

3. The interest rate is high.
4. The uncertainty about the project is high.

In particular, the fourth of these, a high degree of uncertainty about the project, will mean that the postponement criterion (18) is too stringent. With much uncertainty, the asset as a growth opportunity has a high value, so that profitable projects whose net present values are eroding faster than the interest on the investment required may still be optimally postponed.

COMPETITIVE ASSUMPTIONS

In the previous section, the way in which competitive advantage (positive NPV) is eroded through time was seen to play a crucial part in the investment decision. This section shows the impact of a specific realistic assumption about this process on optimal investment decisions. To do this, we will once again consider an individual asset, which may be bought at time t or retained as a growth opportunity until time T.

Investing in the project now gives a value of

$$E(t) - I(t),$$

where $E(t) = A(t, t)$, the value of the asset in place at time t.

Retaining the investment as a growth opportunity has the value of

$$G(t, T) = A(t, T)N(d_1) - I(T)e^{-rt}N(d_2),$$

where

$A(t, T)$ is the value at time T of the unconditional asset value at time T;
$I(T)$ is the investment required at time T.

If we plot the value of the growth opportunity against the value of its underlying asset $(A(t, T))$, we get the line (GG) in Figure 1. This is the value of the asset as a growth opportunity.

The line (UU) gives the net present value at time t of the asset created unconditionally at time T. This value is equal to

$$U(t, T) = A(t, T) - I(T)e^{-rt}. \tag{19}$$

If competition erodes net present value, this will be less than the corresponding net present value of the asset created now:

$$NPV(t) = E(t) - I(t). \tag{20}$$

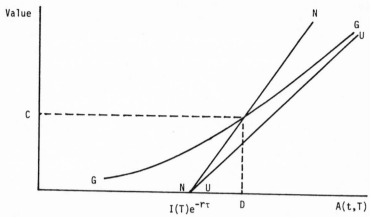

Figure 1. Asset Values

Furthermore, the higher the current net present value, the more it will be eroded between now and time T, so that the difference between NPV(t) and $U(t)$ will increase with the level of NPV(t). Finally, if NPV(t) is zero, so that the project is only marginal, we expect no erosion of net present value over time.

These assumptions about competitive forces are depicted by the line (NN) in Figure 1. The comparison that is relevant to capital budgeting decisions is that between the net present value of the project created now (NN) and the value of the project as a growth opportunity (GG). Above a net present value of C, the investment should be made immediately; below that level, it should be postponed. There is thus a single cutoff criterion for the investment, given these reasonable assumptions about competition, but that cutoff rate is at a net present value greater than zero.[5]

CONCLUSIONS

We have shown that there are two significant biases introduced into capital budgeting decisions by ignoring growth opportunities. Market-measured betas are biased upward for growth companies. A simple adjustment can be made to give, in principle, a correct beta for use in capital budgeting. Accepting all projects with positive net present value ignores the opportunity to keep the asset as a growth option. Under a reasonable set of assumptions about competitive forces, there is a single optimal cutoff point for investment in a project, but it is at a level of NPV greater than zero.

NOTES

1. A less restrictive assumption would be to make z stochastic, so that

$$I(T) = \bar{I}(T) + (1 - \tilde{z})A(T).$$

Then the acceptance criterion is

$$\tilde{z}A(T) > \bar{I}(T),$$

and the underlying asset must be interpreted as the value of a claim on the payoff $zA(T)$. The adjustment to beta remains the same as long as $\tilde{z}$ is independent of the return to the market portfolio. The variance σ^2 in equation (1) would then include the variance of $\tilde{z}$, as well as the variance of $A(t)$.

2. See, for example, Galai and Masulis [3].

3. To the extent that maintenance and replacement of existing assets is optional, this investment should also be included in $PV_t(\bar{I})$.

4. This result uses the fact that

$$A(t, T)f(d_1^T) = I(T)e^{-rt}f(d_2^T).$$

5. Figure 1 refers to the choice between investing at time t and investing at some specific future date, T. The argument may be generalized to allow for exercise of the growth opportunity at any optimal future date, and the conclusions are the same.

REFERENCES

[1] Black, F., and Scholes, M. "The Pricing of Options and Corporate L Liabilities," *Journal of Political Economy* 81 (1973), pp. 637–654.

[2] Franks, J.R., and Broyles, J.E. *Modern Managerial Finance.* New York: John Wiley & Sons, 1979.

[3] Galai, D., and Masulis, R.W. "The Option Pricing Model and the Risk Factor of Stock," *Journal of Financial Economics* 3 (1976), pp. 53–81.

[4] Myers, S.C. "Determinants of Corporate Borrowing," *Journal of Financial Economics* 5 (1977), pp. 147–175.

7 A MULTIPERIOD COST OF CAPITAL CONCEPT AND ITS IMPACT ON THE FORMULATION OF FINANCIAL POLICY

A. I. Diepenhorst
Erasmus University Rotterdam, The Netherlands

The concept of the firm's cost of capital (FCOC) has proved to be a useful device for both elementary and advanced teaching. In addition, it is generally held in high esteem as a powerful analytical tool for both theoretical and practical research. Theories of financial structure and FCOC generally employ a cash-flow stream of a perpetual form, which simplifies its capitalization. As seen in Table 1, when such cash flows (CFs) are conceived to be uncertain, the uncertainty involves only the level on which the perpetuities are realized.

With the help of this kind of model, a number of relations between the several cash flows, between their appropriate capitalization rates, and between their corresponding market values are formulated in this paper. From these, conclusions are reached regarding the impact of financial leverage on the market value of the firm and on the firm's cost of capital, both with and without a corporate tax. In translating these conclusions to cash flows of a nonperpetual form, it is seen that some of the derived formulas have to be adapted. This may give rise to a deeper understanding of the relations involved. This adaptation is also worthwhile because financial managers (usually having to cope with

119

Table 1. Uncertain Perpetuity Cash Flows

State of Nature	Probability	t_1	t_2
a	p_a	CF_a	CF_a
b	p_b	CF_b	CF_b

nonperpetuities) are starting to take a growing interest in such matters, an interest that may be easily frustrated by a misapplication. In this paper, we attempt to clarify these issues by giving as uniformly as possible a presentation of the perpetuity model, the single-period model, and the multiperiod model.

Starting with implicit definitional equations for k_u and k_0, the principal relations between k_0, k_e, k_i, k_u, V, and V_u are derived. (The notation and some of the identities used are defined in the appendix.) It becomes clear that for the multiperiod model the concept of the degree of financial leverage measured in accounting values (L) has both theoretical and practical advantages, in comparison to the customary measurement in market values (λ).

PERPETUITIES

We start first with the derivation of the firm's cost of capital for the case of a perpetual cash-flow stream. In this and the following section, the subscript for the point of time has no use and is therefore omitted.

$$V_u = \frac{CF_u}{k_u}. \tag{1}$$

$$V = \frac{CF}{k_0}. \tag{2}$$

From $S = (1 - \lambda) V$ and

$$CF = k_0 V = (1 - \lambda) k_e V + \lambda k_i V$$

follows

$$k_0 = (1 - \lambda) k_e + \lambda k_i. \tag{3}$$

From $CF = CF_u + bk_i \lambda V$ follows, after capitalization of the individual terms,

$$V = V_u + \frac{bk_i \lambda V}{k_i} = V_u + b\lambda V$$

$$V = \frac{V_u}{1 - b\lambda}$$

$$k_0 = \frac{CF}{V} = \frac{CF_u + b\lambda k_i V}{V} = \frac{CF_u}{V} + b\lambda k_i. \tag{4}$$

Substitution of (4) leads to

$$k_0 = \frac{CF_u(1 - b\lambda)}{V_u} + b\lambda k_i = k_u(1 - b\lambda) + b\lambda k_i$$

$$k_0 = k_u - b\lambda(k_u - k_i). \tag{5}$$

From (3),

$$k_e = \frac{k_0 - \lambda k_i}{1 - \lambda}.$$

By combining this result with (5) we get

$$k_e = \frac{k_u - b(k_u - k_i)\lambda - \lambda k_i}{1 - \lambda} = \frac{k_u - \lambda k_u + \lambda k_u - b\lambda k_u + b\lambda k_i - \lambda k_i}{1 - \lambda}$$

$$= \frac{(1 - \lambda)k_u + (1 - b)\lambda(k_u - k_i)}{1 - \lambda}$$

$$k_e = k_u + \frac{(1 - b)\lambda(k_u - k_i)}{1 - \lambda} \tag{6}$$

$$k_0' = \frac{CF'}{V} = \frac{CF}{V} - \frac{b\lambda k_i V}{V} = k_0 - b\lambda k_i = (1 - \lambda)k_e + \lambda k_i - b\lambda k_i$$

$$k_0' = (1 - \lambda)k_e + (1 - b)\lambda k_i. \tag{7}$$

From this, by substitution of (6),

$$k_0' = (1 - \lambda)k_u + (1 - b)(k_u - k_i)\lambda + (1 - b)\lambda k_i$$

$$k_0' = (1 - \lambda)k_u + (1 - b)\lambda k_u = (1 - b\lambda)k_u. \tag{8}$$

THE SINGLE-PERIOD MODEL

We now focus attention on the case in which there is only a single period rather than a perpetuity.

$$V_u = \frac{CF_u}{1 + k_u}. \tag{9}$$

$$V = \frac{CF}{1 + k_0}. \tag{10}$$

From $V = (1 - \lambda)V + \lambda V$ and

$$CF = (1 + k_0)V = (1 - \lambda)(1 + k_e)V + \lambda(1 + k_i)V$$

follows

$$k_0 = (1 - \lambda)k_e + \lambda k_i. \tag{11}$$

From $CF = CF_u + b\lambda_i \lambda V$ follows, after capitalization of the individual terms,

$$V = V_u + \frac{bk_i \lambda V}{1 + k_i}$$

$$V = \frac{(1 + k_i)V_u}{1 + (1 - b\lambda)k_i} \tag{12}$$

$$k_0 = \frac{CF - V}{V}$$

$$1 + k_0 = \frac{CF}{V} = \frac{CF_u + b\lambda k_i V}{V} = \frac{CF_u}{V} + b\lambda k_i.$$

Substitution of (12) leads to

$$1 + k_0 = \frac{CF_u(1 + k_i - b\lambda k_i)}{(1 + k_i)V_u} + b\lambda k_i = \frac{(1 + k_u)(1 + k_i - b\lambda k_i)}{1 + k_i} + b\lambda k_i$$

$$= 1 + k_u - \frac{(1 + k_u)b\lambda k_i}{1 + k_i} + b\lambda k_i$$

$$= 1 + k_u - \frac{(1 + k_u - 1 - k_i)b\lambda k_i}{1 + k_i}$$

$$1 + k_0 = 1 + k_u - \frac{(k_u - k_i)b\lambda k_i}{1 + k_i}$$

$$k_0 = k_u - b\lambda(k_u - k_i)\frac{k_i}{1 + k_i}. \tag{13}$$

From (11) follows

$$k_e = \frac{k_0 - \lambda k_i}{1 - \lambda}.$$

By substitution of (13),

$$k_e = \frac{k_u - \dfrac{(k_u - k_i) b \lambda k_i}{1 + k_i} - \lambda k_i}{1 - \lambda}$$

$$= \frac{k_u - \lambda k_u + \lambda k_u - \dfrac{(k_u - k_i) b \lambda k_i}{1 + k_i} - \lambda k_i}{1 - \lambda}$$

$$= k_u + \frac{(1 + k_i) \lambda (k_u - k_i) - b k_i \lambda (k_u - k_i)}{(1 - \lambda)(1 + k_i)}$$

$$= k_u + \frac{\{1 + k_i - b k_i\} \{\lambda (k_u - k_i)\}}{(1 - \lambda)(1 + k_i)}$$

$$k_e = k_u + \frac{[1 + (1 - b) k_i] \lambda (k_u - k_i)}{(1 - \lambda)(1 + k_i)} \tag{14}$$

$$k_0' = \frac{CF' - V}{V}$$

$$1 + k_0' = \frac{CF'}{V} = \frac{CF}{V} - \frac{b \lambda k_i V}{V} = 1 + k_0 - b \lambda k_i$$

$$k_0' = k_0 - b \lambda k_i = (1 - \lambda) k_e + \lambda k_i - b \lambda k_i.$$

Substitution of (11) leads to

$$k_0' = (1 - \lambda) k_e + (1 - b) \lambda k_i, \tag{15}$$

while substitution of (13) gives

$$k_0' = k_u - b \lambda (k_u - k_i) \frac{k_i}{1 + k_i} - b \lambda k_i,$$

which leads to[1]

$$k_0' = k_u - b \lambda k_i \frac{1 + k_u}{1 + k_i}. \tag{16}$$

THE MULTIPERIOD MODEL: INTRODUCTION

As should be clear to the reader, the formulas that differ in the single-period model from those in the perpetual case are apt to increase in complexity when derived for the multiperiod model. It would lead to considerable trouble if we tried to express them in a form that would reveal clearly all similarities and differences in the corresponding formulas. Fortunately, working along those lines is not necessary. There are two methods that can be employed to design the multiperiod model as an aggregation of single-period models. The first method consists of connecting successive one-period models with uniform period length in series, and the second of connecting in parallel one-period models with different period length.

Take, for instance, the following cash flow and the corresponding capital values V:

$$\text{At: } t_0 \quad \text{CF}(t_0) < 0 \quad V(t_0),$$

$$t_1 \quad \text{CF}(t_1) > 0 \quad V(t_1),$$

$$t_2 \quad \text{CF}(t_2) > 0.$$

The first method considers $V(t_0)$ as the amount invested during the first period, with a terminal value $\text{CF}(t_1) + V(t_1)$; during the next period, $V(t_1)$ is considered to be invested, with $\text{CF}(t_2)$ as a result. We will call this the successive connection (SUCCO).

The other method has to distinguish from the outset between two investments, each with its own $V(t_0)$. The first investment covers only the period from t_0 to t_1 and results in $\text{CF}(t_1)$; the second runs from t_0 to t_2, resulting in $\text{CF}(t_2)$. We will call this the parallel connection (PARCO).

The SUCCO Routine: The Final Period

Here we will use a rollback method. Starting with the cash flow and the capital values as noted above, the application of the single-period model to the second and final period leads to the following results:

$$V_u(t_1) = \frac{\text{CF}_u(t_2)}{1 + k_u} \tag{17}$$

$$V(t_1) = \frac{\text{CF}(t_2)}{1 + k_0} \tag{18}$$

$$k_0(t_1 - t_2) = (1 - \lambda)k_e + \lambda k_i \tag{19}$$

$$V(t_1) = \frac{(1 + k_i)V_u(t_1)}{1 + (1 - b\lambda)k_i} \tag{20}$$

$$k_0(t_1 - t_2) = k_u - \frac{(k_u - k_i)b\lambda k_i}{1 + k_i} \tag{21}$$

$$k_e(t_1 - t_2) = k_u + \frac{(1 + (1 - b)k_i)\lambda(k_u - k_i)}{(1 - \lambda)(1 + k_i)} \tag{22}$$

$$k_0'(t_1 - t_2) = (1 - \lambda)k_e + \lambda(1 - b)k_i \tag{23}$$

$$k_0'(t_1 - t_2) = k_u - b\lambda k_i \frac{1 + k_u}{1 + k_i}. \tag{24}$$

The SUCCO Routine: The First Period

From the single-period model, we derive

$$V_u(t_0) = \frac{CF_u(t_1) + V_u(t_1)}{1 + k_u} \tag{25}$$

$$V(t_0) = \frac{CF(t_1) + V(t_1)}{1 + k_0(t_0 - t_1)} \tag{26}$$

$$k_0(t_0 - t_1) = (1 - \lambda)k_e(t_0 - t_1) + \lambda k_i. \tag{27}$$

For $V(t_0)$, we can write

$$V(t_0) = V_u(t_0) + \frac{bk_i\lambda V(t_0)}{1 + k_i} + \frac{bk_i\lambda V(t_1)}{(1 + k_i)^2}$$

$$V(t_0) = \frac{(1 + k_i)V_u(t_0) + \dfrac{bk_i\lambda V(t_1)}{1 + k_i}}{1 + (1 - b\lambda)k_i}.$$

Substitution of (12) leads to

$$V(t_0) = \frac{(1 + k_i)V_u(t_0)}{1 + (1 - b\lambda)k_i} + \frac{bk_i V_u(t_1)}{[1 + (1 - b\lambda)k_i]^2}$$

$$1 + k_0(t_0 - t_1) = \frac{CF(t_1) + V(t_1)}{V(t_0)} = \frac{CF_u(t_1) + bk_i\lambda V(t_0) + V(t_1)}{V(t_0)}. \tag{28}$$

From this follows, considering (20) and (12),

$$1 + k_0(t_0 - t_1) = \frac{CF_u(t_1) + f\{b, k_i, \lambda, V_u(t_0), V_u(t_1)\}}{f\{b, k_i, \lambda, V_u(t_0), V_u(t_1)\}}.$$ (29)

The same holds for $k_e(t_0 - t_1)$ and $k_0'(t_0 - t_1)$.

The PARCO Routine

For this method it is necessary to split up the investment at t_0 into one initial expense to be matched with the cash flow at t_1, and another one taken as leading to the cash flow at t_2. This is purely arbitrary. A foothold may be found in using the depreciation amounts charged at the end of each period. In order to be able to do this, we rewrite the cash-flow series of the fourth section as follows:

Investment A	Investment B
t_0 $CF(A, t_0) = -D(t_1)$	t_0 $CF(B, t_0) = -D(t_2)$
t_1 $CF(A, t_1) = CF(t_1)$	t_2 $CF(B, t_2) = CF(t_2)$

For investment A, the single-period model is adequate; for investment B, the SUCCO routine can be followed, with $CF(B, t_1) = 0$.

CONCLUSIONS

The formulas

$$k_0 = (1 - \lambda)k_e + \lambda k_i$$

and

$$k_0' = (1 - \lambda)k_e + (1 - b)\lambda k_i$$

apply both for perpetuities and single-period investments. For multiperiod investments, they apply only per period, to the effect that $k_0(t_0 - t_1)$ does not need to equal $k_0(t_1 - t_2)$, and so on. This implies that the overall value for k_0, which encompasses the whole duration of the life of the investment and which may be calculated as the internal rate of return of the present value $V(t_0)$ and the after-tax cash flows CF_t for $t = 1, \ldots, n$, is not exclusively determined by k_u, λ, and b.

In evaluating investment projects that have risk characteristics identical to the corporate investment already under exploitation, it will generally not be appropriate to use the actual corporate k_0, even if management wants to maintain λ. This procedure would only be justified if the additional cash flow, before taxes, would equal the future cash flow of the existing investment in all aspects, up to a scale factor.

If management wishes to maintain the financial structure measured at market values (i.e., λ) for the evaluation of additional investments, k_u will serve as a point of departure. With the rollback method, the after-tax cash flows and the net present value of the project can then be determined. When using the internal rate of return as a screening device, this rate may be derived from the after-tax cash flows and the initial investment amount. The rate should then be compared with the "overall" k_0 mentioned earlier.

Maintaining (or varying deliberately) the financial structure measured at book values gives rise, of course, to a much simpler procedure for deriving cash flows after taxes from before-tax flows. The net present value and the internal rate of return are easy to calculate:

$$CF(t_n) = (1 - b)CF_{VB}(t_n) + b_i LI_0(t_n) \tag{30}$$

leads to the internal rate of return, while

$$V = V_u + \sum_{n=1}^{N} \frac{br_i LI_0(t_n)}{(1 + k_i)^n} \tag{31}$$

gives expression to the gross present value.

Moreover, maintaining the book value capital structure, L, or at least controlling its level, is much easier to do than is the case for the market value capital structure, λ. In [1], we have pictured the difficulties encountered while managing λ. They were considerable. Since again and again the impression is given that managers, as well as investors, are primarily oriented toward book values, the ideas launched here may contribute to a welcome change in the formulation of the theory. The familiar maxim: Stockholders' wealth does not need to be endangered by this formal modification.

APPENDIX: NOTATION

S	Equity at market value
B	Debt at market value
$V = S + B$	Market value of the firm
$\lambda = B/V$	Degree of leverage at market values
I_e	Equity at book value

I_i — Debt at book value

$I_0 = I_e + I_i$ — Book value of the firm

L — Degree of leverage at book value

b — Corporate income tax (CIT) rate

k_e — Cost of equity at market value

k_i — Cost of debt at market value

CF_{VB} — Cash flow before CIT

$CF_t = (1 - b)(CF_{VB} - D_t - k_iB) + k_iB + D_t$ — Cash flow for the levered firm after CIT

$CF_t' = (1 - b)(CF_{VB} - D_t) + D_t$ — Counterpart of the cash flow, for the levered firm as if unlevered, after CIT

$CF_{u_t} = (1 - b)(CF_{VB} - D_t) + D_t$ — Cash flow for the unlevered firm, after CIT

k_0 — FCOC to be applied to CF

k_0' — Counterpart of the FCOC, to be applied to CF'

k_u — FCOC to be applied to CF_u

D — Depreciation

t_n — Point of time n

$t_{n-1} - t_n$ — Period between t_{n-1} and t_n

r_i — Nominal rate of interest

NOTES

1. The same formula is to be found in [2, p. 11].

REFERENCES

[1] Diepenhorst, A.I. *Cost of and Return to Capital, Financial Structure, and Financial Policy 1976*. Centrum voor Bedrijfseconomisch Onderzoek, CBO reprint 15/F, 1976 (only available in Dutch).
[2] Myers, S.C. "Interactions of Corporate Financing and Investment Decisions: Implications for Capital Budgeting," *Journal of Finance* (1974), p. 11.

8 INEFFICIENT CAPITAL MARKETS AND THEIR IMPLICATIONS

John M. Samuels
Tulane University and Birmingham University, Great Britain

In this paper the point is made that most of the academic literature on the subject of private sector financial management assumes the existence of efficient capital markets. The theory of the subject, the financial strategies that result, and the recommended techniques of corporate resource allocation all revolve around efficient markets. Yet, in terms of the number of capital markets, if not in terms of the quantity of money involved, the vast majority of capital markets are not efficient.

The existence of an inefficient capital market can lead to companies' adopting investment strategies and techniques different from those that are suitable in an efficient market. It cannot be assumed that the stock market prices fully reflect all available information; it cannot be assumed that investors will correctly interpret the information that is released; and it cannot be assumed that insiders cannot operate on a scale sufficient to influence the price. The corporation, on the one hand, has greater potential to influence its own stock market price, and yet, on the other hand, there is a greater possibility that its price will move about in a manner not justified by the information available. The less than effi-

129

cient market will at most times be out of equilibrium. In the 1980s, it is to be hoped that the subject of financial management will become more concerned than it has been with corporate resource allocation where less than efficient capital markets exist.

The assumption of an efficient capital market allows intellectually satisfying decision-making techniques to be developed that will, if followed, enable managers to make optimal financing and investment decisions. However, where markets are less than efficient, the "currently promoted" decision-making techniques may not be appropriate. The existing literature on cost of capital, international portfolio investment, and international direct investment will be shown to be less than adequate when it comes to dealing with inefficient capital markets. More research is necessary into the possible application of already developed resource allocation techniques to the situation in small and developing capital markets.[1]

Most readers will be aware of the vast amount of literature that covers the testing of the efficient market hypothesis. The evidence appears to indicate that in most respects the markets in New York are efficient [14, 16, 17, 19]. However, in the majority of countries with capital markets, the evidence suggests that the markets are not efficient in all respects. Such capital markets vary from cases where there are only minor efficiency problems to ones where there is every reason to believe the market is far from efficient, with resulting distribution and decision-making problems. Nevertheless, the financial decision-making techniques appropriate only to efficient markets are exported to these countries.

It is incorrect to classify a market as efficient or inefficient; there is a whole spectrum of possibilities, with efficiency being the extreme at one end and inefficiency the extreme at the other end. The United States has the most efficient markets, and the developing countries the least efficient. In between come countries such as the United Kingdom, Germany, Spain, and Sweden. This point will be returned to later in the paper. At this stage, all that need be said is that the financial techniques developed for such purposes as measuring the corporate cost of capital are only applicable in the markets at the more efficient end of the spectrum.

In case the U.S. reader should feel that the rest of this paper is not of relevance to him, it should be pointed out that not all the capital markets in the United States have been proven to be efficient. As Dyckman, Downes, and Magee have pointed out, "The issue is not whether the market, the NYSE, is efficient or not, but rather . . . how efficient is this market and of what importance is the efficiency. Moreover, different markets will be characterized by different degrees of efficiency. Regional stock exchanges and the over the counter market may have different and, possibly, lower degrees of efficiency when compared to the NYSE" [12].

This paper is divided into four sections. The next section looks at the evidence on the efficiency of the capital markets in a number of countries. The second section is concerned with the financial conditions that typically are associated with a capital market in a developing country. The third section looks at certain aspects of financial management that lead to problems when applied to less than efficient markets, and finally, in the fourth section, another, perhaps more serious, problem is considered: the effect on the secondary distribution of resources of an inefficient market.

THE THEORY

Technically, for a market to be classed as efficient, it needs to be complete – that is, it must satisfy three necessary and sufficient conditions. First is homogeneous expectations: All investors have the same expectations with regard to the income and risk of each security. Second is that the market must be large enough so that there are a sufficient number of securities being offered to allow all investors to obtain, if they so wish, a perfectly balanced portfolio. Each investor should be able to obtain a combination of stocks and bonds that enables him to obtain a portfolio and to satisfy his expectations. To ascertain whether this is so, it is necessary to compare the number of securities with the number of states of the world – that is, the number of possible outcomes. This points to a problem for any small capital market: There are just not sufficient securities or possible combinations of securities to enable all investors to obtain the portfolios they require. The third condition for a complete market is that all investors' utility functions belong to the same class; this means that they all have a similar attitude to the tradeoff between possible risk and return. It means that some investors do not have an "irrational" attitude toward returns and risk compared to others.

It is, of course, accepted that all these conditions are not met in any capital market. Different markets are characterized by different degrees of efficiency and completeness. The important question in any market is how important the movements away from efficiency are.

In this paper we will classify the possible inefficiencies into five groups. First, inefficiencies due to the size of the capital market: The smaller the market, the more difficult it becomes for an investor to obtain the portfolio of his choosing. This inefficiency is lack of size, breadth, and depth in the market. Second, inefficiencies due to different risk preferences of investors, which can arise in a comparatively new capital market where the attitudes of investors to security investments can vary widely, there being no history of security investment and a poor understanding of the role of a capital market. A third inefficiency can arise due to lack of adequate market regulation and to variable standards of financial disclosure by corporations. A fourth area of inefficiency arises when there is a poor communication system in a country and it can take a long time for information to reach certain regions of the country. A fifth problem area is when there are only a few people in the country who know how to analyze and interpret the information that is released. For the market to be efficient, there need to be analysts who continually monitor company performance, and who are either active themselves or who advise others who are active in the marketplace. These last three problem areas can result in investors in a market having differing expectations with regard to the performance and risk of the securities quoted. It is a market where the securities do not reflect all the available information.

It is accepted that in all but a few markets there are restrictions on the sets of attainable distributions of income because there are a limited number of securities available. It is accepted that investors do not all agree on the expected profits of a company. It is accepted that individuals have different choice preferences; they do not all have the same utility functions. But how great are the differences in expectation? How great are the differences in utility function? Are the differences sufficient to allow us to conclude that the market is inefficient and that techniques applicable in efficient markets are no longer the ones that should be employed?

With regard to investors' preferences, Mossin has argued and demonstrated that "any reasonable set of preferences should induce a fairly well diversified portfolio. Therefore regardless of the individual's preferences he will select a portfolio that is for all practical purposes efficient. This in turn means that the conditions for market optimality may be satisfied" [27, 28]. This is the case for capital markets in developed countries. There are reasons to believe that it would not be so in a new capital market. The preferences of investors in developing countries may not be as close together as those of investors in developed countries.

When one comes to the conditions covering expectations and the range of possible investment opportunities, there are stronger grounds for believing that the smaller and newer capital markets will fail to meet the sufficient and necessary conditions. Mossin, when referring to the homogeneity of expectations assumption, suggests that it may not be too much of an unrealistic assumption. He is, however, referring to the case where the number of individual investors is large, and therefore where it is reasonable to expect that individual deviations from some average of individuals' probability estimates are of minor importance. He is also dealing with the situation where there are a number of sophisticated investors who exercise a discipline over price movements. Where the number of investors is small and where the communication of information about companies is poor, it could well be the case that the deviation from the average expectation is considerable, and significant enough to affect the efficiency of the market.

Sharpe, in his textbook on the subject, agrees that individual expectations can differ [33]. But he argues that in an efficient market, one expects the consensus opinion to reflect as "good a set of estimates of risk and returns" as one can find. The ill-informed investor might depress or inflate a particular company's stock price for a while, but the effect is small, and the informed investor will bring the market back in line [8]. If, however, the importance of the ill-informed investors is high relative to that of the informed investors and trading activity is low, then this adjustment process will take time to have an effect, and the stock prices will not reflect good estimates of risk and return. The capital market line of the Capital Asset Pricing Model (CAPM) will be meaningless in such markets.

It has also been pointed out many times that the quality of disclosure is likely to affect the price of a security. Inadequate corporate disclosure is likely to lead to a range of expectations by investors and therefore increase the fluctuations in the market price of a share. Investment decisions are being made by investors who have different knowledge and expectations about the financial position of a company. The market in such situations is not efficient from either an investment or a distribution point of view.

The Evidence

Jennergren and Korsvold advance the hypothesis that small capital markets are less efficient than large capital markets [18]. One reason for this, they suggest, is that smaller markets are "thin"; there are not many companies quoted, and usually there is not a lot of trading in the stocks of a large proportion of the quoted companies. Usually the companies quoted are small, and so there are not many shares in any one company, with the result that trading in just a few shares can affect the price significantly. Even sophisticated investors cannot be sure of being able to obtain the shares they wish to buy at the time they want them, and it has been shown that for a market to be efficient, it is necessary for the sophisticated investor to be able to act to iron out fluctuations in the random movement of prices. A second reason for the lower level of efficiency in small markets is that they are less well organized technically.

This tightness of the market and the lack of technical organizations are characteristics of the newer capital markets in developing countries. In Nigeria, for example, in addition to the problem of only a few companies with a quotation, there is a reluctance on the part of shareholders to sell the securities that they have obtained. This reluctance to trade means that the quoted price of a share is less likely to reflect its true worth based on the information available to the market than it would in a market with a great deal of trading activity. This nonreflection of available information occurs because investors are reluctant to trade.

Jennergren and Korsvold test their hypothesis that the larger the market, the greater the efficiency. They compare the markets of New York, London, Frankfurt, and Norway and Sweden. In Norway, there are approximately 175 companies listed on the Oslo exchange, and in Sweden, 150 on the Stockholm exchange. The less efficient market is less likely to show a random walk in share price movement. This is the weak form test of the efficient market hypothesis. For a market to be classed as efficient, it should at least satisfy this test. It is the easiest hurdle for a market to overcome in being tested for efficiency. If it is found that over time share prices move in a random manner, it does not prove that the market is efficient, but if there is no random movement, it does indicate that the market is less than efficient. Jennergren and Korsvold conclude that the random walk hypothesis is not a very accurate description of share price behavior on the Norwegian and Swedish stock markets.

In a study by Solnik, it was found that deviation from random walk was more apparent in the behavior of stock prices in each of eight European capital markets than in stock prices in the U.S. markets [34, 35]. The serial correlation results for each of the European exchanges were quite different from those found for the United States and would indicate a lesser efficiency for most European stock markets. Only in the case of London did Solnik find no serial correlation, thus indicating a "fairly efficient" market. Only in the United Kingdom were prices found to behave much like those in the United States. Solnik points out that at the time of the study, 1970, the market value of outstanding shares in London was more than the value for all other European markets put together; this, together with a technically advanced trading system, created a deep market.

Solnik suggests possible reasons for the lower levels of efficiency in the European exchanges. One explanation is thinness of market, and another discontinuity in trading. This is somewhat surprising, as the markets he examined, other than the United Kingdom's, were those of France, Germany, Italy, the Netherlands, Belgium, Switzerland, and Sweden, and in each country, the companies included in the sample were the largest in terms of market value. It has been found by a number of researchers that there is serial correlation in the price behavior of infrequently traded shares, but to find this in relatively large markets, such as those of France and Germany, when considering the largest companies in these countries, suggests that there are strong grounds for doubting the efficiency of smaller capital markets. Solnik studied the most extensively traded shares in each of his European markets, but points out that with the exception of the London market, the level of such trading is very thin compared to that in a typical U.S. quoted stock.

Other explanations for the inefficiencies suggested by Solnik include slow adjustment to new information and poor information systems combined with the existence of inside information and insider trading.

The biggest markets in Europe are to be found in the United Kingdom and Germany. If there is going to be efficiency in the European capital markets, we would expect to find it at least in these two countries. The evidence on the London stock exchange does indicate that it is reasonably efficient, although not as efficient as New York. Tests on the random walk hypothesis by Kendall, Alexander, Dryden, and Kemp and Reid find support for the independence of successive price changes, although Dryden has found some deviations from randomness [2, 11, 21, 22]. Using the weak form test, these researchers find the London capital market to be efficient. In the United Kingdom, as in all other countries outside the United States, tests using the semistrong form of the model are extremely rare, perhaps because of the absence of data in a convenient Compustat form.

The evidence on the stock markets in Germany indicates that they are not always efficient. Solnik's results have already been mentioned, but unfortunately there are not many other studies on the subject. One such study, by Conrad and Juttner, examines the price behavior of fifty-four stocks over the period 1968 to 1971 and concludes that "the empirical evidence we produced does not stand up well to the theory that stocks are being traded in an efficient market which is well organised and highly competitive, fully reflecting purely available information" [7]. They suggest that available and relevant information on economic factors that should help to determine company profits is not assessed correctly by the market. What is surprising is that this conclusion is based on a study of the fifty-four most actively traded stocks in Germany. Active trading was the criterion used for selecting the sample, and it is in the pricing of such stocks that one would have expected the market to be efficient.

However, in another study, by Kahnert, it was found that in certain phases of the economic cycle, the stock market was efficient, but in other phases of the cycle it was inefficient [20]. The results obtained from employing the weak form test of the efficient market hypothesis depended on the period that was studied. One can conclude that the West German stock markets are not always efficient.

What of other European exchanges? Niarchos found, using spectral analysis, that the random walk hypothesis holds for the Greek stock exchange except for lightly traded stocks [29]. Theil and Leenders found the Amsterdam market to be less than efficient [38]. In a study of the Spanish stock markets, where there are three exchanges with 500 companies listed, Palacios concluded that the market has become increasingly efficient [30]. He attributed this improvement in efficiency to the increasing activities of unit trust (mutual fund) investment managers, who are sophisticated investors, and who, if shares are available, can bring shares in line with the "true" value.

If the European exchanges (excluding London) are found to have technical and institutional characteristics that result in departure from a random walk in stock prices, and so a departure from efficiency, what of markets elsewhere in the world? Ang and Pohlman suggest that if "the degree of structure or organisation affects the degree of conformity to the random walk process, then we should expect countries whose stock exchanges are not as organised as the European exchanges to exhibit greater deviation from a random walk process" [3]. Ang and Pohlman examined five Far Eastern capital markets—those of Australia, Hong Kong, Japan, the Philippines, and Singapore. The Japanese market, which is a very large, active market, was found to have a serial correlation coefficient similar to those of the United States and London, indicating a high level of efficiency. The serial correlation results for the other four markets are similar to those found for the seven European exchanges (excluding London). However, in these four Far Eastern markets, a greater departure from the normal distribution of returns was found than in Europe, with high standard deviations and high serial correlation coefficients for some individual stocks. This indicates the possibility of some very profitable trading opportunities. Since only a small number of companies were examined in this study, and these were the largest companies in the respective countries, there could well be even more profitable trading opportunities among the smaller, less frequently traded companies quoted.

Another test on the Australian capital market found that there was autocorrelation between price movements. The random walk hypothesis did not hold [31]. Granger has suggested that this is perhaps because there are a number of shares quoted in Australia, which are included in Praetz's study [31], in which the trading activity is only light [17].

The problems of a thin market have been referred to a number of times in this review. One of the other problems of a new market is highlighted in a study by Drake of the new issue boom in Malaya and Singapore [10]. It was found that although the embryonic market was able to meet the very high demand for capital during an economic boom period, tighter supervision of the market was needed in the future if the public were to be reassured that the market was not just one for wild speculations. Drake commented that the stock markets concerned were much more outlets for gamblers than were the stock markets in industrialized capitalist economies. Perhaps this is what is required in the early years of a capital market; at least in providing opportunities for big gains, the markets do provide those companies seeking funds with the money that is much needed for investment. However, meeting the demand for funds does not mean that the markets are efficient. One can perhaps argue that the early teething problems of developing capital markets can be soon overcome. But history does not show that to be the case, for it has taken the U.S. and U.K. markets over one hundred years to get to their present levels of efficiency, and although newer markets may be quicker, ten to twenty years is a very short time in an industrialization process.

One study that did attempt a weak form test on markets other than in the United States is that by Deakin and Smith [9]. They looked at the impact of earnings information on security prices in Toronto and Johannesburg. For South Africa, it was found that there were significant price changes during the earnings announcement week. The results for the Canadian exchange were found to be less conclusive.

Another finding relating to Toronto that would suggest a less than efficient market was produced in a study by Kryzanowski [23]. This study was concerned with regulations and insider dealing and found there were ample opportunities for insiders to undertake profitable dealings.

So much for the evidence on the comparatively well organized markets in Europe and the Far East. What of the markets in the less developed countries?

INVESTORS' INFORMATION AND EXPECTATIONS

The empirical evidence indicates, therefore, that the smaller and newer markets are less than efficient. In developing countries, in addition to the problem of the "thinness" of the market, there is the more serious problem of investors' expectations and access to information.

We will now concern ourselves with the knowledge and information typically available to investors in developing countries and the way in which this is interpreted. We will use Nigeria as an example. First, in that country there is a Capital Issues Committee, which, at the time of a new issue, has as one of its tasks to ensure that the new shares are distributed as widely as possible among shareholders, so that many people have a stake in the company. When a new issue comes to the market, there has been, in the recent economic conditions of that country, an excess demand for the shares. They have been allocated under the committee's supervision to ensure that no one individual or group receives large holdings of the shares. This is good from the point of view of dispersing ownership, but it does mean that the management of such companies has little to worry about from shareholder power. It is more difficult to organize widely dispersed shareholders to complain about management than to organize a concentrated group of shareholders.

The shares are distributed to many individuals. This leads to a problem — namely, that not all shareholders have the latest information relating to the economy, the industry, or the company. This is because of communication problems in a country as vast as Nigeria and at the state of development of Nigeria. The leading capital markets of the world are not by accident situated where the communication system is at its best. The Eurocurrency and Eurobank markets have no marketplace; they are just a number of centers in different countries connected by an efficient telephone system. Iran in the early 1970s had ambitions to be the financial center for the vast amount of petrodollars that were flowing through the Middle East. One reason why that could not be was because of a poor communication system.

The importance to capital and money markets of a good communication system should not be overlooked. The efficient market hypothesis assumes that markets adjust quickly to new information. In developing countries, this is not possible. It would be quite possible for an investor in, say, Lagos to hear some bad news about a company in the morning, to fly to Kano, and to act on that news by selling his shares to an investor in that town, and for the buyer not to have heard the relevant news at the time of the transaction. The assumption that all investors have the same knowledge is not justified in many developing countries. The expected profits from the use of information is not zero. On the contrary, early access to information is a way of making money.

Do all investors in Nigeria place the same interpretation on information received? The answer would again appear to be no. In recent years in Nigeria, there has been a reluctance to sell shares. If shares are allotted to investors at the time of a new issue, there is a tendency for that person to hold onto the shares. All stock markets experience times of rising prices and times of falling prices. The knowledgeable investor sells his shares just before the market begins to fall. In Nigeria, where many shareholders are new to the ways of portfolio investment, there seems a reluctance to accept that share prices can fall. It is not generally accepted that the pieces of paper, the share certificates, are worth nothing in themselves, that they are only worth what somebody is prepared to pay you for them. It is no good holding onto these pieces of paper when bad news starts to come to the market. The point being made is that in any stock market, some investors know more about the way the market behaves than other investors do. In Nigeria, because the market is relatively new and many shareholders have only recently acquired shares, there are many investors who do not know how to interpret financial information. Financial accounts are hard enough to interpret, even by experts. Standards of disclosure are not high in most developing countries, and this, combined with high levels of inflation, makes it difficult to ascertain the real performance of a company. For the market to be efficient, companies have to disclose a great deal about their performance and financial position.

Of course, there are investors in Nigeria, as in many other countries, who do obtain information early and who know how to interpret it correctly. There are important and serious implications in a society where a small group of experts obtain information early and can interpret the importance of information. They will be able to use this ability to make gains at other investors' expense and to redistribute wealth in their direction. It must be made clear that we are not talking about "insiders" using information to make gains. Insiders are a problem in all capital markets, efficient and inefficient, developed and developing. Legislation is usually introduced to restrict the activities of possible insiders. The point being made is that in a developing capital market, which it can be argued in its early years is almost bound to be inefficient, there are people who because of the positions they occupy or where they are located, or because they are experts at interpreting information, can quite easily and legally make regular gains at the expense of other investors.

Because of the information problem, in certain countries the investment "group" has developed. This is a type of mini capital market; it is a multienterprise firm that obtains its funds from within the group. The people who own the firm may be linked by family, commercial, tribal, or ethnic relations. The information available within the group is far better than the information available to people outside the group. On the basis of this internal information, the group is able to make better (more informed) investment decisions than are those outside the group; it is better able to allocate its capital funds. The firms inside the group tend, therefore, to move funds about between firms in the group. This group may have developed before the creation of a capital market and may continue with its superior information even after a capital market has been created [25].

The existence of such "groups" tends to confirm a point made at a theoretical level by those economists concerned with Information Theory. They have argued that the existence of one giant firm should be more efficient from a capital allocation point of view than the existence of dozens of smaller firms obtaining funds through a capital market. This would be so even with an efficient capital market because there is still information loss between the firm and the market and there are still problems of interpreting the available information.

"Groups" have been found to exist in countries in South America and Central America, as well as in Nigeria, Korea, the Philippines, and Pakistan. Qureshi, in an article entitled "Economic Development, Social Justice and Financial Reporting: Pakistan's Experience with Private Enterprise," points to the problem of inadequate information. Meaningful financial reporting is necessary for a number of reasons, one being to give investors confidence. It was found that in Pakistan there were "several deficiencies in terms of timeliness, quantity, quality, and readability of company financial data as portrayed in annual financial reports." It was found that the general investing public, the potential investors, did not have an information system that they could trust [32]. No wonder, therefore, that in such situations groups exist and flourish despite the existence of a stock market.

DECISION-MAKING PROBLEMS

In this section, we will look at certain of the areas of corporate resource decision making, where the literature on the subject usually assumes the existence of efficient markets. It is suggested that the techniques leave something to be desired when the stock markets turn out to be less than efficient. The three problem areas that are considered, which are chosen for illustrative purposes, are cost of capital, international portfolio diversification, and multinational company investment.

The cost of capital is basic to all capital investment decision making. A necessary condition for accepting any investment proposal is that the expected return exceeds the cost of capital. The funds for the investment can come from a number of different sources, each of which will have its own separate cost. It is the cost of equity funds that is the hardest to determine. In theory, the cost of such capital is equal to the minimum rate of return a company needs to earn to satisfy its stockholders. At this point, when the company invests equity funds in any new project, the value of the equity shares after the announcement of the project and its expected returns should be equal to the value of the shares before the announcement.

The key to estimating this minimum rate of return is to ascertain what returns the investors expect the company to make. What are the expectations of those who operate in the stock market? The technique for determining this is to assume that the stock market price on any day is an equilibrium price and that it conveys information about investors' expectations.

There are two main approaches to measuring the cost of capital. The newer approach is based on the Capital Asset Pricing Model, and it implies that the return that investors require on a stock is equal to a risk-free rate plus a premium for risk. Risk is a function of (1) the expected returns from the market portfolio, (2) the returns from the security being considered, (3) the variance of these two returns, and (4) the covariance between these two returns. If the historical relationship between these variables is a reasonable proxy for the future relationship, then we are able to estimate the well-known beta coefficients. The returns used to estimate beta are the changes in share price over time. These are the returns the stockholder has obtained as a result of holding stock in a particular corporation.

Now, for some problems, the Capital Asset Pricing Model assumes that the stock prices obtained are generated by a perfect capital market. If the market in the past was not in equilibrium, if the true relationship between the risk of a particular company and that of this market portfolio was not established, there is no reason to believe the basic CAPM formula is correct. The return obtained from investing in a stock will not be the risk-free rate plus the true premium for risk. There is also no reason to believe that the coefficients obtained from measuring the past relationships will hold for future periods. The market price at any time will not be the equilibrium price, and there will not be stability in the estimated coefficients needed in the model.

As you relax the assumption of the CAPM to make it more appropriate to inefficient markets, the greater becomes the residual risk, which cannot be measured. Yet this unsystematic risk also influences the expected, the required, rate of return, which is needed to measure the cost of capital.

Is the second approach to measuring the cost of equity capital any more promising in inefficient markets than the first? The answer is unfortunately no. There are a number of models that enable us to estimate a "true" value for a share. One of the simplest is that the value of a share is the discounted sum of future dividends. This model rearranged enables us to estimate the cost of equity capital; it is the market rate of discount that equates the present value of future dividends per share with the current market price of the share. It is the current dividend yield plus the expected growth rate of dividends. Again, it is based on the assumption that the current market price is an equilibrium price that tells us something about shareholders' expectation. If the capital market is inefficient, it is dangerous and incorrect to base future investment decisions on a cost of capital, based on the dividend yield at one point in time. The price, the denominator in the dividend yield calculation, is not an equilibrium price.

The same criticism can be made about the other models, based on earnings yield and dividend yields, that are used to estimate the cost of capital. The yields are based on stock market prices that cannot in an inefficient market be assumed to be free from bias.

Van Horne, in one of the more popular texts on the subject, points out that the methods for determining the cost of capital of corporations in the United States are inexact and that our confidence in the estimates obtained should vary according to the type of corporation for which we are trying to establish the cost. For large corporations whose stock is actively traded on the New York Exchange, our estimates will be reasonable; for smaller corporations whose shares are traded on the over-the-counter market, our confidence in the estimates will be less. "We must live with the inexactness of the measurement process and try to do as good a job as possible" [40]. The point of this paper is that the inexactness in an inefficient market can be so great that we need to change the technique of measurement. One possibility is to obtain measures of risk based on accounting data [4, 5, 6]. This approach is being tried, but the published accounting information often leaves something to be desired.

A second area of financial management that turns out to be not very useful once the assumption of efficient capital markets is removed is international portfolio investment. A number of studies have looked at the possibilities of reducing risk in a portfolio by international diversification. Unfortunately, these studies do not usually examine whether the capital markets in which they wish to invest are efficient. Consequently, the results they obtain are open to question, because they are based on the CAPM, which does require a certain level of efficiency, which is unproven.

Unfortunately, although these studies are strong on mathematics, the data they use are very limited, and usually the efficiency of the markets from which the price data are obtained is not considered. The international diversification articles are concerned with the returns that can be obtained from investing in different capital markets, where returns equal dividend yields plus the changes in stock market prices. Whether the prices they use are equilibrium prices is not disclosed. Typically, either a stock market price index for the country or individual company stock prices are used to obtain the capital gains. Where the individual stock prices are used, they are for the largest and most well-traded companies in the respective stock exchanges.

It has been demonstrated in the literature that if intercountry correlation between returns is low and stable, then a necessary, although not necessarily a sufficient, condition for international diversification exists. The correlation between the returns from investing in different countries is measured for past periods, and if these correlations have been stable in the past, this gives a confidence that they will hold in the future. The point being made in this paper is that less than efficient markets are not in equilibrium, and so a certain amount of the price movement of an individual company share or the movement of the index is caused by the market's trying to adjust to previously released information, to the prices moving to reflect all available information.

There might well be an identifiable correlation between the performance of one country's economy and that of another, but this will only partly be picked up by observing the movement of stock market prices or indices. The international portfolio diversification researchers are hoping to find "a degree of stationarity in the international capital markets." They have no reason to expect to find this when looking for a correlation either between an efficient capital market and an inefficient capital market or between two inefficient capital markets.

There is another problem in this international portfolio diversification literature—namely, in which shares do you invest to obtain the balanced portfolio required? The research, which measures correlation between one stock market index and another, ignores this point. Presumably, the researchers are assuming that one can select a portfolio within any country that, in terms of return and risk, will behave as the index. However, in markets that are not in equilibrium, there is less reason to assume that betas will remain stable over time than there is in efficient markets. Although the literature may claim to show that there are possibilities of gain from international diversification, it begs the question of how to realize that gain. Portfolio theory, with the CAPM approach to investment decision making, may be all right in the New York or London Stock exchanges, but academics in their eagerness to publish should not assume that it can be applied in all capital markets.

The more restrained researcher only considers diversification in the capital markets in developed countries, this being because the stock market prices and data obtained from capital markets in developing countries is often of "doubtful quality, consistency, and reliability" [13]. But it must be remembered that only three or four capital markets in the world have been found to be efficient. The majority of even developed countries' markets are less than efficient.

One of the four capital markets that appears to be efficient is the Tokyo market. A study by Lau, Quay, and Ramsey found that the risk assumptions of the Capital Asset Pricing Model were justified in the Tokyo capital market. They found investors were compensated for bearing systematic risk. The returns above the risk-free rate from holding a stock were related to the risk of the individual company. The investors were found to be risk averse [24]. Similar studies have been made of the CAPM and the London Stock Exchange [37]. It is such studies that should be undertaken before the advantages of international portfolio diversification are considered.

Solnik, who has written extensively on international portfolio diversifications, has pointed to the problem of size in a capital market. In the United States an investor on Wall Street, because of the large number of securities quoted, can "get rid of all but 27% of the typical risk of individual securities by diversifying" [36]. In West Germany, 44 percent of the risk cannot be diversified away, and West Germany is the fourth biggest capital market in the world in terms of the number of companies quoted and is one of the four that show some indications of being efficient.

The third area where problems arise when markets are not efficient is international direct investment. It is here that the problems of the corporate cost of capital and portfolio risk come together.

Much of the literature on multinational long-run financial decisions still prescribes the use for investment decision making of either a global-weighted average cost of capital or the foreign subsidiaries' own weighted average cost of capital based on the local capital leverage. Alder and Dumas criticize these two approaches and suggest a value-maximization model. Their approach recognizes the problems of efficiency in foreign financial and capital markets. They conclude that "the multinational company's required yield on its domestic projects will generally differ from its required yield on foreign projects and both will differ from the required yield of a foreign firm facing the same foreign projects" [1].

The difficulty of finding an appropriate discount rate for evaluating foreign investment projects is illustrated in the two papers on this topic included in the other volume of these proceedings. Folks makes the point that from the local (host country) viewpoint the foreign investment project should at least earn a return sufficient to meet the cost of capital in local terms committed to it; the local cost of capital should approximate the economic return that the local society expects from investment projects [15]. Lessard, taking a different approach to the measurement of cost of capital, emphasizes how at a practical level this is very difficult to obtain [26]. He argues that the cash flows arising from a project should be discounted at the "real rate of interest plus a risk premium reflecting their systematic risk. However, determining this systematic risk represents a major challenge." He gives a number of reasons why it will be difficult to obtain estimates of beta and raises the intriguing question of whether the systematic risk should be measured relative to the investing firm's home country market portfolio or relative to the world market portfolio. In either case, one has the problem already mentioned above—namely, how meaningful our existing attempts to measure systematic risk with international portfolio diversification have been.

Theoretically, we can say how foreign investment projects should be evaluated, but we have not really looked at the problem in the way of implementing the suggested techniques. We need to consider the estimation problems that arise when many capital markets are not efficient and the Capital Asset Pricing Model cannot be applied.

SECOND-PERIOD INEFFICIENCY

The basic question is whether the existence of a capital market in a small or developing country is desirable; are the social returns greater than the social costs? It has been argued that there are reasons to believe that the small and the new capital markets are likely to be inefficient. Indeed, there is empirical evidence that this is so. This inefficiency has implications for the distribution of returns resulting from the investments. At this point, we are concerned with the results of inefficiency in the distribution of the returns to the stockholders, with what is known as second-period efficiency.

A capital market is not responsible for any inequalities in the initial distribution of wealth and income in an economy. Indeed, it is not part of its role to be concerned with such problems. However, the introduction of a capital market, which has a strong chance of being inefficient, will create conditions that will lead to increasing inequality in the distribution of wealth. This is not one of the objectives of those encouraging the development of a capital market in a country, but it can be one of the results.

This increase in inequality at a time when many people in developing countries are expecting to see signs of a reduction in inequality can lead to social unrest. This danger should be taken into account when the introduction and development of a capital market is being considered as a means of improving the flow of funds in an economy. Resulting increases in inequalities, with the accompanying social and political dangers, can perhaps be justified if the social returns from the development of a market are greater than the social cost. However, the claims for benefits need to be looked at carefully. Capital markets in both developed and developing countries have been found to provide only a small proportion of the funds needed each year by a company. Further, the disciplinary aspect of a capital market, where a company is continually having to justify its performance in the marketplace, is now well advanced in developing countries.

On the supply side, a market is efficient in all respects when it is not possible for any investor to gain systematically from knowing something about the economy, an industry, or the position of a company that is not known to other investors. For the market to be efficient, no investor has to have a greater chance than any other of making a gain. Each investor is entering a fair game, with no player having initial advantages. No player can systematically gain at the expense of another. Of course, an investor can gain at somebody else's expense from good fortune, but not from superior knowledge.

In an efficient market, although the investors may initially have different levels of wealth or income, there is no reason to believe that the income resulting from the investment of their funds will increase or decrease the inequality in the distribution of wealth and income. The investors begin the game with funds available for investment. The funds are allocated in the so-called first period to the companies. The companies have announced their past results and their investment plans. The individual investors have made their decisions on whether to consume or to invest. The individuals' preference-ordering between first-period consumption or second-period income is determined by their expected utility. The problem is that it is not a fair game; some investors have a greater chance than others of making a gain.

Should we be concerned with second-period inefficiency? Is it still worth going ahead and developing a capital market even though it is inefficient in certain aspects? The advantages are that savings may be channeled to support investments that would otherwise have found it difficult to obtain funds. The capital market does provide long-term finance. It is equity finance, which is difficult to obtain from other sources. If information is good, the disclosure requirements good, and the market well controlled, it is still possible that the funds are allocated efficiently, that the funds are channeled to those companies that can use them to make the highest returns.

The arguments against such a market are, first, it provides only a very small amount of new capital for companies. A large amount of the activities of a stock market is secondary activity, one investor selling to another, which does not benefit companies at all. It does, however, give the possibility of a redistribution of wealth.

Development finance books urge the setting up of capital markets in order to help support investment. An efficient market is undoubtedly useful. For a market to be efficient, there need to be stringent disclosure requirements, control of inside traders, an active and reasonably sized market, no discontinuities in trading, and a good communication system. If these conditions are not met in a country, a capital market can add to inequalities in the distribution of wealth. This can be acceptable in some political climates, but not in others.

"A vigorous capital market can exist only in a supportive social, political and legal as well as economic environment" [39]. The problem is that although the economic environment might be right, in the early days of a capital market, it will in most developing countries be inefficient, which, because of the wealth redistribution effect, can disrupt or destroy the social and political environment.

NOTES

1. Research into certain aspects of this problem is at present being undertaken by the author and K. Boudreaux of Tulane University.

REFERENCES

[1]   Adler, M., and Dumas, B. "The Long Term Financial Decisions of the Multinational Corporation," in E.J. Elton and M.J. Gruber, eds., *International Capital Markets.* Amsterdam: North-Holland Publishing Company, 1975.

[2]   Alexander, S.S. "Price Movements in Speculative Markets: Trend or Random Walks," *Industrial Management Review* 2 (1961), pp. 7–26.

[3]   Ang, J.S., and Pohlman, R.A. "A Note on the Price Behavior of Far Eastern Stocks," *Journal of International Business Studies* (Spring/Summer 1978).

[4]   Ball, R., and Brown, P. "Portfolio Theory and Accounting," *Journal of Accounting Research* (Autumn 1969).

[5]   Beaver, W.H., and Manecold, J. "The Association between Market Determined and Accounting Determined Measures of Systematic Risk: Some Further Evidence," *Journal of Financial and Quantitative Analysis* (June 1975).

[6]   Bildersee, J.S. "Market Determined and Alternative Measures of Risk," *Accounting Review* (January 1975).

[7]   Conrad, K., and Juttner, D.J. "Recent Behaviour of Stock Market Prices in Germany and the Random Walk Hypothesis," *Kyklos* 26 (1973), pp. 576–599.

[8]   Cootner, P. "Stock Prices – Random v. Systematic Changes," *Industrial Management Review* (Spring 1962).

[9]   Deakin, E.B., and Smith, C.H. "The Impact of Earnings Information on Selected Foreign Securities Markets," *Journal of International Business* (Fall 1978).

[10] Drake, P.J. "The New Issue Boom in Malaya and Singapore," *Economic Development and Cultural Change* (October 1969).

[11] Dryden, M.M. "A Statistical Study of U.K. Share Prices," *Scottish Journal of Political Economy* 27 (1970), pp. 369–389, and "Filter Tests of U.K. Share Prices," *Applied Economics* 1 (1970), pp. 261–275.

[12] Dyckman, T.R.; Downes, D.H.; and Magee, R.P. *Efficient Capital Markets and Accounting – A Critical Analysis.* Englewood Cliffs, N.J.: Prentice-Hall, 1975, p. 84.

[13] Errunza, V.R. "Gains from Portfolio Diversification into Less Developed Countries' Securities," *Journal of International Business* (Fall/Winter 1977).

[14] Fama, E.F. "Efficient Capital Markets: A Review of Theory and Empirical Work," *Journal of Finance* 25 (1970), pp. 383–417.

[15] Folks, W.R. "Critical Assumptions in Evaluating Foreign Investment Projects," in Roy L. Crum and Frans G.J. Derkinderen, eds., *Capital Budgeting under Conditions of Uncertainty.* Boston: Martinus Nijhoff Publishing, 1981.

[16] Granger, C.W.J., and Morgenstern, O. *Predictability of Stock Market Prices.* Lexington, Mass.: Lexington Books, 1970.

[17] Granger, C.W.J. "A Survey of Empirical Studies on Capital Markets," in E.J. Elton and M.J. Gruber, eds., *International Capital Markets.* Amsterdam: North-Holland Publishing Company, 1975.

[18] Jennergren, L.P., and Korsvold, P.E. "The Non-Random Character of Norwegian and Swedish Market Prices," in E.J. Elton and M.J. Gruber, eds., *International Capital Markets.* Amsterdam: North-Holland Publishing Company, 1975.

[19] Jensen, M.C. "Capital Markets: Theory and Evidence," *Bell Journal of Economics and Management Science* 3 (1972), pp. 357–398.

[20] Kahnert, A. *Irrfahrtprozesse und Trendverläufe im Aktienmarkt der Bundesrepublik.* Göttingen: Vandenhoeck und Ruprecht, 1972.

[21] Kemp, A.G., and Reid, G.C. "The Random Walk Hypothesis and the Recent Behaviour of Equity Prices in Britain," *Economica* 38 (1971), pp. 28–51.

[22] Kendall, M.G. "The Analysis of Economic Time-Series – I: Prices," *Journal of the Royal Statistics Society* 96 (1953), pp. 11–25.

[23] Kryzanowski, L. "Misinformation and Regulatory Actions in the Canadian Capital Markets: Some Empirical Evidence," *Bell Journal of Economics* (Autumn 1978).

[24] Lau, S.C.; Quay, S.R.; and Ramsey, C.M. "The Tokyo Stock Exchange and the CAPM," *Journal of Finance* (May 1974).

[25] Leff, N.H. "Capital Markets in the Less Developed Countries: The Group Principle," in R.I. McKinnon, ed., *Money and Finance in Economic Growth and Development.* New York: Dekker, 1976.

[26] Lessard, D. "Evaluating Foreign Projects: An Adjusted Present Value Approach," in Roy L. Crum and Frans G.J. Derkinderen, eds., *Capital Bud-

geting under Conditions of Uncertainty. Boston: Martinus Nijhoff Publishing, 1981.

[27] Mossin, J. *Theory of Financial Markets.* Englewood Cliffs, N.J.: Prentice-Hall, 1973.

[28] Mossin, J. *The Economic Efficiency of Financial Markets.* Lexington, Mass.: Lexington Books, 1977.

[29] Niarchos, N.A. "Statistical Analysis of Transactions of the Athens Stock Exchange," Ph.D. thesis, Nottingham, 1971.

[30] Palacios, J.A. "The Stock Market in Spain: Tests of Efficiency and Capital Market Theory," in E.J. Elton and M.J. Gruber, eds., *International Capital Markets.* Amsterdam: North-Holland Publishing Company, 1975.

[31] Praetz, P.D. "Australian Share Prices and the Random Walk Hypothesis," *Australian Journal of Statistics* 11 (1969), pp. 123–139.

[32] Qureshi, M. "Economic Development, Social Justice and Financial Reporting: Pakistan's Experience with Private Enterprise," *Management International Review* 15 (June 1975).

[33] Sharpe, W.F. *Investments.* Englewood Cliffs, N.J.: Prentice-Hall, 1978.

[34] Solnik, B.H. "Note on the Validity of the Random Walk for European Stock Prices," *Journal of Finance* (1973), pp. 1151–1159.

[35] Solnik, B.H. *European Capital Markets.* Lexington, Mass.: Lexington Books, 1973.

[36] Solnik, B.H. "The International Pricing of Risk: An Empirical Investigation of the World Capital Market Structure," *Journal of Finance* (May 1974).

[37] Taylor, B. *Readings in Investment Analysis and Portfolio Management.* London: Elek Books, 1970.

[38] Theil, H., and Leenders, C.T. "Tomorrow on the Amsterdam Stock Exchange," *Journal of Business* (July 1965).

[39] Tun Wai, U., and Patrick, H.T. *Stock and Bond Issues and Capital Markets in Less Developed Countries.* I.M.F. Staff Papers.

[40] Van Horne, J.C. *Financial Management and Policy,* 3rd ed. Englewood Cliffs, N.J.: Prentice-Hall, 1974.

9 AN INVESTMENT DECISION MODEL FOR SMALL BUSINESS

Ernest W. Walker
University of Texas at Austin

In the majority of cases, small businesses have not utilized the more sophisticated methods when making investments in assets; on the other hand, many large firms have employed such techniques as internal rate of return, net present value, and the Capital Asset Pricing Model when selecting among alternative investments. It is the contention of this writer that none of these methods is applicable to the manager of the small business, since they require the knowledge of a single investment criterion which, in most, if not all, cases, cannot be ascertained with any degree of confidence.

The purpose of this paper is to present an investment model that employs the concept of discounted cash flow and does not require a single investment criterion. Not only does the model allow the manager to select the most desirable investment; it also "informs" the decision maker which optimum financing method should be used, thus eliminating the necessity of the manager's knowing the firm's optimum capital structure prior to making the investment decision.

The model also informs the manager of the effects that changes in the asset mix have on the "returns" to the various suppliers of capital, as well as on the

149

"return" on total capital. Information of this nature allows the owner-manager to select the optimum investments from various types of investments—for example, an investment in a retail establishment rather than in a manufacturing firm.

ADJUSTED INTERNAL RETURN METHOD

The adjusted internal rate of return (AIRR) technique requires at least two adjustments to be made in the firm's data. First, the capital account should be divided into debt and equity sources. If leases are used in the financing process, they should be isolated from traditional sources of debt, and the internal rate of return on this capital should be computed. To accomplish these adjustments requires knowledge not only of the capital structure of the firm, but of the asset mix as well. Incidentally, a change in either the asset mix or debt/equity mix affects the flow of funds, which, in turn, causes the internal rate of return of each supplier to change. Moreover, a change in the firm's asset mix will cause the internal rate of return (IRR) on all capital either to increase or decrease, but a change in the debt/equity mix will not cause the IRR on total capital to change. Second, the firm's total cash flows should be divided in such a way that management can ascertain the internal rate of return on (1) debt capital (IRR_d) and (2) equity capital (IRR_e). The firm's cash flows are defined mathematically as follows:

$$(EBIDT - D - I)(1 - TR) + I(1 - TR) + D + W/C + S \qquad (1)$$

[Total cash flow (CF_t) = profit (less taxes) + interest (less taxes)
+ depreciation + working capital (W/C) + scrap] ;

stated differently,

$$CF_t = (EBIDT - I)(1 - TR) + I(1 - TR) + D(TR) + W/C + S, \qquad (2)$$

where EBIDT is defined as earnings before interest, depreciation, and taxes, and TR is equal to the firm's tax rate.

Total cash flow (CF_t) is divided into three major components: cash flow to equity holders (CF_e), creditors (CF_d), and lessors (CF_l).

$$CF_e = \text{profit after taxes} + (1 - \alpha)\text{ depreciation} + (1 - \alpha)\text{ working capital} + (1 - \alpha)\text{ scrap,} \qquad (3)$$

$$CF_d = \text{interest } (1 - TR) + (\alpha)\text{ depreciation} + (\alpha)\text{ working capital} + (\alpha)\text{ scrap, and} \qquad (4)$$

$$CF_l = \text{lease payments only,} \qquad (5)$$

where α is equal to the ratio of debt plus equity, debt/(debt + equity). Therefore,

$$CF_t = CF_e + CF_d + CF_l. \tag{6}$$

Employing the data of a hypothetical company, we are able to illustrate
these adjustments. Assume that the ABC Company's cash flows and balance
sheet data are depicted in Table 1. The allocation of the cash flows based on
the above criteria between creditors and the owners is provided in Table 2. In
viewing the table, the cash flows associated with the creditor's portion of the
investment, CF_d, consists of interest adjusted by the tax rate of the firm plus
the amount of the capital provided by the creditors. The latter amount is represented in the cash flow as depreciation, return of working capital, and scrap
value. The amount of depreciation, working capital, and scrap allocated to each
supplier is based on the ratio of debt to debt plus equity, α. In the above example, since the creditors financed one-half of the investment, it is presumed
the cash flow allocated to them will consist of one-half ($\alpha = 0.5$) of the depreciation plus one-half of the working capital plus one-half of the scrap value. On
the other hand, if the creditors had financed only one-fourth of the investment,
they would have received only one-fourth of the depreciation, working capital,
and scrap (i.e., $\alpha = 0.25$). It should be emphasized that while the principal
owed to the creditors will not actually be repaid in this manner, it is "earned"
in this way. Cash flows related to the owners' investment (CF_e), on the other
hand, include earnings (less taxes) plus the amount of capital provided by the
equity investors. In this case, they, like the creditors, receive one-half ($1 - \alpha$)
of the depreciation, working capital, and scrap.

After CF_d and CF_e have been determined, we are able to calculate the
internal rate of return (IRR_d) on debt capital by solving the following equation:

$$\sum_{t=1}^{n} \frac{(CF_d)_t}{(1+r)^t} - \sum_{t=0}^{n-1} \frac{(CO_d)_t}{(1+r)^t} = 0, \tag{7}$$

where CF_d is the cash flow "earned" for the creditors in period t, CO_d is the
amount of capital supplied by *all* creditors, and r is the rate that equates the
present value of the future CF_d to the present value of investment provided
by the creditors. In other words, r is the internal rate of return (IRR_d) on the
amount of debt capital invested by all creditors.

The internal rate of return on equity (IRR_e) may be determined by solving
the following equation:

$$\sum_{t=1}^{n} \frac{(CF_e)_t}{(1+r)^t} - \sum_{t=0}^{n-1} \frac{(CO_e)_t}{(1+r)^t} = 0, \tag{8}$$

Table 1.   The ABC Company: Balance Sheet Data and Income Data

Balance Sheet Data

Assets	
Current assets	
Cash	$ 10,000
Receivables	20,000
Inventories	20,000
Fixed assets	50,000
Total	$100,000
Liabilities and net worth	
Current liabilities	
Notes payable	$ 15,000
Accounts payable	15,000
Long-term note	20,000
Net worth	
Common stock – 50,000 shares	50,000
Total	$100,000

Income Data

	Year				
	1	2	3	4	5
Expected EBIDT[a]	$24,500	$25,000	$26,000	$25,500	$27,000
Expected interest payment[b]	4,600	5,200	5,000	5,400	5,800
Depreciation	9,000	9,000	9,000	9,000	9,000
Expected earnings before taxes	10,900	10,800	12,000	11,100	12,200
Taxes (20%)	2,180	2,160	2,400	2,220	2,440
Profit after tax	8,720	8,640	9,600	8,880	9,760

[a]EBIDT means earnings before interest, depreciation, and taxes.
[b]Change in totals resulted from changing interest rates, not amount borrowed.

where CF_e represents the cash flow earned for the equity investors, CO_e is the amount of capital supplied by the equity investors, and r is the rate that equates the present values of future CF_e to the present value of the investment provided by the equity investors; that is, r is the internal rate of return (IRR_e) on equity capital.

Table 2. The ABC Company: Allocation of Cash Flows to Creditors and Owners

	Cash Flow Allocated to Creditors								
Years	Interest (1 − TR)	+	0.50 (Depre- ciation)	+	0.50 (Working Capital)	+	0.50 (Scrap)	=	CF_d
1	$ 3,680	+	$ 4,500	+	$ 0	+	$ 0	=	$ 8,180
2	4,160	+	4,500	+	0	+	0	=	8,660
3	4,000	+	4,500	+	0	+	0	=	8,500
4	4,320	+	4,500	+	0	+	0	=	8,820
5	4,640	+	4,500	+	25,000	+	2,500	=	36,640
	$20,800	+	$22,500	+	$25,000	+	$2,500	=	$70,800

	Cash Flow Allocated to Owners								
Years	Earnings	+	0.50 (Depre- ciation)	+	0.50 (Working Capital)	+	0.50 (Scrap)	=	CF_e
1	$ 8,720	+	$ 4,500	+	$ 0	+	$ 0	=	$13,220
2	8,640	+	4,500	+	0	+	0	=	13,140
3	9,600	+	4,500	+	0	+	0	=	14,100
4	8,880	+	4,500	+	0	+	0	=	13,380
5	9,760	+	4,500	+	25,000	+	2,500	=	41,760
	$45,600		$22,500		$25,000		$2,500		$95,600

The internal rate of return on leased capital (IRR$_l$) may be determined by solving the following equation:

$$\sum_{t=1}^{n} \frac{(CF_l)_t}{(1 + r)^t} - \sum_{t=0}^{n-1} \frac{(CO_l)^t}{(1 + r)^t} = 0, \qquad (9)$$

where CF$_l$ represents the cash flow earned for the lessor, CO$_l$ is the amount of capital supplied by the lessor, and r is the rate that equates the present values of future CF$_l$ to the present value of the investment provided by the lessor; that is, r is the internal rate of return (IRR$_l$) on leased equipment.

Using the adjusted data of the ABC Company, we are able to calculate the IRR$_d$ and IRR$_e$ for the investors of debt and equity capital. Table 3 depicts these calculations.[1]

Table 3. The ABC Company: Calculations of IRR_d and IRR_e

			Calculation of IRR_d			
				Present Values		
Years	CF_d	CO_e	PVIF at 8%	$	PVIF at 10%	$
0	$ 0	$50,000	1.000	-$50,000	1.000	-$50,000
1	8,180	0	0.926	7,575	0.909	7,436
2	8,660	0	0.857	7,422	0.826	7,153
3	8,500	0	0.794	6,749	0.751	6,384
4	8,820	0	0.735	6,483	0.683	6,024
5	36,640	0	0.681	24,952	0.621	22,753
				$ 3,181		-$ 250

Interpolate: $\dfrac{\$3,181}{\$3,431} \times 2.00 = 1.85\% + 8.00\% = 9.85\%$

$IRR_d = 9.85\%$

			Calculation of IRR_e			
				Present Values		
Years	CF_e	CO_e	PVIF at 20%	$	PVIF at 22%	$
0	$ 0	$50,000	1.000	-$50,000	1.000	-$50,000
1	13,220	0	0.833	11,012	0.820	10,840
2	13,140	0	0.694	9,119	0.672	8,830
3	14,100	0	0.579	8,164	0.551	7,769
4	13,380	0	0.482	6,449	0.451	6,034
5	41,760	0	0.402	16,787	0.370	15,451
				$ 1,531		-$ 1,076

Interpolate: $\dfrac{\$1,531}{\$2,607} \times 2.00 = 1.17\% + 20.00\% = 21.17\%$

$IRR_e = 21.17\%$

From the preceding example, it may be seen that by determining the internal rate of return for debt and equity capital we are able to provide management with information that is essential to a sound investment decision. First, the investment of $100,000 ($50,000 from debt and $50,000 from equity sources) is returned in full and is available for reinvestment. Second, the return of the total number of dollars paid to creditors is covered in excess of five times in total, as well as annually. Third, the after-tax weighted average return (cost of debt) on all types of debt equals 9.85 percent. Finally, equity investors know that the firm is earning 21.17 percent on their investment. This knowledge makes it possible for them to compare this return with returns from other investment opportunities, as well as with their expectations. If the latter criterion is met, the investment is acceptable.

The adjusted internal rate of return has several advantages when compared to the NPV and IRR techniques. First, and probably the most important, is that the equity investors are able to determine the return on their invested capital. This figure is unavailable in the other methods. Second, it does not require a knowledge of the firm's "weighted cost of capital." Finally, it is a vehicle by which the internal rate of return on total capital may be calculated. For example, in the above case, we know that the firm's IRR will be 15.51 percent (21.17 × 0.50 + 9.85 × 0.50 = 15.51 percent) if the project is undertaken. (The internal rate of return on CF_t is equal to 15.56 percent, and the difference between the 15.51 and 15.56 is the result of rounding.)[2]

IMPACT OF A CHANGE IN THE METHOD OF FINANCING

The reader knows, of course, that a firm can increase the return to equity by employing more debt, provided the return on total capital exceeds the borrowing rate. Not only will the return on equity increase, but IRR_e *will also increase.* The following example reveals this fact. Assume that debt is increased to 60 percent, equity is decreased to 40 percent, and the asset mix consists of $50,000 in fixed assets and $50,000 in working capital. The debt mix remains the same; also, interest rates remain the same. Liabilities under these conditions are as follows: notes payable, $18,000; accounts payable, $18,000; and long-term debt, $24,000. Interest costs are $5520, $6240, $6000, $6480, and $6690, respectively. CF_d and CF_e for each of the five years are as follows (see Table 4):

Years	CF_d	CF_e
1	$ 9,816	$11,584
2	10,392	11,408
3	10,200	12,400
4	10,584	11,616
5	43,968	34,432

Substituting the preceding data in equations (7) and (8), we find that IRR_d

Table 4.   The ABC Company: Calculations of CF_d and CF_e

		Debt/Equity Ratio 60/40			
EBIDT	$24,500	$25,000	$26,000	$25,500	$27,000
Expected interest	5,520	6,240	6,000	6,480	6,960
EBDT	$18,980	$18,760	$20,000	$19,020	$20,040
Depreciation	9,000	9,000	9,000	9,000	9,000
EBT	$ 9,980	$ 9,760	$11,000	$10,020	$11,040
Taxes	1,996	1,952	2,200	2,004	2,208
EAT	$ 7,984	$ 7,808	$ 8,800	$ 8,016	$ 8,832
Effective interest	$ 4,416	$ 4,992	$ 4,800	$ 5,184	$ 5,568

Calculation of CF_d

Years	Interest $(1 - TR)$	+	0.60 (Depreciation)	+	0.60 (Working Capital)	+	0.60 (Scrap)	=	CF_d
1	$ 4,416	+	$ 5,400	+	$ 0	+	$ 0	=	$ 9,816
2	4,992	+	5,400	+	0	+	0	=	10,392
3	4,800	+	5,400	+	0	+	0	=	10,200
4	5,184	+	5,400	+	0	+	0	=	10,584
5	5,568	+	5,400	+	30,000	+	3,000	=	43,968
	$24,960		$27,000		$30,000		$3,000		$84,960

Calculation of CF_e

Years	Earnings	+	0.40 (Depreciation)	+	0.40 (Working Capital)	+	0.40 (Scrap)	=	CF_e
1	$ 7,984	+	$ 3,600	+	$ 0	+	$ 0	=	$11,584
2	7,808	+	3,600	+	0	+	0	=	11,408
3	8,800	+	3,600	+	0	+	0	=	12,400
4	8,016	+	3,600	+	0	+	0	=	11,616
5	8,832	+	3,600	+	20,000	+	2,000	=	34,432
	$41,440		$18,000		$20,000		$2,000		$81,440

equals 9.85 percent and IRR_e equals 23.91 percent, which is 13 percent higher than when we financed the project with 50 percent debt and 50 percent equity (see Table 5). It should be noted that in this case, IRR_t remains the same under the adjusted internal return technique (9.85 × 0.6 + 23.91 × 0.4 = 15.47). If cash flows that exclude interest (earnings + depreciation + working capital + scrap) are used in the analysis, a change in the debt/equity structure will cause a *decrease* in IRR_t, and a decrease in the debt to equity ratio will cause an *increase* in IRR_t. This seems to be in direct conflict with the traditional average concept—in the above case, IRR_t would have equaled 9.66 percent rather than 10.82 percent when the debt/equity ratio equaled 50/50; that is, IRR_t would have decreased 10.8 percent when more debt was used even though the return to equity would have increased. This is very important information since the analyst would calculate an incorrect IRR_t for each project evaluated unless, of course, the optimum capital structure is employed. While many authorities

Table 5. The ABC Company: Calculations of IRR_d and IRR_e

	Cash Flows		Present Value of CF_d		Present Value of CF_e	
Years	CF_d	CF_e	at 8%	at 10%	at 20%	at 24%
1	$ 9,816	$11,584	$ 9,090	$ 8,923	$ 9,649	$ 9,337
2	10,392	11,408	8,906	8,584	7,917	7,415
3	10,200	12,400	8,099	7,660	7,180	6,498
4	10,584	11,616	7,779	7,229	5,599	4,914
5	43,968	34,432	29,942	27,304	13,761	11,741
Present value of CF_d and CF_e			$63,816	$59,700	$44,106	$39,905
Present value of investment			60,000	60,000	40,000	40,000
			$ 3,816	($ 300)	$ 4,106	($ 95)

$$IRR_d \text{ interpolation: } \frac{\$3,816}{\$4,116} \times 2.0 = 1.85\% + 8.00\% = 9.85\%$$

$$IRR_d = 9.85\%$$

$$IRR_e \text{ interpolation: } \frac{\$4,106}{\$4,201} \times 4.0 = 3.91\% + 20.00\% = 23.91\%$$

$$IRR_e = 23.91\%$$

158   ERNEST W. WALKER

argue that the optimum capital structure is known before the investment analysis
is computed, this writer is of the opinion that it is impossible to know which
capital structure is optimum prior to the analysis since one is actually the
function of the other.

It is believed that the AIRR technique permits the owner-manager to select
the "correct" project, as well as the most effective capital structure.

The simultaneous selection of the firm's optimum capital structure and
correct investment project is accomplished by calculating the IRR_d, IRR_e,
and IRR_t for a particular project at various debt/equity structures. Let us assume that it is possible to produce the following expected EBIDT on a particular project for the duration of its life:

Years	Expected EBIDT
1	$24,500
2	25,000
3	26,000
4	25,500
5	27,000

Let us further assume that the total amount of interest paid on debt increases
10 percent for each increment in debt of 10 percent after the 20 percent level
is reached. Further assume that total interest increases 20 percent for each
increase in debt of 10 percent between the 60 percent level and 80 percent level.
The amounts of interest shown in Table 6 would result from the varying debt/
equity ratios described there.

Table 6.   Interest Cost at Varying Debt/Equity Ratios

			Years		
D/E Ratios	1	2	3	4	5
20/80	$ 1,382	$ 1,563	$ 1,503	$ 1,623	$ 1,743
30/70	2,281	2,579	2,480	2,678	2,876
40/60	3,345	3,782	3,636	3,927	4,218
50/50	4,600	5,200	5,000	5,400	5,800
60/40	6,071	6,864	6,600	7,128	7,657
70/30	8,500	9,610	9,240	9,072	10,719
80/20	11,658	13,179	12,672	12,442	14,701

Table 7 depicts the cash flows that would be "earned" for the suppliers of capital (creditors and owners) if the firm operated at different debt levels.

The internal rates of return earned on debt and equity capital for the various debt/equity ratios for the company are shown in Table 8.

It is my belief that the firm's optimum capital structure is *that point where*

Table 7. CF_t, CF_d, and CF_e for Various Debt/Equity Levels

	Years				
D/E Ratios	1	2	3	4	5
20/80					
CF_d	$ 4,565	$ 4,926	$ 4,806	$ 5,046	$16,286
CF_e	18,494	18,750	19,598	19,102	64,206
CF_t	21,400	21,800	22,600	22,200	78,400
30/70					
CF_d	$ 4,525	$ 4,763	$ 4,684	$ 4,842	$21,501
CF_e	16,875	17,037	17,916	17,358	56,899
CF_t	21,400	21,800	22,600	22,200	78,400
40/60					
CF_d	$ 6,276	$ 6,626	$ 6,509	$ 6,742	$28,974
CF_e	15,124	15,174	16,091	15,458	49,426
CF_t	21,400	21,800	22,600	22,200	78,400
50/50					
CF_d	$ 8,180	$ 8,660	$ 8,500	$ 8,820	$36,640
CF_e	13,220	13,140	14,100	13,380	41,760
CF_t	21,400	21,800	22,600	22,200	78,400
60/40					
CF_d	$10,257	$10,891	$10,680	$11,102	$44,526
CF_e	11,143	10,909	11,920	11,098	33,874
CF_t	21,400	21,800	22,600	22,200	78,400
70/30					
CF_d	$13,100	$13,988	$13,692	$13,558	$53,375
CF_e	8,300	7,812	8,908	8,642	25,025
CF_t	21,400	21,800	22,600	22,200	78,400
80/20					
CF_d	$16,526	$17,743	$17,338	$17,154	$62,961
CF_e	4,874	4,057	5,262	5,046	15,439
CF_t	21,400	21,800	22,600	22,200	78,400

Table 8. IRR_t, IRR_d, and IRR_e at Various Debt/Equity Ratios

	Debt/Equity Ratios						
	20/80	30/70	40/60	50/50	60/40	70/30	80/20
IRR_t	15.55%	15.55%	15.55%	15.55%	15.55%	15.55%	15.55%
IRR_d	7.45	8.18	8.98	9.85	10.81	12.68	15.13
IRR_e	17.54	18.65	19.96	21.16	22.56	22.15	17.27
Difference	10.09	10.47	10.88	11.31	11.75	9.47	2.14

the marginal increase in IRR_e is equal to the marginal increase in IRR_d. Stated differently, it is the point where the difference between IRR_e and IRR_d is the greatest, but not necessarily where IRR_e is the highest. The logic behind this conclusion is that the value of the firm will increase until this "point" is reached; thereafter, the value of the firm will decline since the marginal cost of debt rises at a faster rate than the marginal increase in the return on equity capital, thus causing the risk for all subsequent returns on equity capital to be excessive.

It is believed that this is the same point as that suggested by Solomon when he said that a firm's optimum capital structure is that "point where the rising marginal cost of borrowing is equal to the average overall cost of capital" [1].

This method of calculating a firm's capital structure is much simpler than the techniques recommended by Modigliani and Miller (M & M) and Solomon in that it is only necessary to calculate the internal rates of return on debt and equity capital at different debt/equity ratios. It is true that it is difficult to estimate debt costs at changing debt structures; however, it should be noted that M & M and Solomon are required to estimate changes in debt costs. In addition, they must calculate the "cost of equity capital," which, in my opinion, is most difficult, if not impossible, to do.

It is believed that we have shown that not only is it possible to calculate whether a firm should undertake a project, but also which capital structure will produce the highest market value for the firm.

IMPACT OF A CHANGING ASSET MIX

It was mentioned earlier that a change in the asset mix will cause the IRR_t, IRR_d, and IRR_e to change. To illustrate, assume that another firm is able to produce the same EBIDT with an asset mix of 70 percent working capital and

Table 9.   The XYZ Company: Balance Sheet Data

Assets		Liabilities and Net Worth	
Cash	$ 15,000	Notes payable	$ 15,000
Receivables	25,000	Accounts payable	15,000
Inventories	30,000	Long-term note	20,000
Fixed assets	30,000	Common stock	50,000
	$100,000		$100,000

30 percent fixed assets, rather than 50 percent working capital and 50 percent fixed assets. The balance sheet and profit and loss data are as shown in Tables 9 and 10.

The reader recalls that IRR_d and IRR_e may be determined by solving equations (6) and (7). Substituting the data from Table 7 in these equations, we find that IRR_d equals 9.18 percent and IRR_e equals 25.97 percent (see Table 11). As a result of the changes in asset mix, the "return" on equity capital increased from 21.16 percent to 25.97 percent, an increase of 23 percent. The principal reason for the increase is the decrease in depreciation, which, of course, is an expense. Since expenses were smaller, earnings were greater, resulting in a higher return. This increase was reduced somewhat by the fact that a larger amount of the investment was in working capital rather than fixed capital. Since working capital is normally recovered later in the project's life than is fixed capital (through depreciation), it has less value; however, the loss in value resulting from the time value of funds concept was insufficient to offset the increase in the return resulting from reduced expenses (depreciation).

As mentioned earlier, a change in the asset mix will not only cause the return to each contributor of capital to change, *but will also cause total IRR to change.* In the above case, total IRR increased from 15.47 to 17.57 percent, a gain of approximately 13.5 percent; IRR_e changed to 25.97 percent from 21.17 percent; and IRR_d changed from 9.78 percent to 9.18 percent. It should be noted, however, that, generally speaking, as the time horizon increases, the effect of working capital on total IRR will be less.

In summary, it can be said that the debt/equity ratio and asset mix definitely affect the internal rate of return on equity. That is to say, the IRR_e increases in direct relation to an increase in working capital and debt capital. This is important to the small business manager since small businesses employ more working capital and debt capital than do their larger counterparts.

Table 10. The XYZ Company: Income Data and Allocation of Cash Flows to Creditors and Owners

			Income Data		
Years	1	2	3	4	5
EBIDT	$24,500	$25,000	$26,000	$25,500	$27,000
Interest	4,600	5,200	5,000	5,400	5,800
Depreciation	5,400	5,400	5,400	5,400	5,400
PBT	$14,500	$14,400	$15,600	$14,700	$15,800
Taxes	2,900	2,880	3,120	2,940	3,160
PAT	$11,600	$11,520	$12,480	$11,760	$12,640

Cash Flows Allocated to Creditors

Years	Interest $(1 - TR)$	+ .50($27,000)	+ .50($70,000)	+ .50($3,000) =	CF_d
1	$ 3,680	+ $ 2,700	+ $ 0	+ $ 0 =	$ 6,380
2	4,160	+ 2,700	+ 0	+ 0 =	6,860
3	4,000	+ 2,700	+ 0	+ 0 =	6,700
4	4,320	+ 2,700	+ 0	+ 0 =	7,020
5	4,640	+ 2,700	+ 35,000	+ 1,500 =	43,840
	$20,800	+ $13,500	+ $35,000	+ $1,500 =	$70,800

Cash Flows Allocated to Owners

Years	Earnings	+ .50($27,000)	+ .50($70,000)	+ .50($3,000) =	CF_e
1	$11,600	+ $ 2,700	+ $ 0	+ $ 0 =	$14,300
2	11,520	+ 2,700	+ 0	+ 0 =	14,220
3	12,480	+ 2,700	+ 0	+ 0 =	15,180
4	11,760	+ 2,700	+ 0	+ 0 =	14,460
5	12,640	+ 2,700	+ 35,000	+ 1,500 =	51,840
	$60,000	+ $13,500	+ $35,000	+ $1,500 =	$110,000

Table 11. The XYZ Company: Calculations of IRR_d and IRR_e

Years	Cash Flows		Present Value of CF_d		Present Value of CF_e	
	CF_d	CF_e	at 8%	at 10%	at 24%	at 26%
1	$ 6,380	$14,300	$ 5,908	$ 5,799	$11,526	$11,354
2	6,860	14,220	5,879	5,666	9,243	8,959
3	6,700	15,180	5,320	5,032	7,954	7,590
4	7,020	14,460	5,160	4,795	6,117	5,741
5	43,840	51,840	29,855	27,225	17,677	16,330
			$52,122	$48,517	$52,517	$49,974
			50,000	50,000	50,000	50,000
			$ 2,122	($ 1,483)	$ 2,517	($ 26)

$$IRR_d \text{ Interpolation: } \frac{\$2122}{\$3605} \times 2.0 = 1.18\% + 8.0\% = 9.18\%$$

$$IRR_d = 9.18\%$$

$$IRR_e \text{ Interpolation: } \frac{\$2517}{\$3605} \times 2.0 = 1.97\% + 24.00\% = 25.97\%$$

$$IRR_e = 25.97\%$$

NOTES

1. ABC does not lease any of its equipment; therefore, IRR_l is not computed in this example.

2. When the definition of cash flows (E + D + W/C + S) is used, the IRR would equal 10.82 percent. The difference results from the exclusion of interest (1 − TR) from the flows.

REFERENCES

[1] Solomon, Ezra. *The Theory of Financial Management*. New York: Columbia University Press, 1963, p. 97.

III FINANCING THE INVESTMENT OF CAPITAL

10 ON WORKING CAPITAL AS AN INVESTMENT BY THE FIRM

Keith V. Smith
Purdue University

Working capital is well recognized as an important decision area within the firm. Yet working capital does not seem to occupy a very prominent place within the academic field of finance. While a gap between theory and practice persists in many areas of management decision making, it would seem to be especially so for working capital management.

This paper suggests that the gap between theory and practice may not be so serious if working capital is given an appropriate decision-making context. Specifically, it is argued that working capital ought to be viewed as an investment and that changes in working capital policies ought to be included in the capital budgeting process of the firm. The next section offers an overall review of the working capital literature, while the following section focuses on the standard theoretical development. The results of a recent survey of working capital practices are then presented, together with some aggregate statistics on working capital investments. Next, the major arguments of the paper are presented in two sections. They are followed by a numerical illustration. Brief implications are offered in the last section.

REVIEW OF THE LITERATURE

Much of the literature on working capital can be categorized in terms of the balance sheet of the firm. The following representation of a typical balance sheet will be helpful in briefly reviewing the literature:

Current assets $a = \displaystyle\sum_j a_j$	Current liabilities $l = \displaystyle\sum_j l_j$
Fixed assets $A = \displaystyle\sum_j A_j$	Long-term debt $L = \displaystyle\sum_j L_j$
	Equity $E = \displaystyle\sum_j E_j$
Total assets $\quad a + A$	Total sources $\quad l + L + E$

Using this representation, working capital is given by a, net working capital by $a - l$, while the balance sheet equation is $a + A = l + L + E$.

One plausible reason why developments in working capital management have seemed to lag behind those of other areas of finance is that the subject has emerged as a series of independent technologies rather than as a comprehensive subject. In introductory finance textbooks, such as those by Weston and Brigham [32] and Van Horne [28], the unifying treatment for working capital is aggregate guidelines—that is, marketable securities a_j^* for investing surplus funds and short-term borrowing l_j^* for covering fund deficits. More detailed treatment in these and other introductory textbooks, however, is to discuss and to illustrate such individual technologies as credit scoring, lockboxes, and economic order quantities for managing individual current assets a_j and current liabilities l_j.

In contrast, the more advanced finance textbooks hardly mention working capital at all. In the preface to their book, Fama and Miller [8] admit that they pass over some of the standard topics, such as cash-flow forecasting, cash budgeting, and credit management, in developing a theory of finance. Haley and Schall [12] do not even mention that working capital management is excluded from their theoretical development. Mao [17] talks about the investment that a firm makes in cash, accounts receivable, and inventory, but more as a springboard for his discussion of how quantitative approaches can be used in those decisions.

Within the professional journals, there has been considerable treatment of the individual technologies—that is, of how individual current assets or current liabilities should be managed. Examples include Searby [25] on float management, Mehta [18] on credit analysis, Gitman, Forrester, and Forrester [10] on cash disbursements, Magee [15] on inventory control, and Conover [6] on short-term bank borrowing.

At the same time, there have been attempts to discuss the interrelationships or linkages between certain working capital accounts. For example, Miller and Orr [19] treat cash and marketable securities, Schiff [24] considers accounts receivable and inventory, Beranek [2] examines inventory and bank credit, Haley and Higgins [11] focus on inventory and trade credit, and Maier and Vanderweide [16] interrelate cash collections with cash disbursements.

Mathematical programming models also have been useful in capturing some of the linkages between working capital accounts. Examples include the papers by Pogue, Faucett, and Bussard [22], which focuses on cash management; Orgler [21], whose perspective extends to other working capital accounts; and Robicheck, Teichroew, and Jones [23], which centers on the short-term financing decisions of the firm.

There have been varying—albeit less satisfying—attempts to integrate working capital into the mainstream theory of finance. An earlier, introductory text by Walker [30] presents four principles that constitute a theoretical basis for working capital management. Walker focuses on the risk-return tradeoffs in each working capital account, a_j, and how the firm ought to view each account as an investment. Friedland [9] suggests a portfolio theoretic approach to managing the firm's portfolio of asset accounts. In so doing, he examines the covariance, $cov(a_i, a_j)$, between each pair of asset accounts. The popular Capital Asset Pricing Model has been applied to accounts receivable by Copeland and Khoury [7], to linking working capital with financial structure by Bierman, Chopra, and Thomas [3], and to overall consideration of working capital management by Cohn and Pringle [5]. More recently, option pricing theory has been used by Levasseur [14] to develop a concept of firm liquidity.

THEORETICAL ANTECEDENTS

Both the theory of the firm and the theory of finance have had something to say about working capital. We begin with the theory of the firm. Following Vickers [29], we recall the profit-maximizing decision for an all-equity firm as

$$\text{Maximize} \quad \Pi = P(Q)f(X, Y) - \gamma_1 X - \gamma_2 Y - b \tag{1}$$

$$\text{Subject to:} \quad \alpha X + \beta Y + a(Q) \leqslant E, \tag{2}$$

where

Π = profit;
P = price;
Q = quantity;
X, Y = input factors of production;
$f(X, Y)$ = production function;
γ_1, γ_2 = unit costs of X and Y, respectively;
b = fixed cost of production;
α, β = capital requirement coefficient of factors X and Y, respectively;
$a(Q)$ = working capital requirement;
E = total equity.

The appropriate Lagrangian function for this formulation is

$$L(X, Y, \mu) \equiv P(Q)f(X, Y) - \gamma_1 X - \gamma_2 Y - b + \mu[E - \alpha X - \beta Y - a(Q)], \quad (3)$$

where μ is the Lagrangian multiplier.

The first-order condition is given by

$$\frac{\partial L}{\partial X} = \left(P + Q\frac{dP}{dQ}\right)f_X - \gamma_1 - \mu\alpha - \mu a'(Q)f_X, \quad (4)$$

where f_X is the marginal physical product of input X and $a'(Q)$ is the rate of change of the firm's working capital requirement. Setting expression (4) equal to zero leads to

$$\left[P + Q\frac{dP}{dQ} - \mu a'(Q)\right]f_X = \gamma_1 + \mu\alpha. \quad (5)$$

The bracketed quantity is marginal revenue net of the cost of working capital, while the right-hand side is marginal resource cost. Note that working capital is costed at the firm's rate of return on equity (i.e., $\mu = d\Pi/dE$). Using expression (5) plus a comparable relationship for input Y, one obtains the familiar result

$$\frac{f_X}{f_Y} = \frac{\gamma_1 + \mu\alpha}{\gamma_2 + \mu\beta}. \quad (6)$$

Although this is the same result that is obtained without consideration of working capital, the solution for each input *does* depend on working capital, as seen in the bracketed quantity in expression (5).

The theory of finance provides further perspective. In particular, we consider net present value, the accepted criterion for evaluating long-term investment projects of the firm. For a given project, net present value is given by

$$\text{NPV(project)} = -C_0 + \sum_{t=1}^{n} \frac{B_t - C_t}{(1+k)^t}, \tag{7}$$

where

C_0 = initial cash outlay;
C_t = additional cash outlay in period $t = 1, \ldots, n$;
B_t = cash inflow in period t;
k = the firm's average cost of capital.

Many authors, particularly Bierman and Smidt [4], carefully point out that the cash inflows and outlays should reflect working capital (wc)—that is, both initial and subsequent cash outlays should include necessary investments in current assets, a_t, while the final cash outflow, B_n, should include recovery of working capital at the end of the project. For the simplest case, where $a_0 = a_n = a$ and there are no interim adjustments to working capital, we can write an expression for the project plus its working capital implications as follows:

$$\text{NPV(project + wc)} = -(C_0 + a) + \sum_{t=1}^{n} \frac{B_t - C_t}{(1+k)^t} + \frac{a}{(1+k)^n}. \tag{8}$$

For this case, the total project can be broken down into two major components:

$$\text{NPV(project + wc)} = \text{NPV(project)} + \text{NPV(wc)}. \tag{9}$$

Hence, for just the working capital investment, we have

$$\text{NPV(wc)} = -a + \frac{a}{(1+k)^n} = -a \left[1 - \frac{1}{(1+k)^n} \right]. \tag{10}$$

Alternatively, if the firm makes adjustments (i.e., $\pm a_t$) to the working capital associated with a given project in each year of the project horizon, then the working capital investment would be given by

$$\text{NPV(wc)} = -a_0 + \sum_{t=1}^{n} \frac{a_t}{(1+k)^t}, \tag{11}$$

which is seen to be analogous to expression (7), the standard formulation for a capital budgeting project *without* explicit consideration of working capital. In other words, working capital can be logically viewed as a separate project.

FURTHER PERSPECTIVE

The foregoing review demonstrates that working capital can be viewed in a variety of ways. From a theoretical standpoint, it is clear that working capital is a variable that should be considered by financial managers, as well as from the perspective of the entire firm. To offer additional perspective on working capital as an investment, we provide two additional, though independent, viewpoints.

First, it is helpful to see how changes in working capital accounts compare to long-run investment projects made by the firm. One way to make that comparison is to examine year-to-year changes in certain balance sheet accounts. Using data from Standard and Poor's Compustat tapes, it was possible to calculate the absolute changes in accounts receivable, inventory, and gross plant as a percentage of total firm assets. Absolute changes were measured since some changes in working capital policies (e.g., a tighter credit policy) may result in lower investment levels. Table 1 presents the average changes of a sample of 2000 firms for each year from 1968 through 1977. The findings demonstrate that changes in both receivables and inventory have been substantial relative to changes in gross plant. Moreover, the total change in receivables and inventory exceeded the change in gross plant for each year.

Second, it also is helpful to see if financial managers view working capital as an investment. A recent survey by Smith and Sell [27] investigated current

Table 1. Average Absolute Changes in Selected Assets as a Percentage of Change in Total Assets, Annually 1968-1977

Year	Receivables	Inventory	Receivables plus Inventory	Gross Plant
1968	28.1%	31.2%	59.3%	58.0%
1969	31.1	33.9	65.0	60.6
1970	31.7	37.7	69.4	63.8
1971	30.8	35.4	66.2	57.9
1972	35.6	34.7	70.3	54.9
1973	31.5	41.4	72.9	50.6
1974	29.9	48.4	78.3	50.4
1975	32.5	44.0	76.5	57.2
1976	32.5	39.6	72.1	54.8
1977	34.1	36.7	70.8	60.1

Note: Calculations are based on the first 2000 firms for which complete data were available on Standard and Poor's Compustat annual industrial tape.

Table 2. Ranking of Criteria Used in Evaluating Credit Terms Changes

Criterion	Number of Responses	Number Assigning Rank				Weighted Response
		1	2	3	4	
Effect on firm sales	161	53	50	43	15	2.12
Effect on level of receivables	147	29	36	39	43	2.65
Effect on firm profits	159	71	49	31	8	1.85
Effect on return on investment	136	36	36	29	35	2.46

practices in the management of working capital by America's largest industrial firms. Questionnaires were sent to a population of 653 firms, selected on the basis of both size and profitability, from the annual *Fortune* listing of industrial corporations. Completed questionnaires were returned by 210 firms, for a response rate of 32.2 percent. The survey instrument included both single-answer and ranked-response questions. Certain of the findings are pertinent here.

Two ranked-response questions focused on the criteria used in managing individual working capital accounts. With respect to criteria used in evaluating proposed changes in credit terms (Table 2), "return on investment" (i.e., ROI) received fewer responses than the other possible answers. In terms of a weighted-rank response (which infers a cardinality scale on the part of the financial manager), ROI was ranked below both firm profits and firm sales. With respect to criteria used in evaluating changes in inventory policy (Table 3), ROI received slightly fewer responses than either inventory level or firm profits as a criterion. For the weighted-rank response, however, the ROI response was second only to firm profits. Clearly, return on investment is a prominent concept in the minds of managers responsible for both receivables and inventory.

Table 3. Ranking of Criteria Used in Evaluating Inventory Policy Changes

Criterion	Number of Responses	Number Assigning Rank				Weighted Response
		1	2	3	4	
Effect on inventory costs	139	24	39	51	25	2.55
Effect on level of inventory	148	43	34	36	35	2.42
Effect on firm profits	154	68	54	27	5	1.79
Effect on return on investment	142	50	43	17	32	2.22

Table 4. The Use of Return-on-Investment Criterion in Evaluating Possible Changes in Working Capital Components (In Percentage)

Usage	Total Sample	Larger-Sized	Smaller-Sized	More Profitable	Less Profitable
Never	12.5%	12.5%	19.2%	14.5%	11.1%
Sometimes	51.0	54.2	50.0	45.2	51.4
Always	36.5	33.3	30.8	40.3	37.5

Three single-answer questions probed further on the issue of working capital as an investment. We asked financial managers if they use an ROI criterion in evaluating proposed changes in working capital components (Table 4). Almost 90 percent of those responding indicated that they sometimes or always use ROI. The percentage response to "always use ROI" was slightly higher for the larger-sized and more profitable subsamples.[1] When asked if working capital implications are included in the evaluation of capital budgeting projects (Table 5), two-thirds of the responding firms indicated that they always do so, while only 5.7 percent indicated that they never do so. A greater proportion of the larger-sized firms, as well as the less profitable firms, "always" reflect the working capital implications of capital projects.

Finally, and most apropos to this paper, we asked if changes in working capital components (e.g., easier credit terms, lower inventory levels) are considered *along* with other projects in the firm's capital budgeting process (Table 6). Less than 20 percent of the total sample "never" do so, while 33 percent "always" do so. As for the subsample comparisons, a smaller fraction of both the larger and the less profitable firms do not consider working capital changes as investment projects.

Table 5. Working Capital Implications in Capital Budgeting Decisions (In Percentage)

Usage	Total Sample	Larger-Sized	Smaller-Sized	More Profitable	Less Profitable
Never	5.7%	2.7%	11.3%	12.7%	1.4%
Sometimes	27.6	27.4	32.1	25.4	33.3
Always	66.7	69.9	56.6	61.9	65.3

Table 6. Changes in Working Capital Components as Projects in Capital Budgeting Decisions (In Percentage)

Usage	Total Sample	Larger-Sized	Smaller-Sized	More Profitable	Less Profitable
Never	19.1%	12.5%	20.8%	47.5%	30.0%
Sometimes	47.8	55.6	47.2	39.7	46.5
Always	33.0	31.9	32.1	30.2	36.6

FINANCIAL CONTROL

In view of the relative size of working capital changes, and also the finding that many firms do indeed view such changes as investment projects, it is well to consider more closely the relationship of working capital decisions to other financial decisions made by the firm. In my opinion, the relationship is found in financial control. While control is well known to be one of the key functions of management, it would appear to have received considerably less treatment than planning, at least in the financial literature. But just as control without adequate planning will likely be futile, planning without followup control will prove frustrating.

A first dimension of financial control that has been well documented is to monitor the financial progress of the firm over time. This usually takes the form of tracking selected financial ratios, and thereby assessing both the current status and likely future prospects of the organization. If attention is limited to single ratios for just profitability and liquidity, then financial control is relatively straightforward. If, instead, management tracks a larger number of financial ratios, then financial control is more complex as tradeoffs must be made. In general, if there are N measures being tracked, any investment project or change in policy will result in 2^N possible changes in the status of the firm: one change favorable for all N measures, one change unfavorable for all N measures, and 2^N-2 changes involving tradeoffs. Obviously, the number 2^N-2 quickly becomes large as N is increased. One way to handle the complexity of multiple ratios is with composite measures, such as the duPont system [13] or the Altman bankruptcy test [1].

A second dimension of financial control is to consider corrective actions that can be taken when firm progress departs from firm plans. For example, if the liquidity position of the organization appears to be worsening, management may decide to issue either bonds or stocks in order to reduce short-term financial obligations. Alternatively, management may decide to reduce inventory levels and/or to expand credit if the profitability goal of the firm is not being achieved. Many possible corrective actions pertain to the current assets and current liabilities of the firm, and thus working capital adjustments can be an important part of overall financial control within the organization.

WORKING CAPITAL INVESTMENTS

A logical extension of this idea is to view corrective actions as investments made by the firm. Just as investments are routinely made by the firm in capital projects, so too should the firm routinely consider changes in working capital accounts as investment projects. Viewed in this way, each investment in working capital is an attempt to move the firm closer to its expressed goals. This view, it should be noted, is different from just including working capital implications with each capital project being considered. It is also a view that is consistent with the theory of the firm, the theory of finance, and apparently the current practices of many large industrial firms.

A list of possible corrective actions having to do with working capital is presented in Table 7. The list, which is representative rather than exhaustive, is organized into six groups that correspond to certain current assets and current liabilities normally found on the balance sheet. Some of the changes result from internal decisions by firm management, while the effects of other changes depend on the actions of external constituencies, such as customers or suppliers. Certain changes reflect management's willingness to assume risk. Other changes are an attempt to influence float.

Not all of the corrective actions in Table 7 would be feasible, let alone desirable, for a given firm at a particular point in time. For each corrective action that is feasible, financial managers should identify the expected benefits and costs to evaluate whether the action would help the firm move toward its expressed goals. Corrective action 7, for example, is a change in the cash discounts that the firm offers to its credit customers. A cash discount is tantamount to a reduction in price. Suppose the discount is increased. To the extent that customers take advantage of the larger discount by paying their bills sooner, the firm's investment in accounts receivable is reduced. The expected dollar benefit of corrective action 7 therefore should reflect the extent of the discount that is offered, the proportion of credit customers that are expected to take the discount, and the resulting decrease in the receivable investment. The expected dollar cost of corrective action 7 is the reduced profit to the firm as a result of credit customers that avail themselves of the larger discount.

Based on past experience with customer response to changing credit terms, the credit manager ought to be able to make reasonable estimates of the ex-

Table 7. Possible Corrective Actions Involving Working Capital

---

Cash:
   1. Change collection network.
   2. Change disbursement network.
   3. Change size of operating cash balance.

Marketable Securities:
   4. Change method of investing surplus cash.
   5. Change method of transferring funds between cash account and marketable securities portfolio.

Accounts Receivable:
   6. Change cutoff score for credit applications.
   7. Change discounts offered customers.
   8. Change frequency of followup payment notices.

Inventory:
   9. Change inventory valuation methods.
  10. Change inventory order quantities.
  11. Change inventory safety stocks.
  12. Change distribution network.

Payables and Accruals:
  13. Change suppliers used.
  14. Change response to supplier discounts.
  15. Change payroll procedures.

Short-Term Borrowing:
  16. Change lenders used.
  17. Change payment methods.
  18. Change collateral arrangements.

---

pected benefit and cost to the firm of offering customers a larger cash discount. Expected benefit and cost can then be combined to calculate a "return on investment" for the proposed corrective action. If a similar procedure is also followed for each corrective action being considered (such as those in Table 7), then each corrective action can be viewed as a proposed investment project by the firm—and evaluated within the context of the capital budgeting process. Again, this would seem to be consistent with both received theory and current management practice.

AN ILLUSTRATION

Using an illustration,[2] we complete the suggestion of evaluating working capital changes as investment projects. Suppose that financial executives for a particular firm are considering four corrective actions that involve working capital from the

Table 8. Illustration of Four Proposed Changes in Working Capital

Change	Description	Estimated Benefit	Estimated Cost	Return on Investment
1.	Change Collection Network: Implement lockbox collection system in five metropolitan areas.	Reduced average collection time of one week. $50,000 lower investment in negative float.	Service fees to five banks for managing lockboxes. $7,000 annual fee.	$\dfrac{(\$7,000)}{(\$50,000)} = 14\%^a$
4.	Change Method of Investing Surplus Cash: Hire manager for firm's portfolio of marketable securities.	Increased average yield on surplus cash balances. $(1.5\%)(\$2,400,000) = \$36,000$ annually.	Total compensation package of added manager. $30,000 annually.	$\dfrac{\$36,000-30,000}{\$30,000} = 20\%$
6.	Change Cutoff Score for Credit Applications: Relax credit by decreasing credit cutoff score.	Increased profit from added sales, net of likely increased bad debts. $54,000 annually.	Added investment in accounts receivable and inventory. $300,000.	$\dfrac{\$54,000}{\$300,000} = 18\%$
10.	Change Inventory Order Quantity: Increase purchase quantities for parts used in manufacturing in response to supplier quantity discounts.	Increased profits (decreased total costs) associated with acquiring the parts. $13,000 annually.	Increased average inventory and hence investment in inventory. $100,000.	$\dfrac{\$13,000}{\$100,000} = 13\%$

[a]When both numerator and denominator are negative, a lower ratio is preferable to a higher ratio.

178

previous list (1, 4, 6, and 10). Table 8 includes for each change a brief description, a qualitative assessment and a quantitative estimate of both its benefits and costs, and the calculation of a return on investment.

Before looking at the investment decision to be made, it is useful to pinpoint certain features of the changes summarized in Table 8. Changes 6 and 10 are relatively straightforward in that additional investments in current assets are expected to lead to increased annual profits (i.e., cash flows) to the firm. In addition, change 6 reflects an important linkage in that the estimated cost includes additional investment in both accounts receivable and inventory. For change 1, a reduced investment in a current asset (i.e., cash) is made possible through an annual expense and hence a reduced profit to the firm. For "reduced investments" of this sort, the associated return on investment must be *less* than the firm's cost of capital in order to be attractive to the firm. For change 4, an annual compensation expense leads to an annual expected increase in additional revenue (i.e., yield) to the firm. Since the firm must make an advance commitment for the new position, it is appropriate to think of the $30,000 salary as an annual "investment," just as with the other three proposed changes.

Suppose that the firm's cost of capital is estimated to be 15 percent. If the four proposed corrective actions are judged to be independent, and if no investment constraint is imposed by the firm, then changes 1, 4, and 6 would be acceptable according to the usual criterion of return on investment exceeding cost of capital. However, if management imposes a dollar investment constraint on the changes that can be made, then the projects must be considered in combination.

Table 9 is a complete enumeration of all combinations of the four proposed changes for the illustration. For four proposed projects, there are $2^4 = 16$ combinations reflected in Table 9. Without any changes, the firm is expected to earn 15 percent on its investment (i.e., total assets) of $1 million. The optimal choice of projects is indicated for each of several selected investment constraints. For investment constraints of $1,050,000 (5 percent growth in firm size) and $1,150,000 (15 percent growth), changes 1 and 4 should be implemented. For a constraint of $1,250,000 (25 percent growth), the combination of changes 1 and 6 is optimal. For a constraint of $1,350,000 (35 percent growth), the combination of changes 1, 4, and 6 is optimal. If there is no investment constraint imposed by management, then changes 1, 4, and 6 should all be implemented. The aggregate result of those three changes in working capital would be to increase the return on investment of the firm from 15.00 percent to 15.86 percent.

But what if working capital changes were evaluated alongside the long-term capital projects of the firm? Would it change the optimal solution available to

Table 9. Optimal Choice of Working Capital Projects for Selected Capital Constraints

Projects	Return[a]	Investment[a]	Return on Investment	Investment Constraint[a]				
				1,050	1,150	1,250	1,350	Unlimited
None	150	1,000	15.00%					
1	143	950	15.05					
4	156	1,030	15.15					
6	204	1,300	15.69	No[b]	No	No		
10	163	1,100	14.82	No				
1,4	149	980	15.20	Optimal	Optimal			
1,6	197	1,250	15.76	No	No	Optimal		
1,10	156	1,050	14.86					
4,6	210	1,330	15.79	No	No	No		
4,10	169	1,130	14.96	No				
6,10	217	1,400	15.50	No	No	No	No	
1,4,6	203	1,280	15.86	No	No	No	Optimal	Optimal
1,4,10	162	1,080	15.00	No				
1,6,10	210	1,350	15.56	No	No	No		
4,6,10	223	1,430	15.59	No	No	No	No	
1,4,6,10	216	1,380	15.65	No	No	No	No	

[a] In thousands of dollars.
[b] No = project combination not feasible under constraint.

management? To answer these questions, suppose that financial executives also are asked to consider a *single* capital budgeting project—namely, the introduction of a new product for the firm. It is described as a twenty-year project for which the immediate investment of $200,000 is expected to increase after-tax cash flows by $36,500 per year. The internal rate of return for that twenty-year project is approximately 17 percent, and thus the project would be *acceptable* given the firm's 15 percent cost of capital.

Again assuming independent projects, Table 10 shows how the optimal solution would change for each level of investment constraint. For simplicity, the twenty-year capital project is referred to as project 20. There are now five projects being evaluated, and hence there are $2^5 = 32$ combinations under consideration. Table 10 indicates that the optimal choice among the thirty-two combinations is different for a growth constraint of 15 percent, and also if there is no investment constraint. It is also seen that without a capital constraint, the optimal choice (projects 1, 4, 6, and 20) increases the total firm return from 15.86 percent to 16.18 percent. Though clearly simplistic, the illustration demonstrates that management is led to different solutions when working capital changes are considered alongside capital projects. To do otherwise is to suboptimize—especially if investment constraints are imposed by management.

IMPLICATIONS

This paper has dealt with working capital as an investment. Investigation included a brief review of the literature, a special focus on how working capital is treated in the theory of the firm and the theory of finance, empirical evidence

Table 10. Optimal Choice of Working Capital and Capital Budgeting Projects for Selected Capital Constraints

Investment Constraint[a]	Working Capital Projects Alone[b]	Working Capital and Capital Projects[b]	Comparison of Solution
1,050	1, 4 (15.20%)	1, 4 (15.20%)	Same
1,150	1, 4 (15.20%)	1, 20 (15.61%)	Different
1,250	1, 6 (15.76%)	1, 6 (15.76%)	Same
1,350	1, 4, 6 (15.86%)	1, 4, 6 (15.86%)	Same
Unlimited	1, 4, 6 (15.86%)	1, 4, 6, 20 (16.18%)	Different

[a]In thousands of dollars.

[b]The value in parentheses for each case is the overall rate of return to the firm for that combination of accepted projects.

on how annual changes in receivables and inventory have exceeded annual changes in gross plant for a large sample of industrial firms, and a look at current management practices with regard to working capital.

This led to a suggestion that working capital should not be treated as just a set of independent topics—as often is done in introductory finance textbooks —but rather as a set of investment projects. As part of overall financial control, each working capital project should be viewed as a corrective action in helping to move the firm toward its expressed goals. Emphasis should be on relative changes—instead of absolute levels—for each working capital investment.

Furthermore, working capital projects should be evaluated alongside long-term investment projects as part of the firm's capital budgeting process. Each working capital project should reflect, where appropriate, linkage to other working capital accounts, just as the projected cash flows for a long-term investment project should reflect necessary changes in receivables, inventory, and so on.

Two limitations to these suggestions should be mentioned. First, the illustration assumed that all projects being considered were independent. Such an assumption is at odds with one observation made repeatedly in the paper, that all relevant linkages between working capital accounts should be considered. While some attention was given to the importance of linkages—especially for corrective action 6 in the illustration—we really did not come to grips with possible interrelationships. For example, in the second part of the illustration, we did not consider how the working capital implications of the capital project 20 might impact on the benefits and costs of the other four working capital projects being considered. In pursuing such interrelationships between projects, discussion comes full circle to the gap between theory and practice—since a portfolio view of financial management has been suggested in the literature [9], though probably not incorporated by very many firms.

Second, many readers probably observed that liquidity and risk were conspicuously absent from the literature. The usual caveat, that the firm's cost of capital ought to reflect the relative risk of the projects being considered, is not very satisfying. Still, if risk and liquidity can somehow be formulated as further constraints to the investment decision problem of the firm, the suggestions of this paper would still hold; that is, an investment framework should be appropriate for evaluating both the proposed working capital and investment projects of the firm, subject to all constraints that are identified. That decision problem, of course, has been well developed by several authors, especially Weingartner [31].

If an investment view of working capital is taken, then working capital becomes a more logical part of finance, rather than just a subsidiary topic.

Moreover, it can be argued that an investment view of working capital provides a useful framework for integrating the seemingly disparate literature. Among the current assets and liabilities of the firm, only accounts receivable has consistently been viewed from an investment perspective [20]. Cash has tended to be viewed mainly from the perspective of reducing float, while inventory has been largely approached via a square root formula. Accounts payable has centered on the percentage cost of not taking cash discounts offered by suppliers, while discussions of short-term borrowing often have examined how compensating balances and/or commitment fees on credit lines effectively increase the annual percentage cost of the borrowing. By looking at each working capital account as an investment—and, in particular, at relative changes in the investment level of each—working capital seems to begin to come together as a more coherent subject.

This paper began with an observation that there is a gap between the theory and practice of working capital. While academicians typically believe that their work is in advance of what occurs in practice, working capital may well be a decision area where practice has tended to lead theory; we have seen that many firms do think of working capital as an investment, and many do evaluate working capital changes in a capital budgeting context. It is hoped that the suggestion of working capital as an investment by the firm—developed and illustrated here—will help to redirect the thrust of subsequent research on working capital management to be even more relevant to those who deal with working capital decisions in practice.

NOTES

1. The "larger-sized" subsample consisted of seventy-three firms having an average sales of $4.7 billion, while the "smaller-sized" subsample included fifty-three firms with an average sales of $130 million. The "more profitable" subsample consisted of sixty-three firms with an average five-year return on equity of 11.6 percent; the "less profitable" subsample included seventy-two firms with an average return on equity of −4.8 percent.

2. An earlier version of this illustration appeared in Smith [26].

REFERENCES

[1] Altman, E.I. "Financial Ratios, Discriminant Analysis, and the Prediction of Corporate Bankruptcy," *Journal of Finance* (September 1968), pp. 589–609.

[2] Beranek, W. "Financial Implications of Lot-Size Inventory Models," *Management Science* (April 1967), pp. 28–33.

[3] Bierman, H.; Chopra, K.; and Thomas, J. "Ruin Considerations: Optimal Working Capital and Capital Structure," *Journal of Financial and Quantitative Analysis* (March 1975), pp. 119–128.

[4] Bierman, H., and Smidt, S. *The Capital Budgeting Decision,* 4th ed. New York: Macmillan Publishing Company, 1975, p. 137.

[5] Cohn, R., and Pringle, J.J. "Steps toward an Integration of Corporate Financial Theory," in K.V. Smith, ed., *Readings on the Management of Working Capital.* St. Paul, Minn.: West Publishing Company, 1974, pp. 369–375.

[6] Conover, C.T. "The Case of the Costly Credit Agreement," *Financial Executive* (September 1971), pp. 40–48.

[7] Copeland, T.E., and Khoury, Nabil T. "Analysis Credit Extensions in a World of Uncertainty," unpublished manuscript, July 1977.

[8] Fama, E.F., and Miller, M.H. *The Theory of Finance.* New York: Holt, Rinehart and Winston, 1972, Preface.

[9] Friedland, S. *The Economics of Corporate Finance.* Englewood Cliffs, N.J.: Prentice-Hall, 1966.

[10] Gitman, L.J.; Forrester, D.K.; and Forrester, J.R., Jr. "Maximizing Cash Disbursement Float," *Financial Management* (Summer 1976), pp. 15–24.

[11] Haley, C., and Higgins, R.C. "Inventory Control Theory and Trade Credit Financing," *Management Science* (December 1973), Parts I and II, pp. 464–471.

[12] Haley, C., and Schall, L.D. *The Theory of Financial Decisions.* New York: McGraw-Hill Book Company, 1973.

[13] Helfert, E.A. *Techniques of Financial Analysis,* 4th ed. Homewood, Ill.: Richard D. Irwin, 1977, Chap. 2.

[14] Levasseur, M.G. "An Option Model Approach to Firm Liquidity Management," *Journal of Banking and Finance* (1977), pp. 13–28.

[15] Magee, J.F. "Guides to Inventory Policy: Problems of Uncertainty," *Harvard Business Review* (March–April 1956), pp. 103–116.

[16] Maier, S.F., and Vanderweide, J.H. "A Unified Location Model for Cash Disbursements and Lock-Box Collections," *Management Science* (Summer 1976), pp. 166–172.

[17] Mao, J.C.T. *Quantitative Analysis of Financial Decisions.* New York: Macmillan Publishing Company, 1969, Chap. 13.

[18] Mehta, D. "The Formulation of Credit Policy Models," *Management Science* (October 1968), pp. B-30–B-50.

[19] Miller, M., and Orr, D. "Mathematical Models for Financial Management," Selected Paper 23, University of Chicago, Graduate School of Business, pp. 1–20.

[20] Oh, J.S. "Opportunity Cost in the Evaluation of Investment in Accounts Receivable," *Financial Management* (Summer 1976), pp. 32–36.

[21] Orgler, Y.E. "An Unequal-Period Model for Cash Management Decisions," *Management Science* (October 1969), pp. B-77–B-92.

[22] Pogue, G.; Faucett, R.; and Bussard, R. "Cash Management: A Systems Approach," *Industrial Management Review* (Winter 1970), pp. 55–74.

[23] Robichek, A.; Teichroew, D.; and Jones, J.M. "Optimal Short Term Financing Decision," *Management Science* (September 1965), pp. 1–36.

[24] Schiff, M. "Credit and Inventory Management – Separate or Together," *Financial Executive* (November 1972), pp. 28–33.

[25] Searby, F.W. "Use Your Hidden Cash Resources," *Harvard Business Review* (March–April 1968), pp. 71–80.

[26] Smith, K.V. *Guide to Working Capital Management.* New York: McGraw-Hill Book Company, 1979, Chap. 9.

[27] Smith, K.V., and Sell, S.B. "Working Capital Management in Practice," unpublished manuscript, 1979.

[28] Van Horne, J.C. *Financial Management and Policy,* 4th ed. Englewood Cliffs, N.J.: Prentice-Hall, 1977.

[29] Vickers, D. *The Theory of the Firm: Production, Capital, and Finance.* New York: McGraw-Hill Book Company, 1968.

[30] Walker, E.W. *Essentials of Financial Management,* 2nd ed. Englewood Cliffs, N.J.: Prentice-Hall, 1971, Chap. 7.

[31] Weingartner, H.M. *Mathematical Programming and the Analysis of Capital Budgeting Problems.* Chicago: Markham Publishing Company, 1967.

[32] Weston, J.F., and Brigham, E.F. *Managerial Finance,* 6th ed. Hinsdale, Ill.: Dryden Press, 1978, Chap. 6.

11 CAPITAL BUDGETING PROPOSALS WITH NEGATIVE SALVAGE VALUES

Sandor Asztély
University of Gothenburg, Sweden

Continued expansion of nuclear power facilities to satisfy future energy needs or nuclear power as a source of energy on the whole are topics too gigantic to lend themselves to a thorough discussion in a short paper. In their extension appears the complexity of environmental problems or, to state it differently, the problematic relationship between man and nature—a question as important as, if not more important than, the relationship between labor and capital. This discussion shall instead be limited to the special problem of negative salvage values as a part of capital budgeting theory. The problem could hitherto be regarded as peripheral, to be almost a matter of curiosity. However, in connection with the construction of new nuclear power facilities and the discontinuation of old ones or indeed with environmentally sensitive projects in general, the special problem of negative salvage values has become sufficiently important to warrant a discussion.

The cash-flow pattern of a conventional investment proposal shows a major capital outlay (G) at the beginning, a stream of benefits during the useful life of the project $a(t)$, $t = 1, 2, \ldots, n$, and some income because of eventual salvage values, a secondhand—or possibly only scrap—value, at the end, $S(n)$. With little loss in accuracy, the continuous stream of benefits over time can be converted into discrete annual amounts, assigned to the ends of the years, a_t, $t = 1, 2, \ldots, n$. (See Figure 1.) As a further practical simplification, salvage values are often disregarded because of their highly uncertain character and their realization in a remote future, which means a substantial reduction of their discounted present values.

As a consequence of increasingly stringent requirements during recent years for satisfactory environmental protection and restoration, salvage values for projects of a certain character can easily turn negative. Such is the case with loam and gravel pits, as exploitation licenses for them involve the obligation to restore the landscape. Similar problems arise for mining operations, alone or in combination with concentration activities, because of the resulting cavities in the ground and considerable slag mounds. The question of negative salvage values has become increasingly interesting owing to ardent, and sometimes rather emotional, discussions about the costs and side effects of nuclear technology. These discussions deal not only with decontamination of spent nuclear fuel and radioactive waste, but also with the decommissioning of time-expired, contaminated structures and the restoration of their sites. Decontamination, safe storage, and transportation of spent nuclear fuel have been discussed in considerable detail. The discussion has become more intensive and has alternated between technical, economic, and ethical-political arguments. On the other hand, the question of decommissioning time-expired nuclear plants is a relatively new one [18, p. 25]. The International Atomic Energy Agency (IAEA) in Vienna held a consultants meeting in October 1973 to examine decommissioning and issued tentative recommendations two years later [5, p. 5]. Since then,

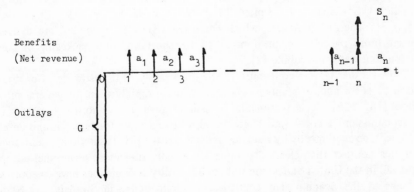

Figure 1. Cash-Flow Pattern of a Conventional Investment Proposal when Outlays in General Occur *before* Revenues

several studies on decommissioning have been published, mostly by consulting organizations [2, 13, 14, 17, 18, 23]. I began to look into the matter when some colleagues from Lund University asked my advice on drawing up a study of the financial aspects of decommissioning [4].

Decommissioning is the process of assuring that risks for radioactive exposure from nuclear power plants that have been in operation a long time remain within acceptable limits. Decommissioning means either confinement of the plant on its site (safe storage) or the dismantling of components to such an extent that the use of the site is no longer subject to restrictions because of radiation risks [6, p. 117; 14, p. 69]. Dismantling can take place immediately after closing down the power plant, or it can be deferred with previous interim confinement for ten, thirty, fifty, or even a hundred years. The principal incentive for deferment comes from the reduction of radiation exposure that can be achieved. This amounts to about 40 percent after ten years or 60 percent after thirty years [23, p. ii]. After forty years of interim confinement, there is no further appreciable reduction [2, p. 47].

Between 1960 and 1976, a total of sixty-five nuclear reactors, situated mostly in the United States, have been or were in the process of being decommissioned. Most of these reactors were for demonstration, test, or research purposes. All of them were comparatively small, with a capacity below 100 MW, and operated only for a short time. Thus a wealth of experience exists regarding technical methods and equipment, and there seems to be no major technical impediment to successful decommissioning of large reactors (500–1300 MW) now normally in use all over the world [23, Section 3]. As decommissioning costs cannot be assumed to be proportional to size, we cannot extrapolate cost findings from historical decommissionings. For reactors of normal size, we must instead rely on estimates of projected costs based on engineering studies. These estimates, which generally include 20–25 percent contingencies, vary between 45 and 90 million U.S. dollars in 1978 prices [4, p. 22; 14, p. 45; 17, pp. 21ff.; 23, Section 8, p. 3]. The higher figures, which come from German estimates, are derived using more rigorous assumptions as to transportation and packaging of contaminated waste and rubble [2].

Many other factors contribute to the uncertainty of the estimates. Construction costs for nuclear plants increase much more rapidly than the general price level [18, p. 2]. It is reasonable to assume analogous abnormal increases in decommissioning costs, too. There are also hidden costs for research and development, covered mostly by state and federal grants [18]. It should be mentioned in this context that electricity rates are usually subject to governmental approval. In the United States, the state public utility commissions have to approve them; in the Scandinavian countries, a public body—in Sweden, the State Waterpower Board—has to authorize changes in electricity rates to domestic consumers. With regard to including expected decommissioning outlays in power costs from nuclear reactors, the official attitude is apparently changing. Previously, as long as nuclear power was assumed to be the energy answer for the future, the authorities wanted to protect the public against excessively high rates. They wanted "to minimize the overall cost" to the *present* electricity consumer.[1] They were unwilling to accept "speculations as to what decommissioning might cost in 30 years" [18, p. 23]. An expected shortage of uranium and the side effects of nuclear technology are, however, coming more and more into focus, and nuclear power is increasingly regarded as merely an interlude in the energy supply. Opinion is changing gradually. The present issue seems to be that the cost of decommissioning should not place an unfair burden on *future* generations, electricity consumers or taxpayers. This change in philosophy has an impact on the choice among feasible alternatives for solving practical problems.

It is maintained here that irrespective of ownership—commercial, municipal, or state, or perhaps some combined ownership—future generations should not bear the costs of cleaning up after activities that satisfy today's energy requirements. Intergenerational subsidies should, as far as possible, be avoided. This means that

1. Power rates from nuclear reactors should cover all expenses, including those caused by the necessity of cleaning up after a shutdown. We can call this the *cost problem*.
2. Some portion of the revenues from sales of electricity needed to cover decommissioning costs should be accumulated so that they are free for disposal when decommissioning finally takes place. We can call this the *financial problem*.

The useful life of nuclear power stations is generally estimated to be about thirty to forty years, assuming normal operations [14, p. i; 23, Section 2, p. 6]. This relatively long useful life reduces the present value of future decommissioning costs to some fraction of one cent per kwh electricity sold [4, p. 22; 14, p. 97; 23, Section 6, p. 2]. However, major accidents (Harrisburg) and reversal in public opinion (plebiscites) imply appreciable risks for premature termination of operations. It is interesting to note the difference in emphasis concerning risks for major accidents between the opinion of the majority of members and of the dissidents, respectively, stated in the main report of the Swedish Energy Commission. The majority proposed

> . . . that various imaginable sequences which may lead to a core meltdown in a nuclear reactor be studied further, and that various measures which may reduce the probability and effects of reactor accidents be developed for both new and existing reactors. [6, p. 26]

One third of the committee members maintained that

> ... the theoretical risk estimates imply a substantial probability that a core meltdown will occur in Sweden during the normal operating time that has been planned. There is great probability that a core meltdown will cover large land areas with radioactivity ... lead to a great many cancer cases ... and under unfavourable circumstances to acute deaths. [6, p. 27]

The main report is dated six months *before* the Harrisburg disaster!

Sizable sums, 1 to 2 million U.S. dollars, must be earmarked and accumulated annually during the years of operation in order to accrue the sum needed for decommissioning. The financial problem is thus of great importance.

THE COST PROBLEM

Negative salvage values of considerable magnitude change the cash-flow pattern of an investment proposal. The stream of benefits over time should not only cover interest and amortization of the initial capital outlay, but also accumulate to cover decommissioning costs at the end. A considerable expenditure occurs *after* revenues. Projects with a cash-flow pattern similar to that shown in Figure 2 are a combination of a conventional and nonconventional investment [1, p. 25]. The present value of net revenues during the years 0–k is to be compared with the initial capital outlay at the time 0, and the accumulated value of net revenues during the years k–n with the decommissioning outlays at the time n. The building of the facilities and the time for planning and preparations require several years. Although twelve years, as mentioned in the twenty-third report on hearings at the House of Representatives in Washington [18, p. 4], might

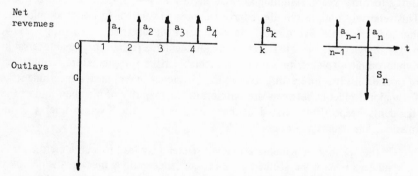

Figure 2. Cash-Flow Pattern of an Investment Proposal with a Negative Salvage Value of Some Import

be rather on the high side, political and administrative procedures can cause considerable prolongations, as recent events in Sweden and elsewhere have shown. Time requirements for decommissioning depend on the alternative chosen: about six years for immediate dismantling, including two years of planning during the last years of operations, or three years for interim confinement (mothballing), including one and a half years for planning. In the latter case, dismantling is deferred by ten, thirty, fifty or even a hundred years [23, Section 2, p. 1]. A third alternative, partial dismantling with secure residual confinement (permanent entombment) of a reactor that has been operated for twenty to thirty years or more, was found to be unsatisfactory. Radiation within the reactor vessel remains in that case well above unrestricted release levels ad infinitum [23, p. ii]. The Swedish Energy Commission's main report on health hazards, risks of major accidents, and sabotage [6, p. 117] also refers to U.S. estimates of three and six years, respectively. The Norwegian Scandpower estimates are based upon the assumption that dismantling is deferred for fifty years [14, p. 79].

Although neither building nor decommissioning of nuclear facilities occurs at a certain point of time, but takes place over a rather long period, this does not alter the model presented in this paper. In the case of a combined conventional/nonconventional investment project, a higher rate of discount has the following consequences: Net revenues, discounted at the higher rate, are needed from *more* years than before to cover initial capital outlays, and net revenues, accumulated at this higher rate, are needed from *fewer* years to cover future decommissioning expenses. The point k on the time axis in Figure 2 shifts to the right in the case of an increased discount rate, and vice versa. This has to be considered when choosing the appropriate rate of discount.

Irrespective of ownership, power stations are usually heavily bond-financed. The long-term financing of the Swedish Forsmark Power Group may serve as an illustration. Its composition as of February 15, 1979 [10, p. ii] in billions of Swedish crowns was as follows:

External borrowing in Sweden and abroad	4.1	67%
Borrowings from owners (State Water Power Board 75%, private Central Swedish Power Corporation 25%)	1.8	28%
	5.9	95%
Shareholders' equity	0.3	5%
Total	6.2	100%

1 Swedish crown = about 23 U.S. cents.

Shareholders' equity amounts to only 5 percent of the long-term capitalization. The predominant part of it carries claims on fixed yield. Returns on borrowing from owners, as well as on share capital, should reasonably exceed and under no circumstances fall below claims from holders of bonds. This means that the rate of discount should somewhat exceed the effective external borrowing rate. Consequently, electricity rates should be fixed at a level that yields an internal rate of return for the whole project—negative salvage values taken into consideration—not falling below the external borrowing rate.

Future decommissioning costs can possibly be covered by insurance or by fiscally deductible reservations combined with compulsory payments in part to an interest-free account at the Swedish Riksbanken (46 percent as per regulations in Sweden for appropriations to investment funds). Decommissioning costs will then, at the time (n), be balanced largely or entirely by payments from the insurance company or the Riksbanken, payments then subject to income taxation. Insurance premiums, as well as payment into the interest-free account at the Riksbanken, will, of course, reduce annual cash flow. The all-inclusive cashflow pattern reestablishes by any of these means the shape of a conventional investment proposal, as shown in Figure 3.

We can reasonably expect increasingly stringent requirements from the authorities supervising environmental protection. Decommissioning costs will presumably increase for other reasons as well, such as inflationary cost escalations or increasing compensation demands for radiation risks from people engaged in dismantling, cleaning up the sites, and so on. It will be necessary

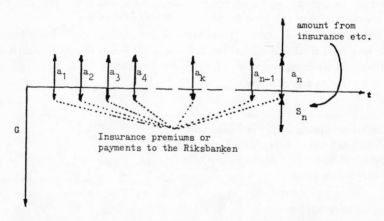

Figure 3. All-Inclusive Cash-Flow Pattern of an Investment Proposal when Negative Salvage Values Are Covered by Insurance or Deductible Payments to an Interest-Free Account at the Riksbanken

therefore to regularly reassess future decommissioning costs, S_n^t, $t = 0, 1, 2, \ldots n$. By means of the sinking-fund factor $i/[(1 + i)^n -1]$, the amount in question should then be distributed equally over the remaining useful life of the facilities. The balance of the sinking fund (reserve for future decommissioning costs) between amounts accumulated until the end of the actual and the previous year should be charged to the year's operations and recovered, together with all other costs, by revenues from electricity sales.

S_n^{t-1} and S_n^t stand for future decommissioning costs, the negative salvage value, reassessed at the time $t -1$ and t, respectively. Sums accumulated in the sinking fund up to the beginning and the end of the actual year amount to

$$\text{opening balance, } S_{t-1} = S_n^{t-1} \cdot \frac{i}{(1 + i)^n - 1} \cdot \frac{(1 + i)^{t-1} -1}{i}$$

$$= S_n^{t-1} \cdot \frac{(1 + i)^{t-1} -1}{(1 + i)^n -1}; \tag{1}$$

$$\text{closing balance, } S_t = S_n^t \cdot \frac{(1 + i)^t -1}{(1 + i)^n -1}. \tag{2}$$

The *difference* to be charged to the year's operations is

$$C = \frac{i}{(1 + i)^n -1} \left\{ S_n^{t-1} \cdot \left[\frac{(1 + i)^t - 1}{i} - \frac{(1 + i)^{t-1} -1}{i} \right] + (S_n^t - S_n^{t-1}) \cdot \frac{(1 + i)^t - 1}{i} \right\}$$

and after reduction

$$C = \frac{i}{(1 + i)^n -1} \cdot \left[S_n^{t-1} (1 + i)^{t-1} + (S_n^t - S_n^{t-1}) \cdot \frac{(1 + i)^t -1}{i} \right]. \tag{3}$$

This expression consists of two factors:

1. The *interest* on the previous year's assessment, S_n^{t-1}, accrued during the year, *and the year's annuity:*

$$i \cdot S_n^{t-1} \cdot \frac{(1 + i)^{t-1} -1}{(1 + i)^n -1} + S_n^{t-1} \cdot \frac{i}{(1 + i)^n -1} = \frac{i}{(1 + i)^n - 1} \cdot S_n^{t-1} (1 + i)^{t-1}.$$

2. The *adjustment* for cost escalation $S_n^t - S_n^{t-1}$, accumulated to the end of the year. If no changes are expected, the second factor is equal to zero. The sinking-fund account with $S_{t-1}, S_t,$ and C is shown in Figure 4.

We assumed above only changing estimates of future decommissioning costs, which makes annual reassessment of S_n^t necessary. Changing the rate of discount

Closing balance, $S_t =$	Opening balance, $S_{t-1} =$
$S_n^t \cdot \dfrac{(1+i)^t - 1}{(1+i)^n - 1}$	$S_n^{t-1} \cdot \dfrac{(1+i)^{t-1} - 1}{(1+i)^n - 1}$
	Charged to operations, $C =$
	$\dfrac{i}{(1+i)^n - 1} \left[S_n^{t-1} \cdot (1+i)^{t-1} \right.$
	$\left. + (S_n^t - S_n^{t-1}) \cdot \dfrac{(1+i)^t - 1}{i} \right]$

Figure 4. Reserve for Future Decommissioning Costs, Adjusted for Cost Escalations

from i to j and the estimated useful life from n to m might, however, also be justified. Under such circumstances the closing balance will be

$$S_t = S_m^t \cdot \frac{(1+j)^t - 1}{(1+j)^m - 1},$$ (2a)

and the difference between S_t and S_{t-1}, to be charged to the year's operations,

$$C = S_m^t \cdot \frac{(1+j)^t - 1}{(1+j)^m - 1} - S_n^{t-1} \cdot \frac{(1+i)^{t-1} - 1}{(1+i)^n - 1}.$$ (3a)

In his study on negative net salvage, Robert Faust also proposes annual reassessment of decommissioning costs [7, pp. 28ff.]. His is, however, a purely accounting approach, focusing on the computation of depreciation charges and thus neglecting the time dimension of monetary claims, essential for the capital budgeting/financing approach in the present paper. Here the interim utilization of annual reservations is considered by using an appropriate rate of discount. Also, the need for accumulated adjustments for previous years $(0 - t - 1)$ is taken into consideration.

THE FINANCING PROBLEM

Decommissioning nuclear facilities will cause considerable outlays, in the magnitude of 45 to 90 million U.S. dollars in terms of 1978 prices. Apart from considering this when establishing the power rates, the equivalent part of sales revenues has to be saved in order to be available when facilities are closed down. Saving in different forms is feasible. These forms involve differing annual amounts because of different fiscal treatment and interest yield on sums set aside. This will be explained below.

1. *Appropriation* of annual amounts in the corporation's books. Figure 4 shows how this "reserve for future decommissioning costs" is treated in accounting. Appropriations are either deductible for income taxes or else they have to be made from retained earnings after taxes. In the latter case, income taxes on appropriations are to be included in charges to operations. If s stands for the income tax rate, charges to operations should amount to $(S_t - S_{t-1})/(1 - s)$.

2. Appropriations as under case one, but in addition a *compulsory guarantee* from a financial institution (bank, insurance company). Costs for this guarantee must also be charged to operations.

3. Appropriations as under case one, deductible from income tax, provided that a certain percentage is *deposited* in an interest-free account *at the Riksbanken.* As mentioned above, similar stipulations exist in Sweden for appropriations to investment funds. According to these, 46 percent of the year's net appropriations has to be deposited. The money deposited can be used only when decommissioning occurs and should then be subject to income taxes. As no interest is paid on these deposits, annual costs increase accordingly. The year's appropriations then have to be

$$0.54 \cdot C + \frac{0.46}{n} \cdot S_n^t + (t-1) \cdot (S_n^t - S_n^{t-1});$$

for the value of C, see formula (3).

4. Payment into an *independent sinking fund,* managed by some financial institution authorized for this function, where the money accrues with interest. The amounts to be paid in correspond to the costs to be charged to operations and depend on the interest paid on the deposits by the financial institution. The interest rate is presumably lower than the corporation's rate of discount/internal rate of return.

5. *Insurance* through an insurance company. The premium, revised annually in accordance with reassessed S_n^t, is to be charged to operations. In cases where payment from the insurance company is subject to income taxation at the outcome (i.e., when decommissioning occurs), the annual premium should be deductible. It should, however, be added that there has been no precedent for this in Sweden until now and that the Central Taxation Board (Riksskatteverket) has not yet examined a pending case.

6. Compulsory *charges into a public fund* in proportion to the capacity of the power station or to the electricity actually delivered, where the fund,

in return, is responsible for financing decommissioning. These deductible fees are to be charged to operations.

In cases one and two, the total funded amounts, but only 54 percent of them in case three, form part of the corporation's working capital until decommissioning occurs. In cases three–six, the money is paid out from the corporation. Only when borrowing back is permitted do the funds contribute to the financing of the corporation.

FUTURE COSTS AND INCOME TAXATION

The Swedish AKA inquiry, a blue book on *Spent Nuclear Fuel and Radioactive Waste* [21], concludes that

> in their cost calculations the power utilities should also include the future costs of reprocessing and terminal storage at the time when nuclear fuel is being used for power production. . . . A sum corresponding to these charges should be reserved in the . . . yearly account and transferred to a special fund from which the costs will be covered when they appear later on. In the meantime the fund may form part of the companies' working capital.
> Another possibility is for the state to levy a charge on energy delivered . . . and thereby assume the responsibility of further handling of spent nuclear fuel. . . . The charges should be credited to a special state equalization fund. . . . [21, p. 81]

Reservation for decommissioning as such is not mentioned here, although earlier in the same blue book it is maintained that

> . . . decommissioning of reactors . . . should be considered at an early stage . . . in order to facilitate a further decommissioning. . . . Certain steps should . . . be taken already during the design and construction phase. . . . We therefore suggest that an acceptable technical description of the planning of any future decommissioning should constitute a precondition for licensing of nuclear facilities. [21, p. 84]

These lines of thought are to a certain extent analogous to legal regulations concerning exploitation of gravel pits. Activities have to be licensed by local government (länsstyrelsen) and a normal precondition is that those pursuing exploitation have to restore the landscape to the utmost possible extent after terminating exploitation. To ensure that restoration will be carried out, the local authorities usually demand security from the licensee [11, p. 606].

The government bill on the deductibility of future expenses proposes that an amount, reserved on the books to cover future expenses for handling spent nuclear fuel, and so on, should be deductible for income taxation [19]. The ensuing law stipulates that deduction is granted only to the extent that the costs of managing spent fuel, and so on, correspond to activities pursued during or prior to the year assessed for income taxes. Deducted sums should be added to the following year's taxable income [15]. In a supplementary decree, the Central Taxation Board is authorized to issue instructions for these deductibles [9]. The Swedish Minister of Industry has recently commissioned Governor Bertil Löfberg "to investigate into the management of radioactive waste – organization and financing" [12, p. 13]. According to the general instructions to the commission, a system of financing future costs should be designed in order to ensure that there will be sufficient funds available as long as expenses may arise. Of the two financing alternatives of the AKA inquiry [21], the emphasis is now on charges to a state fund to cover leftover costs of nuclear power. Reference is also made to the power corporation's possibilities of borrowing from the fund. The general instructions also emphasize the need for alternative calculations of future *decommissioning costs*. These should be estimated both for partial dismantling and total dismantling, as well as for removal of the structures.

It should be added that the comparison with gravel pit exploitation, as discussed earlier, can be of only limited help in throwing light on the handling of decommissioning costs. Deductibility of costs, if in conformity with the accounting ledgers, is in the gravel pit case dependent on volume: "so much of future restoration costs as corresponds to the quantity extracted out of total deposits during all the years past, including the year actually assessed for income taxes" [11, p. 606].

A similar dependence on volume can indeed be established for the future costs of managing nuclear fuel and radioactive waste, whereas decommissioning costs of a nuclear reactor that is out of service are indivisible. After the facilities have been contaminated because of radiation during operations, decommissioning costs will depend less on the number of years of operations or the magnitude of electricity delivered and more on the time frame of the chosen alternative of decommissioning: immediate dismantling or interim confinement with deferred dismantling.

The question of deductibility in Sweden is more important for power corporations established decades ago, such as Sydkraft AB or Skandinaviska Elverk AB, but is of smaller significance for power stations recently set up or still under construction, such as the Forsmark Group. The older corporations' operations are to a considerable extent financed by shareholders' capital. They also have a well-established production from sources other than nuclear power, and their earning capacity is considerable. New power stations, being much heavier bond-financed, have very high effective costs of capital. Their income taxes will presumably consist mainly of property taxes for a good many years, as these are determined as a fixed percentage of property value, independent of what the income statement might show.

INSURANCE AND GUARANTEES

Swedish insurance companies have formed jointly a Nuclear Insurance Pool (Atomförsäkringspoolen, AFP, Birger Jarlsgatan 2, Stockholm) to promote risk-sharing on activities for which experience is scarce. The companies are, via the AFP, engaged in the reinsurance business all over the world. The Swedish share of the costs of the Harrisburg disaster, for example, were about 6.5 million U.S. dollars.

It should be mentioned in this context that the nuclear power industry in Finland is liable by law to make reservations covering the costs of (1) managing radioactive waste and (2) decommissioning nuclear facilities, whereas regulations covering the latter costs are still under consideration in Sweden. Finnish rules also presume the possibility of offering guarantees. In this latter question, interested parties in Finland turned to the Swedish AFP, but could not, until now, obtain any offer.[2]

Individual Swedish insurance companies do not, as mentioned above, insure nuclear risks. It might be added that there exists no practice in Sweden regarding guarantees from insurance companies for environmental restoration in connection with exploitation of gravel pits. The problem was not even discussed in the professional journals.[3]

THE APPROPRIATE DISCOUNT RATE

The question of interest has been touched upon casually before. For power stations, typically capital-intensive projects, the cost of capital is the most important single cost factor—apart from fuel (coal, oil, gas, or uranium).

For *financing*, the external rate of interest, paid to creditors in the capital market, is decisive. The Swedish nuclear power industry is predominantly—between two-thirds and nine-tenths—debt-financed. In the beginning of 1979, the share of debts in long-term financing was for Sydkraft 76 percent, for the Oskarshamn Power group 90 percent, for the Forsmark Power Group 66 percent, or 95 percent including borrowing from owners [7, 20, 22]. The average and marginal cost of capital is thus of central importance for financial planning.

In all types of *economic analysis*, cash flows over many years of construction, operation, and decommissioning have to be made comparable. The proper rate of discount has to be chosen when

1. Appraising the overall profitability of capital budgeting proposals
2. Adding to other costs of fixed assets (buildings, machinery, equipment) the costs of capital during the years of construction until the power station starts to operate
3. Computing the sinking-fund factor, $i/[(1 + i)^n - 1]$, for accumulating funds set aside annually to cover future decommissioning costs

The time necessary for construction amounts to about seven years,[4] the useful life to thirty to forty years, and decommissioning to six to nine years or, in the case of deferment, a much longer time. During this long time span, technology and environmental regulations will change considerably, and prices and wages may double many times over. Under these circumstances, it is very tempting to draw up calculations in stable prices and consequently to disregard inflationary fluctuations also when determining the rate of discount. The nominal external rate of interest (i), oriented toward the capital market, must then be adjusted according to the expected rate of cost escalation (j). The resulting "real" rate of capital, (r), [16, p. 321; 3, p. 87] will then be $r = i-j$ or, carefully computed,

$$\frac{1+i}{1+j} - 1.$$

For the NESP study, "considerations of escalation and discount factors . . . was beyond the . . . scope" [17, p. iv]. In two Swedish studies heavily dependent on NESP, the question of the proper rate of discount is also disregarded [13, App. 3, p. 14, App. 4, pp. 9ff.]. In the German NIS study, an 8 percent rate of inflation and a 12 percent interest rate are assumed [2, p. 47]. The recent U.S. Batelle study states that

> . . . the discount rate (k) should be generally in the 8–10% range. Interest rates obtainable from stable, secure investments are generally several percentage points less than the current discount rates. . . . Where there is little historical basis for projecting inflation rates (j) over long periods of time, there are data, which indicate that the difference between (k) and (j) is relatively constant, at about 4%, independent of the current rate of inflation. Thus for purposes of this study a discount rate of 10% . . . and an inflation rate of 6% have been selected as the base conditions. [23, App. D, p. 10]

When the Swedish Minister of Industry recently commissioned the Norwegian consultants Scandpower A/S to investigate the costs of nuclear power in *Sweden,* part of the commission's general instructions was that a "real" rent of 4 percent should be used [14, p. 3]. In the Scandpower report, data from the American and German studies mentioned above [2, 17, 23], after certain adjustments for local conditions, are applied to six nuclear power stations in operation and five under construction. A useful life of thirty years is assumed, and the facilities are assumed to be fully depreciated within twenty-five years. In calculations in terms of 1978 prices, rates of 4 percent (see general instructions above) and 0 percent are alternatively applied [14, pp. 96ff.], the latter with regard to the relatively low present values resulting from discounting at 4 percent for so many years [14, p. 94].

The underlying assumption of a "real" analysis is, however, that relative prices and costs will remain unchanged over the entire life of the project [16, p. 321]. Clearly, this assumption might easily prove to be unrealistic. If the nominal rate, the effective external rate of interest, occasionally falls below the rate of inflation (this happened repeatedly in Sweden during the postwar years), the "real" rate of interest becomes negative. In this case, evaluating projected cash flows over thirty to forty years or more might produce bizarre consequences. The expedient of a zero rate does not seem to be satisfactory, although computational work is simplified. There are great risks for losing touch with reality when

1. Establishing electricity rates
2. Planning capital and interest service on debt
3. Appropriating means to cover future decommissioning costs

It is safer and more adequate to forecast as carefully as possible future conditions, such as expected prices and costs, and to revise forecasts regularly. At the same time, nominal rates of interest, reflecting inflationary expectations of the capital market, should be applied. In this manner, real outcomes can currently be compared with original forecasts, and the latter can, if necessary, be revised and adjusted.

The object of this discussion is indeed the financing of *decommissioning,* but it would be unwise to disregard the importance of the proper rate of discount for the overall calculations of power rates. There is an apparent risk of ignoring entirely or partly the question of interest, and with that, the time factor, in spite of the long-term character of the analysis. There is, of course, the expedient of a state fund, which should levy charges on power stations and assume responsibility for future decommissioning. But this would be a pseudo-solution only. The objective in view is that *no part of today's energy costs should be charged to coming generations.* In a more general context than the one with decommissioning in focus, excessively low rates of interest might have very serious consequences. For example, if electricity rates yield only 4 percent (eventually 0 percent) on invested capital, while interest payable on two-thirds to nine-tenths of long-term capitalization amounts to about 10 percent or more, considerable annual losses will arise. The deficits would have to be covered by subventions in order to guarantee further operations.

According to the Scandpower report [14, pp. 10ff.], capital outlays for eleven nuclear power stations in Sweden amount to about 5.5 billion U.S. dollars in terms of 1978 prices. The annual cost of capital to be covered by power rates would then on the average amount to,

Computed at 4 percent, 220 million U.S. dollars
Computed at 10 percent, 550 million U.S. dollars
Computed at 12 percent, 660 million U.S. dollars

The subvention needed in the case of 4 percent instead of 10 percent should amount to 330 million U.S. dollars per year on the average. Such enormous subventions in relation to a total population in Sweden of 8 million people would clearly counteract today's general emphasis on the necessity of energy conservation. The result, on the contrary, would be a great waste of energy.

As bonds for financing the reactor power stations generally have to be amortized in twenty years (in some cases fifteen years), the interest portion of the annuity will be much higher in earlier years than the figures shown above and will then diminish gradually. From the financing point of view the focus is on disbursements/capital outlays. This means, of course, the whole annuity on the debt on which capital and interest should be served. If this amounts to two-thirds of the 5.5 billion dollars above, net income before depreciation and interest, payable during the first twenty years of operations, should render it possible to pay out annually,

At 4 percent, 270 million U.S. dollars
At 10 percent, 430 million U.S. dollars
At 12 percent, 490 million U.S. dollars

This has to be considered when negotiating with the authorities on the subject of pricing electrical power.

CONCLUSIONS

Negative salvage values of substantial magnitude—for example, future decommissioning costs of nuclear facilities—should be reckoned with carefully when

1. Evaluating capital budgeting proposals (calculation)
2. Charging corresponding annuities to operations during the facilities' useful life (accounting)
3. Saving and accumulating these annual amounts for future use (financing)

Costs expected in the distant future should be reassessed currently, and the annuity charged to operations adjusted accordingly. Different forms of saving and accumulating, within the organization or outside it, affect the annual amount because of differences in fiscal treatment and interest yield.

The appropriate rate of discount has to be chosen carefully as it affects coverage of capital outlays at the beginning and negative salvage values at the end in opposite ways. The chosen rate should ensure an internal rate of return slightly above the cost of capital. The "practical" expedient of projecting future costs at an unchanged price level and applying a "real" rate of interest is risky. One might easily lose touch with reality. A careful projection of future nominal prices and costs and the application of a nominal rate are more advisable.

NOTES

1. A. Zielinski, Chairman, Public Services Commission, New York State [23, Section 6, p. 1].
2. Information from Gunnar Andersson, AFP.
3. Information from Stig Bäckström, Skandia, Göteburg.
4. See, however, the second section of this paper, "The Cost Problem"; also [18].

REFERENCES

[1] Asztély, S. *Investeringsplanering,* 2nd ed. Stockholm, 1973.
[2] Bardtenschlager a.a., *Decommissioning of Light Water Nuclear Power Plants,* Nuclear Ingenieur Service Ges.m.b.H. (NIS), Frankfurt a/M, Nuclear Engineering and Design Vol. 45. Amsterdam: North-Holland Publishing Company, 1978.
[3] Bergknut, P., and Hentzel, M. *Investering.* Lund, 1977.
[4] Carlberg, G.; Pehrson, P.; and Prahl, S. *Finansiella aspekter på avveckling av uttjänta kärnkraftverk,* mimeogr., Lund, January 1979.
[5] *Decommissioning of Nuclear Facilities,* International Atomic Energy Agency (IAEA), Vienna, 1975.
[6] *Energi. Hälso-, miljö- och säkerhetsrisker.* Energikommissionens slutbetänkande [Energy. Health hazards, risks of major accidents and sabotage. Main Report of the Energy Commission]. Summary in English, pp. 19–28, SOU, Stockholm, 1978:49.
[7] Faust, Robert. "A Positive Rationale for Negative Net Salvage," *Public Utilities Fortnightly* (July 29, 1976).
[8] Ferguson, John S. "Salvage Is Also Important," *Public Utilities Fortnightly* (August 3, 1978).

[9]   Förordning med bemyndigande för riksskatteverket att utfärda föreskrifter för beräkning av avdrag för framtida utgifter för hantering av utbränt kärnbränsle mm, SFS 1979:27.

[10] Forsmarks Kraftgrupp AB, 10 1/4% obligationslån på 200 mkr., emissionsprospekt, April 10, 1979.

[11] Haglund, E. "Om periodisering av klassningskostnader," Svensk skattetidning 1978 nr 9, sid. 597ff.

[12] "Hantering av radioaktivt avfall—organisation och finansiering," Industriministerns direktiv, Från Riksdag och Departement 1979 nr 9, sid. 13.

[13] Kärnkraftens avveckling, utredning åt Energikommissionen (Decommissioning of Nuclear Power), mimeogr., Vattenfall, October 7, 1977.

[14] Kjernkraftens kostnader, utredning, utarbeidet for det svenske industridepartementet, Scandpower S/A, mimeogr., February 1979.

[15] Lag om ändring i kommunalskattelagen (1928:370), SFS 1978:974.

[16] Levy, H., and Sarnat, M. Capital Investment and Financial Decisions. Englewood Cliffs, N.J.: Prentice-Hall, 1978.

[17] Manion, W.J., and La Guardia, T.S. An Engineering Evaluation of Nuclear Power Reactor Decommissioning Alternatives, summary report, National Environmental Studies Project (NSEP), Atomic Industrial Forum, AIF/NESP-009, November 1976.

[18] Nuclear Power Costs, 23rd report by the Committee of Government Operations. Washington, D.C.: U.S. Government Printing Office, April 26, 1978.

[19] Om avdrag för framtida utgifter för hantering av kärnbränsle, Regeringens proposition, 1978/79:39, October 26, 1978.

[20] Oskarshamnsverkets Kraftgrupp AB, 10 1/4% obligationslån på 75 mkr., emissionsprospekt, December 10, 1978.

[21] Spent Nuclear Fuel and Radioactive Waste, a summary of a report given by the Swedish Government Committee on Radioactive Waste (AKA-utredningens betäkande), SOU Stockholm 1976:32.

[22] Sydkraft AB, 10 1/4% obligationslån på 50 mkr., emissionsprospekt, May 10, 1978.·

[23] Technology, Safety and Cost of Decommissioning a Reference PWR Reactor Power Station, prepared by Batelle Pacific Northwest Laboratories (BNWL) for U.S. Nuclear Regulatory Commission, NUREG/CR–0130, Vol. I/II, Richland, Wash., June 1978.

12 THE COST OF FINANCING TO THE FIRM IN FOREIGN EXCHANGE:

Some Empirical Results and Implications

Harald Burmeister
IESE, Spain

This paper tries to fill one of many observable gaps in operationally oriented research. The author sees his role as one of a mediator between theorists and practitioners: The merits of theories as such are not called into question, but they must deliver decision rules that are both practically applicable and functionally good. If theories cannot do this job, they are not yet useful to business, and other decision rules, whether backed by theory or not, must be developed or looked for. While theories without operational decision rules are not rejected by research into these mechanisms, they are rejected as the origin of acceptable decision rules. The criteria for rejection are therefore not necessarily those drawn from the current state of the art of methodology. This paper attempts to make this point clear through a rather simplistic research example.

Any business or economically active institution of some size has a choice of financing its activities in more than one currency, and therefore an obligation to solve the problem of which currency or currencies to choose and use in order to minimize borrowing costs.

Available literature treats this problem as a subtopic of either or both of two main fields:

1. How to optimize currency exposure, including, of course, any liabilities
2. How to minimize the cost of capital, including, of course, any credits in foreign exchange

While this kind of treatment may be sound conceptually, at least *a priori*, it bears little resemblance to how managers look at the problem. The type of research available offers them little hope of doing things better, or of researchers being much help.

One justification for looking at a problem that is perhaps only a part of a larger one is to try to formulate and analyze it as the decision makers seem to do it, rightly or wrongly. The analysis and solution will gain the advantage of their understanding the work done.

Another justification is that our concepts of "science," including our research methodology, are culture- and time-bound. There is reason to believe that our recent efforts at all-inclusive modeling may be a little bit too ambitious and somewhat less successful than anticipated when applied to operations; thus looking at partial problems may after all not be a suboptimal effort worthy of condemnation. Still, do it one way or the other and be damned, either by the businessman or by the economist. This author tentatively prefers the wrath of the latter to that of the former.

For the reasons just mentioned, the form of the data used is taken from the concrete context of business loans: medium-term Euroloans with interests based on LIBOR six months plus a margin (instead of data without a context, which seem to be "abstract" to the manager, like interests on financial assets usually found in research but not used by businesses as debt instruments: government bonds, three-month Eurorates without margin, etc.).

In order not to ask more of the results than the input data can possibly promise, great pains are taken not to claim validity where it is not obvious. This research therefore claims no more than to inform on the costs incurred by businesses and other borrowers had they taken medium-term loans in one or another currency during one or another period of the last nine years. As borrowers have been doing just that in increasing number year after year, this study would seem to be useful, at least to the decision makers on the battlefield.

In the next section, some of the presently available research literature is analyzed in regard to its tenor, substance, and usefulness to the decision maker in order to arrive at a starting point for the research presented here. Following that, the research task is formulated in more detail and with some rigor. The choice of the data used is explained and discussed, as is the choice of measuring techniques. The results are then presented and interpreted, after which some conclusions are drawn as to the usefulness of presently available decision rules and possible substitutes.

PRESENT THEORY AND RESEARCH

A suitable summary and synthesis of present theory and research are contained in Aliber [1], who combines various theories (Law of One Price, PPP, Fisher Closed and Open, Interest Rate Parity) into proportionality propositions that relate prices, interests, and exchange rates—spot and future—in a systematic manner. Of specific interest here is Fisher Open, as it relates interest rates and exchange rates and the changes in these rates. It says in essence that differences in interest rates on similar assets denominated in different currencies are equal to the anticipated exchange rate change. In an efficient market, the forecast of future exchange rates implied in the word "anticipated" cannot be improved upon, and while the "anticipation" derived from the difference in interest rates may be off the target, it is so without bias; if there were a consistent deviation between the anticipated and effective future exchange rate, this would imply inefficiency of the market, a bias speculators could, but do not, exploit. Research [1, 2, 4, 5, 7, 8, 9] has in general confirmed absence of bias; differences between anticipated and effective exchange rates have been substantial, but essentially random.

For good order's sake, the Interest Rate Parity Theorem should be drawn into this argument, since it tries to explain the relation between the difference in interest rates on similar assets and the difference between spot and forward exchange rates. This theory is mentioned here because forward exchange rates are frequently cast as yet another forecast of future spot exchange rates. Research studying this proposition [2, 6, 10] has also resulted in the maintenance of the hypothesis of absence of bias, although the forecasts implied in the forward exchange rate have not always been satisfactory, to put it mildly.[1]

For borrowers, the implication of Fisher Open seems to be clear: It is useless to spend time and money trying to choose the right currency in which to borrow because the lower (or higher) interest rate of one currency will be compensated by a re- (or de-) valuation of that currency, so that the resulting total cost of a credit in (any) foreign exchange will be equal among the currencies. Possible deviations known *ex post facto* cannot be foreseen because they are random.

While Aliber does not go so far as to confirm the operational applicability of the theory, the tenor of his (and others') interpretations of research results and especially of his recommendations for business is quite ambiguous:

> In contemplating its exposure in various currencies, the firm must decide on its confidence in Fisher Open as a systematic central tendency, and whether,

if Fisher holds, there are non-random biases from Fisher. If the managers believe that Fisher Open holds, they can ignore the firm's exposure, as long as it
remains unchanged. [1, p. 140]

The specific results of his research include, for instance, average yearly deviations, from interest rates on U.S. government bonds, of 1.68 (2.07, 2.78, 4.80,
10.64) percent for Swiss government bonds covering a period of twenty-five
(twenty, fifteen, ten, five) years from 1950 to 1975 (1955-1975, 1960-1975,
1965-1975, 1970-1975). Aliber writes that

> . . . for the nine foreign bonds as a group, the rate of return averaged 1.80
> per cent higher per year than the rate of return on dollar bonds on the inclu-
> sive (25 years) period. For the most recent five-year period (1970–1975)
> however, the rate of return on the foreign bonds exceeded that on dollar
> bonds by more than 6% a year. . . . [1, p. 71]

A formulation of the results for the U.S./Swiss bond comparison more relevant for borrowers would probably have been to say that borrowers' cost (or
investors' return) differed by 37.2 (41.3, 50.0, 75.6, 138.4)[2] percent per year
over twenty-five (twenty, fifteen, ten, five) years, instead of giving the absolute
values of the differences cited above.

Interest rates on government bonds are not equal to the financing costs
businesses incur, but they are probably correlated. Let us assume for a moment
that the differences in financing costs for businesses are similar to the above
numbers. No manager could decide that Fisher Open holds if the difference of
cost over twenty-five years would be an average of 37.2 percent per annum!
On the other hand, from Aliber's numbers cited above, it seems to become clear
that a tendency toward convergence exists the more extended the period measured, although the results of the measurement of only one instance per time
period (i.e., for five years only, the period 1970-1975 and not 1950-1955,
1955-1960, 1960-1965, 1965-1970 as well) are cited here. The results, if measured in as many periods as possible throughout the twenty-five years, would
have been much less clear-cut regarding the tendency toward convergence. In any
case, my conclusion is that whatever tendency for convergence of costs, if a
twenty-five-year period shows a yearly difference of 37.2 percent, the convergence is of little consolation to borrowers (and lenders).

On the other hand, it must be admitted that our recent and not so recent
history (say from 1945 to 1979) of exchange and interest rate changes is such
that no harm is done by calling it unusual. Which period is studied is of great
importance for results. The choice of base and terminal years can change results
drastically. Since 1945, we have had wild (1945-1949; 1971-1979) and quiet
(1950-1970) periods. Therefore, it would seem advisable to be prudent in the
interpretation of the data and especially the extrapolation of their validity.
Since we cannot assume that the future will be like, or better than, the past,

we may well have to limit our conclusions to the period studied. If we take this position, it will not allow us to make a positive conclusion on the applicability at all times of the theories (which may or may not be rejected by our studies), but a judgment with such limiting effects in itself must then be taken as a starting point for the need to develop decision rules that take this fact into account. Theories may not be rejectable through results of research; a different but perfectly valid question is, however, if they lead under the best of circumstances to acceptable decision rules for the manager. In the case studied here, this seems not to be so, and the theory is therefore lacking usefulness. Aliber's careful wording of his conclusions expresses this, as well as a lack of concern for what to do next, not atypical, and perhaps justified, for macroeconomists.

RESEARCHING THE COST OF TYPICAL INTERNATIONAL MEDIUM-TERM CREDITS TO BUSINESS BORROWERS

The presently dominant[3] form of borrowing by business (and government) in the international market is the medium-term (approximately three to ten years) credit in dollars, marks, Swiss francs, or, to a lesser degree, pound sterling. The interest formula used is mostly LIBOR six months[4] and a margin; while the margin is fixed for the life of the credit,[5] the basic interest rate (LIBOR) changes every six months. There are other costs to be taken into account, as will be explained later.

Borrowers have a choice regarding the currency or currencies to take,[6] since the international market offers a number of them in practically equal terms of disposability. This choice would not be easy if the only consideration were the interest rate plus margin payable, since the currencies have been carrying ever-changing and also diverging interest rates (while the margin would be the same for all currencies). With a change in interest rates every six months over three to ten years, one could not be sure that an initially low interest rate on, say, the Swiss franc would not be replaced later by a higher interest rate and thus compensate or overcompensate any initial advantage, always in terms relative to the interest rate movements on other currencies available. In practice—although not in theory—the problem is aggravated by the fact that there is an additional and most important cost consideration to be taken into account: exchange rate changes.

It has already been explained that prevailing theory likes to think of the two cost elements mentioned—interest rates and exchange rates and their changes—as compensatory. Business borrowers can hardly share this thinking, as their experiences, as well as research results, do not lend themselves to confirming the postulates of theory in a way satisfactory for decision making.

In the research done here, the aim was to establish the cost of the medium-term credits described in the various currencies in realistic terms, understandable to the businessman, and covering a time span that practically encompasses the whole period during which businesses were able to obtain such credits (1970 onward).

The exchange rates used were obtained from various sources,[7] and represent closing or midday rates of the last working day of each semester. It can only be hoped that no bias is introduced by using closing and midday rates without distinction.[8]

The interest rates are offered rates (i.e., LIBOR) and were obtained from even more varied sources and in some complicated ways.[9] The no-bias hope must be repeated here.[10]

As margin, a 2 percent p.a. was taken. Margins have been varying, according to the quality of the borrower and the liquidity of the market, between .5 percent and 2 percent. As the .5 percent (and even 1 percent) margin is totally unremunerative for banks (they would actually incur a loss when lending at such margins), all kinds of commissions and fees were established: management fee (.25-1 percent), participation fee (.25-.75 percent), agency fee ($5000-$15,000 annually), commitment fee (.25-.75 percent p.a. for credits or parts thereof negotiated but not taken up), legal fees and other out-of-pocket cost (up to $50,000), and so on. The smaller the borrowed sum, the higher perhaps the margin but the less the commissions (as usually one bank would be the lender and not a consortium). There are other expenses such as buy-sell margins and possibly commissions on foreign exchange transactions.[11] It is assumed that the margin of 2 percent assumed for the calculations include, in an annualized form, all these commissions and charges and represent a "typical" cost additional to LIBOR.

It is important to include such a (it is hoped realistic) margin in the calculations, as the difference in costs brought about through interest rates alone or through interest rates plus margin can be affected very seriously: if LIBOR six months for the Swiss franc is 2 percent, and for marks 4 percent, and thus the difference 100 percent, with the margin here assumed of 2 percent the costs convert into 4 percent and 6 percent, respectively, and thus a difference of 50 percent only.

Regarding repayment of the loans, the "bullet" type (i.e., repayment in full at the end of the life of a credit) was assumed in order to avoid complications in calculating partial amortizations. Partial amortizations also exist, in practice, in an infinite variety,[12] and for that reason alone, they cannot be represented usefully by just one form of amortization.

To make calculations easy, a nominal amount of pesetas (pts. 1000,-) was taken and converted into the four currencies at exchange rates prevailing at the starting dates of the calculations. The interest rate for the currencies was that valid on the same date (plus the 2 percent margin), but payment would be effected only six months later and at the exchange rate then valid. After these six months, a new interest rate was fixed, payable six months later at the exchange rate valid on the new payment date, and so on. After establishing a complete cash flow, in pesetas, for all currencies in the way described, the internal rate of return was calculated. The different results in terms of the internal rate of return for all currencies were thus deemed comparable.

Regarding the time periods measured, a total of 9 years—first quarter 1970 to first quarter 1979—was available. The following periods were established:

1. 1st quarter 1970–1st quarter 1979 = 9 years
2. 1st quarter 1970–3rd quarter 1974 = 4½ years
3. 3rd quarter 1974–1st quarter 1979 = 4½ years
4. 1st quarter 1970–1st quarter 1973 = 3 years
5. 1st quarter 1973–1st quarter 1976 = 3 years
6. 1st quarter 1976–1st quarter 1979 = 3 years

The differing length of the periods measured would allow us to establish whether there existed a tendency to converging costs among the currencies from the shorter (three years) to the longer (four and a half years) and longest periods (nine years) measured, although the number of data would be insufficient for statistically significant conclusions.

The possible convergence of costs could be of major importance to firms. While most managers continue looking at loans one by one, there is no doubt that firms use outside funds constantly, although not necessarily at all times in the form of medium-term foreign exchange credits. If convergence existed, a company would enjoy, over time, the compensatory effect between interest rate and exchange rate variations. It could decide to be always indebted in foreign exchange and always in the same currency in order to enjoy the effect. Before doing so, the firm should study what kinds of losses it could suffer from a temporary maximum divergence in costs among the currencies, and if such maximum losses would be bearable. Without tackling the task of establishing the maximum loss sustainable for the firm in order to contrast it with the maximum loss possible through foreign exchange borrowing, it is worth mentioning that this in itself is not an easy problem to solve. On the other hand, financing costs seem not to be among the major costs for many companies, and heavy temporary fluctuations in only one of the many forms of outside financing may therefore not be too important.[13]

The results obtained in the form of internal rates of return were then submitted to a simple comparison of differences in absolute and relative percentages, since the reduced number of data did not allow submission of results to statistical treatment. It is evident that such an evaluation cannot test any hypothesis in the classical sense, but this is less important—within the objectives of this study—than to try to identify whether the decision rules derived from the hypotheses are operational.

PRESENTATION AND INTERPRETATION OF RESULTS

Table 1 contains the interest rate and exchange rate data used. In Table 2, the results for all periods measured are summarized in annual percentages representing internal rates of return. Table 3 identifies the absolute and relative percentage differences existing, using—for the latter—the lowest and highest rates as a basis.

Turning to Table 3, one can easily observe that absolute cost differences are substantial. The dollar turns out to have been the cheapest currency for the nine-year period, closely followed by the pound. Swiss francs and German marks are at the other extreme. The difference for the nine-year period between the cheapest and the most expensive currency to borrow turns out to be 7.63 percent annually, a simply momentous figure in practical terms. The calculations of relative percentage rates put this figure into perspective by telling us that it is 82.8 percent higher than the lowest cost figure (for the dollar) or, vice versa, that the lowest cost is 45.2 percent less than the highest (for the Swiss franc). Between the two four-and-a-half-year periods, huge cost differences continue to prevail. In one case the difference exceeds (9.04 percent) and in the other it is below (6.47 percent) the difference for the 9 years (7.63 percent). Curiously enough, looking at the relative cost differences, the one with the lower absolute cost difference has the higher relative difference: 113.9 percent more than the lowest cost and 53.25 percent less than the highest cost, while the second four-and-a-half-year period with the higher absolute difference shows "only" a 61.8 percent cost excess over the cheapest currency and a 38.2 percent reduction over the most costly currency.

Of the three three-year periods, two have larger and one has a lower absolute cost difference than the nine-year period and, compared to the two four-and-a-half-year periods, two of the three-year periods show less difference and one, a greater one. In relative terms, it again occurs that the period with the least absolute difference has the highest relative difference with a cost above the cheapest of 215.3 percent, while in the other cases the differences are between 80 percent and 90 percent for the more costly currency above the cheapest.

In summary, there is one period of three years and one of four and a half that have lower absolute cost differences than the nine-year period; and there are two

Table 1. Interest Rates (LIBOR Six Months) and Exchange Rates against the Peseta

Currencies Dates End of	U.S. $		DM		Pound		Swiss Franc	
	LIBOR	Exchange Rate	LIBOR	Exchange Rate	LIBOR	Exchange Rate	LIBOR	Exchange Rate
1st quarter '70	8 3/4	70.00	9 1/4	19.19	9 1/4	168.00	8	16.22
3rd quarter '70	8 3/4	70.00	8 3/4	19.28	10 1/8	168.00	6 3/4	16.28
1st quarter '71	6	69.70	6 1/2	19.20	8 1/2	168.46	5 1/8	16.23
3rd quarter '71	7 7/8	68.67	7 1/4	20.70	7 1/8	170.68	3 1/2	17.38
1st quarter '72	6 1/4	64.70	3 7/8	20.42	6 3/8	169.24	2	16.84
3rd quarter '72	6 3/8	63.59	3	19.86	9 1/8	153.89	2 7/8	16.72
1st quarter '73	8 7/8	58.13	7 1/8	20.48	11 3/4	144.05	5 1/8	17.96
3rd quarter '73	10 5/8	56.87	7 1/4	23.50	14 3/4	137.28	6 7/8	18.82
1st quarter '74	10	59.01	10 1/2	23.39	18 5/8	141.27	11	19.67
3rd quarter '74	12 1/4	57.68	10 1/4	21.74	16 1/8	134.51	10 7/8	19.58

1st quarter '75	8	56.06	5 7/8	24.10	13 1/8	135.00	6	22.48
3rd quarter '75	8 7/8	56.72	4 3/4	22.43	12 1/4	122.01	4 3/8	21.73
1st quarter '76	6 1/8	66.53	3 5/8	26.30	10 1/2	128.35	2 1/4	26.29
3rd quarter '76	6	67.67	5	28.38	17.1/2	109.60	2 1/2	28.00
1st quarter '77	5 1/2	68.57	4 1/2	28.75	9 3/4	118.10	3 1/2	27.01
3rd quarter '77	7 1/4	84.67	4	36.98	7 1/4	152.60	2 3/4	37.34
1st quarter '78	7 3/4	80.02	3 1/2	39.39	7 1/4	149.87	1	42.36
3rd quarter '78	9 3/4	72.27	3 3/4	37.27	13 1/4	142.51	1	46.60
1st quarter '79	10 3/4	68.38	5 3/8	36.59	11 7/8	141.43	7/8	40.41

Sources: Credit Suisse-White Weld Ltd.; Euromoney; Harris Bank; International Westminster Bank Ltd.; Mercado de Monedas.

Table 2. Combined Cost of Interest Rates (LIBOR Six Months + 2%) and Exchange Rate Variations, Expressed in Annual Internal Rate-of-Return Percentage against the Peseta

Currencies Period Covered	$	DM	Pound	Swiss Franc
9 years 1st qr. 1st qr. 1970–1979	9.21%	15.30%	10.00%	16.84%
4½ years 1st qr. 3rd qr. 1970–1974	5.68%	12.15%	7.46%	11.94%
4½ years 3rd qr. 1st qr. 1974–1979	14.72%	19.87%	14.63%	23.67%
3 years 1st qr. 1st qr. 1970–1973	3.46%	10.91%	5.70%	10.26%
3 years 1st qr. 1st qr. 1973–1976	15.82%	18.60%	12.16%	22.59%
3 years 1st qr. 1st qr. 1976–1979	10.68%	18.02%	16.16%	19.71%

periods of three years and the other four-and-a-half-year period that have higher cost differences in the absolute form than the nine-year period.[14] Regarding the relative cost differences, two of the three-year periods have practically the same difference in cost between the highest and lowest cost currency as the nine-year period, while the two four-and-a-half-year periods turn out to be above and below the relative cost differences of the nine-year period.[15]

I therefore conclude that no clear tendency evolves. The results are so mixed that it is impossible to discover a trend from looking at these few figures. As statistical treatment is excluded, this is all one can squeeze out as an interpretation.

It is quite clear that the cost differences, in their absolute or relative forms, represent such a deviation from Fisher Open that it would not have been operational for firms to be guided by that theory during any of the periods measured.

For some firms the cash-flow pattern of a credit in foreign exchange may be of importance or of interest. The results for the nine-year period are graphically demonstrated in Figures 1 to 4 for the four different currencies. Looking only at the two extreme cash-flow patterns, those of the Swiss franc and the pound sterling, one can see that the interest rate payments for Swiss francs during the period covered represent a relatively small drain of liquidity, thus providing a relatively large volume of credit during their lifetime, since only at the time of repayment did the major part of the revaluation effect of the Swiss franc come to bear. The horizontal straight line indicates the internal rate of return for the whole period in per annum percentage, while the dented line representing the interest payment converted into pesetas remains well below this mean cost. With the pound sterling the situation is inverted: The interest cost is at all times considerable and exceeds the average cost of the credit. Therefore the volume of credit put at the disposal of the borrower was less than through the credit in Swiss francs, coinciding with the fact that the repayment at the end of the life of the credit was effected at a devalued exchange rate instead of the revalued one for the Swiss franc. If one could identify currencies according to their relative nominal interest rate, then a borrower with preference for a large volume of funds generated by a credit could choose a low interest rate currency, while a borrower indifferent to the volume of a credit during the life of same would not be guided by the nominal interest rate, *ceteris paribus*. These remarks are, however, more anecdotal than of real importance, since it is not possible to deduce from the data obtained that in the future some currencies will have high interest rates and others low, as in the past, although one might be very tempted to do so.[16]

CONCLUSION: NEW DECISION RULES NEEDED

The results of this study, in line with Aliber's and others', confirm my opinion that Fisher Open, while perhaps not rejectable, is operationally useless as a decision rule. Financing costs among currencies, composed of interest rates charged to firms and exchange rate variations, vary widely and without a sufficient tendency toward convergence over the time periods studied here.

An additional reason to abandon Fisher Open as a basis for decision rules is an even more conclusive one: Fisher Open can only hold—if it holds at all—if the exchange risk exposure is held constant (i.e., in the same sums in the same currencies over time). There is practically no business with such a constellation of exchange risk (although an investor may occasionally fulfill this condition). If

Table 3. Maximum Differences (between Highest and Lowest Cost Currencies) in Absolute and Relative Percentage Points

Period and Currencies Highest/Lowest Cost / Percentage Differences	9 Years 1st Qr. '70–1st Qr. '79		4½ Years 1st Qr. '70–3rd Qr. '74		4½ Years 3rd Qr. '74–1st Qr. '79	
	Sw. Fr.	*$*	*DM*	*$*	*Sw. Fr.*	*£*
Absolute between highest and lowest	7.63%		6.47%		9.04%	
Relative above lowest cost	+82.8%		+113.9%		+61.8%	
below highest cost		–45.3%		–53.25%		–38.2%

sums and/or currencies change—a thing sure to happen in the short and long term through normal commercial and/or financial transactions of the firm—Fisher Open is not claimed to hold even by its most ardent defenders. Therefore business has to look for decision rules whose basis cannot possibly be Fisher Open.

After perusing the research results of both Aliber's and this study, there seem to be four alternatives on how to decide:

1. Take loans in dollars and never in Swiss francs.
2. Make your own forecasts of interest and exchange rate movements and decide for the cheapest currency.
3. Arrange loans in a mixture of currencies in order to spread the risk.
4. Take any currency and utilize forward cover at all times.

I will briefly discuss these four alternatives.

The first is a simple derivation from the fact that during the last nine years the dollar has been the cheapest currency to borrow. Underlying the decision rule proposed would be the assumption that the past would repeat itself in the future. On the one hand, it may well be that dollars cost less in real terms in the United States, a mature financial market with a relatively favorable *a priori* savings-investment ratio; on the other, the lesser costs of the dollar in the international market were not caused by interest rates but—if by anything

3 Years 1st Qr. '70–1st Qr. '73		3 Years 1st Qr. '73–1st Qr. '76		3 Years 1st Qr. '76–1st Qr. '79	
DM	$	Sw. Fr.	£	Sw. Fr.	$
7.45%		10.43%		9.05%	
+215.3%		+85.8%		+84.6%	
	−68.3%		−46.2%		−45.8%

identifiable—by major exchange rate movements. The latter have little to do with the argument of mature financial markets. There seems to be no *a priori* reason to assume that the dollar will also be cheaper—always combining interest rates and exchange rate movements—in the future, and it would be difficult to defend this decision rule on rational grounds.[17]

The second alternative involves making forecasts that are better than those implied in the interest and foreign (spot and forward) exchange rates. As these latter forecasts of future spot exchange rates seem to be, operationally speaking, simply inadequate, although perhaps without bias, one is terribly tempted to assume that there must be ways to forecast more successfully, and it is always possible that such ways may be invented. However, if invented, either they will stay secret and therefore not serve as decision rules for firms that depend on publicly available information, or they will become known, in which case their informational value would be fast included in the interest and spot and forward exchange rates and thus lose their independence to these three already existing forecasts. Thus they would not serve firms as separate tools either, although the forecasts inherent in interest and foreign exchange rates might emerge improved. In other words, the second alternative seems to be no more viable than the first.

The third alternative is a simple extension of portfolio theory and is not meant here as a serious optimizing procedure. If a firm has the size and skills to obtain loans in a variety of currencies in proportions to be defined, and to maintain such portfolio without raising the cost of any in its currency-specific terms,

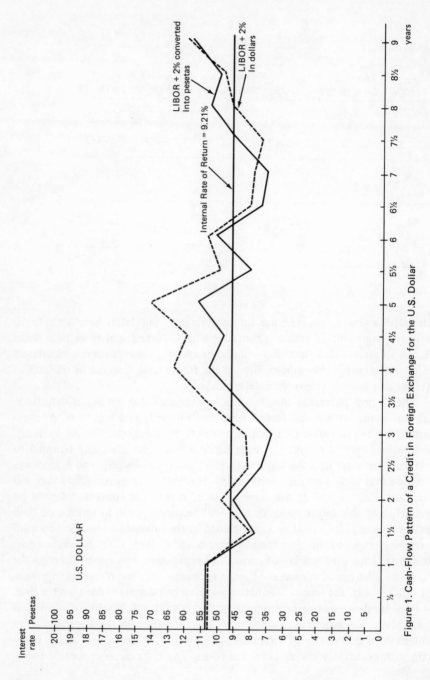

Figure 1. Cash-Flow Pattern of a Credit in Foreign Exchange for the U.S. Dollar

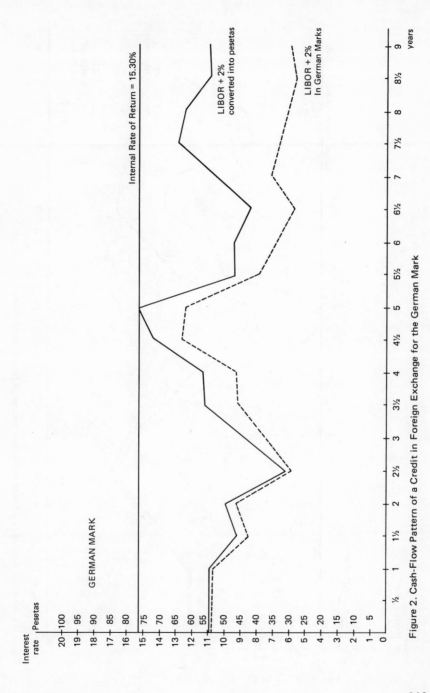

Figure 2. Cash-Flow Pattern of a Credit in Foreign Exchange for the German Mark

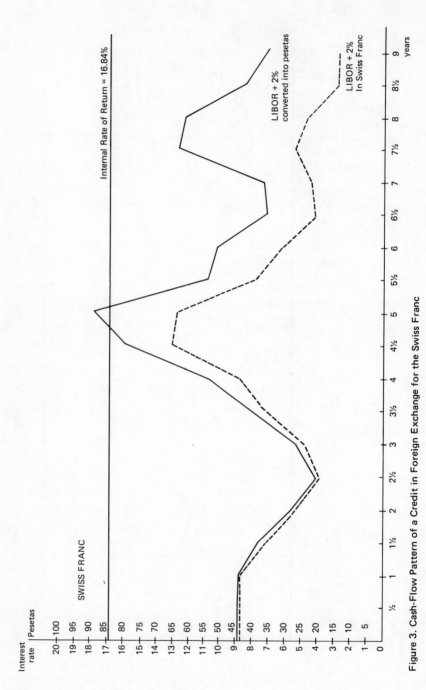

Figure 3. Cash-Flow Pattern of a Credit in Foreign Exchange for the Swiss Franc

220

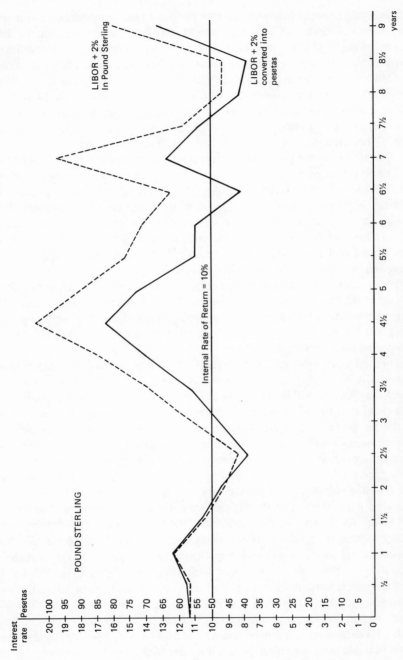

Figure 4. Cash-Flow Pattern of a Credit in Foreign Exchange for the Pound Sterling

221

this procedure should help reduce hefty financing cost fluctuations. How many currencies to include and with what weight seems to be a problem, but one that can be solved in practice. The catch is that few firms will be able to avail themselves of this method. Exposure in foreign currency is a result of specific deals, typically different for each firm and different over time for any one firm, within which taking a loan is one element that may or may not contribute to a better distribution of risks regarding financing costs. In any case, it seems worthwhile thinking and acting along these lines for firms whose liabilities have a volume that allows taking economic-order-size loans in different currencies, although the task of keeping the portfolio constant remains extremely difficult in practice.

The fourth alternative does not pretend to be an optimizing process either. All one can achieve covering the exchange risk through a forward operation is that the borrowing cost for any and all of the currencies under consideration would become the same. In other words, through forward coverage one finally obtains the Fisher Open effect: Interest rates and discounts or premiums of forward on spot rates combine into exactly[18] the same cost for all currencies borrowed. If Fisher Open is the objective, here is the solution.[19]

Firms would thus obtain certainty of borrowing costs in two senses: certainty of cost in the absolute sense for six months (but costs thereafter are unknown as interest rates and forward discounts or premiums will change) and certainty that costs will not exceed those incurred for other currencies not taken if forward cover were always effected.

Forward cover is usually not more costly in transactions cost than a spot transaction, but in this case the forward does not substitute a spot transaction.[20] Therefore these transaction costs (about two per mil each time) must be counted as a (low) cost to pay in order to achieve Fisher Open through Interest Parity.

On the other hand, it may well be worthwhile taking forward cover for another reason. There is little doubt that in the past nine years exchange rate changes have heavily outweighed interest rate differences in importance in establishing the total cost of borrowing in foreign exchange: The Swiss franc has had the lowest nominal interest rates nearly throughout the nine years, the dollar and even more the pound the highest, while the total cost relation has turned out to be just the reverse, thus confirming the extreme weight of exchange rate changes within the total cost of borrowing. One could, of course, doubt whether the future will see the continuation of the relative weight of the two cost components, but there should be little doubt that floating exchange rates will continue undergoing more violent and extensive changes than interest rates. Therefore, if changes in exchange rates can be "domesticated" by forward cover, and if the notion of a maximum loss tolerable to a firm is valid, a firm taking forward cover can reduce cost divergences to more bearable levels. These more bearable levels are indeed identical to that of the domestic interest rates, as the difference between domestic and foreign interest rates will be absorbed through a forward premium if the foreign interest rates are lower, or a discount if they are higher. It sounds reasonable to assume that *a priori* the evolution of interest rates in (any) one country would be more gradual and therefore look less destabilizing to managers through its uncertainty aspects and impact on costs than if a borrower is exposed to the extremes of the combined variations of interest and foreign exchange rates in various currencies.[21] The problem the borrower faces is thus reduced to carrying domestic interest rates also on foreign exchange credits, a situation for which many firms would probably feel they could opt.

A final word of caution should be added regarding tax treatment of foreign exchange losses and profits without forward cover. A general answer to this problem must be left open, as the fiscal treatment is very different from country to country. In some countries, profits and losses are treated as operational results and would therefore not influence a decision to take out forward cover or not. Others assign them the status of capital gains and losses with a lower tax rate than for operational results; for losses this turns out to be unfavorable, and for gains favorable compared to taking cover. A third fiscal posture is to exclude profits and losses from fiscal treatment, a situation that enhances the effect of the second one mentioned. Firms could thus incur heavy losses (or gains) that are not reduced through fiscal effects. Firms operating under any of the latter two fiscal systems might prefer, also for this reason, to take forward cover, as it would reduce uncertainty of costs.

CONCLUSIONS

The aim of this research was to see whether Fisher Open would provide valid operational decision rules for borrowers in the medium-term international market. The concrete context used to derive data and to arrive at results plausible to the manager did not allow the generation of sufficient data for a statistical test of two hypotheses concerning Fisher Open's validity over any term, or at least over the long term.

The concrete results obtained reveal, however, extremely great differences in cost from one currency to another during the period studied (1970–1979). It was not possible to develop even a notion of an increasing usefulness of Fisher Open decision rules the longer the time span covered.

While we cannot exclude that cost differences among currencies could even out over the long term, as Fisher Open claims, the financing cost differences developing over the medium term have been such as to motivate looking elsewhere for decision rules that can limit the extreme fluctuations in financing cost. Additionally, it seems unoperational for firms to try to maintain exposure in the form of a stable portfolio of currencies, a necessary condition for Fisher Open to apply at all; business deals causing exposure and change of exposure and other factors of a practical nature prevent firms from establishing and maintaining stable currency risk portfolios. Therefore the most operational decision seems to be to cover the currency risk forward. The result is that every currency will cost the same in terms of one's own currency, as interest rate parity and therefore equalization of total cost (interest rates and exchange rates changes) come about automatically.

NOTES

1. On the other hand, the Interest Rate Parity Theorem is correct in linking interest rate differentials and spot and forward exchange rates in practically absolute terms for interest rates on interbank deposits in the Euromarket and exchange rates, spot and forward, taking into account (extremely low) transactions costs. This is so simply because a sufficient number of arbitrageurs are busy looking for profit opportunities at all times. Research studying this proposition [2, 10] and not finding it conclusive is surely deluded by errors in the data used (for example, interest rates at midday and exchange rates at the end of the trading day), as any banker familiar with foreign exchange operations would gladly confirm.

2. Taking the U.S. interest rates as basis. The average annual U.S. rate for the period 1950-1975 was 4.52 percent, the average Swiss rate (adjusted for exchange rate charges) 6.20 percent. The difference 1.68 percent divided by 4.52 percent results in 37.2 percent, and so on. Worse results were obtained for Belgian, Dutch, Italian, and Swedish bonds, better for Canadian, British, and French, the best – French franc bonds – being a difference of "only" 21.2 percent annually for the twenty-five-year period!

3. The volume of published new credits of this category, in billions of dollars, is:

1972	1973	1974	1975	1976	1977	1978	1979(4m)
6857	21,851	29,275	20,749	28,850	41,765	70,179	20,141

Source: World Financial Markets, April 1976 and 1979 (Morgan Guaranty Trust Company of New York).

4. LIBOR = London Interbank Offered Rate for time deposits among banks.

5. Some credits have a split margin – for example, 5/8 percent for the first three and 3/4 percent for the last four years.

6. Some credits have a multicurrency clause, allowing the borrower to switch from one to another currency every six months at the date of interest changeovers.

7. See Table 1 for data on sources.

8. The no-bias hope is inherent, but not always expressly mentioned, in so many assumptions, in this and in practically any other paper, that it seems to be superfluous to point it out. If we researchers had more time (and an unlimited supply of energy to be ap-

plied to important- and unimportant-looking problems alike), we could probably eliminate a few no-bias assumptions.

9. See [7] for sources; additionally, some detective work had to be done: While dollar interest rates for six-month deposits were available, this was not so for Swiss francs, marks, and pounds in some instances. Forward rate discounts or premiums between these currencies (information that was available) had to be used to arrive at the interest rates.

10. The location of the sources is, however, of little importance, as long as they all come from Europe (or any other region with little trading time difference), as the markets (foreign exchange and interbank deposit) are totally integrated. Some studies try to explain differences in quotations between, say, London and Paris as due to the catchall called "political" risk; there, differences — very small in any case — are exclusively due to differences in the hour at which they were taken (e.g., 12:00 or 16:00 of the same day). See also note 1.

11. One rate is applicable when changing the foreign exchange proceeds into the borrower's currency, and the other when paying interests and when repaying the principal of the credit.

12. Linear, increasing, or decreasing installments, after a period of grace that can vary from no time to many years.

13. In a recent statistic (the source of which the author forgot), it was said that German firms' (outside) financing costs reached 4 to 5 percent of total production cost. As this is a nominal cost calculation, financing costs would presumably be higher in countries with higher inflation rates (if interest rates reflect inflation) than in Germany and higher or lower due to worse or better ratios between own and outside funds.

14. The absolute costs here identified in percentage p.a. represent costs incurred by a borrower using the proceeds in pesetas. In order to make the results valid for other currencies, the cost differences between each of the currencies are more meaningful than the costs themselves. To obtain borrowing costs for someone using the funds in, say, dollars, one has to add or subtract from the dollar rate p.a. the differences between dollar and other currencies' borrowing costs as established through the calculations. The results would not need any additional interpretation regarding the original research objective (test decision rules and look for new ones if the tested ones fail), as the differences in cost between the currencies remain identical, regardless of the type of currency into which the proceeds of the loan are converted.

15. Calculations covering other interest and exchange rate data (taken midmonth, middle of quarter, etc.) and periods (one year, other three year, etc.) within the nine years studied were made according to availability of data but did not reveal any tendencies, or different tendencies, from the nontendency found in the data published here.

16. It seems tempting to forecast, in continuation of past trends, low nominal interest rates for Swiss francs and high ones for the pound, as the problem of inflation has been handled so differently in the two countries in the past. The reason seems to lie no longer in economic policy differences, but in sociological factors whose rate of change is slow and therefore would allow more confidence in predictions that the future will bring "more of the same" (i.e., of the past).

17. However, not only the results presented here but Aliber's [1] as well confirm lower dollar costs over the period measured by him (twenty-five years). He advances speculative ideas, all usually ending up with the "political" risk factor, to explain this phenomenon. Either the market is not efficient (not enough speculators? Hardly. . .) or the phenomenon is *ex post* and therefore does not lend itself to extrapolation.

18. Or nearly exactly, as the interest rate parity premium or discount will be calculated on LIBOR, while our interest rates charged the hypothetical borrower are 2 percent higher

in each case. There will be a slight difference in the results, the slighter the higher the interest rates involved, which, however, we can in practice forget.

19. Whenever foreign exchange regulations allow access of borrowers to operate in the forward market. In Spain, this has never yet been the case since the forward market started functioning some twelve years ago.

20. Except for the interest part payable every six months and when repayments of the loan become due.

21. Here are the average interest rates p.a. (LIBOR + 2 percent) to confirm this point, at least for the period measured:

	9 Years	4½ Years	4½ Years	3 Years	3 Years	3 Years
$	10.06	10.17	9.94	9.33	11.77	9.06
DM	8.05	9.07	7.03	8.46	9.63	6.06
Sw. fr.	6.75	7.69	5.81	6.71	9.38	4.17
£	13.26	12.63	13.89	10.42	16.44	12.92

REFERENCES

[1]   Aliber, R.Z. *Exchange Risk and Corporate International Finance.* London: Macmillan Press, 1978.

[2]   Aliber, R.Z. "The Interest Rate Parity Theorem: A Reinterpretation," *Journal of Political Economy,* No. 81 (December 1973), pp. 1451–1459.

[3]   Duffy, G., and Giddy, I.H. "Forecasting Exchange Rates in a Floating World," *Euromoney* (November 1975), pp. 28–35.

[4]   Duffy, G., and Giddy, I.H. "The Random Behavior of Flexible Exchange Rates," *Journal of International Business Studies* 6, No. 1 (Spring 1975), pp. 1–32.

[5]   Giddy, I.H. "Why It Doesn't Pay to Make a Habit of Forward Hedging," *Euromoney* (December 1976), pp. 96–100.

[6]   Isard, P. "Exchange Rate Determination: A Survey of Popular Views and Recent Models," *Princeton Studies in International Finance,* No. 42 (May (1978).

[7]   Kohlhagen, S.W. "The Performance of the Foreign Exchange Markets: 1971–1974," *Journal of International Business Studies* 6, No. 2 (Fall 1975).

[8]   Levich, R.M. "On the Efficiency of Markets for Foreign Exchange," New York University Working Paper (October 1977).

[9]   Levich, R.M. "Tests of Forecasting Models and Market Efficiency in the International Money Market," *The Economics of Exchange Rates: Selected Studies.* Reading, Mass.: Addison-Wesley Publishing Company, 1978.

[10] Officer, L.H., and Willet, T.O. "The Covered Arbitrage Schedule: A Critical Survey of Recent Developments," *Journal of Money, Credit and Banking* (May 1970).

13 LEASING:

The Gulf between Theory and Practice

Cyril Tomkins, Julian Lowe, and Eleanor Morgan
University of Bath, Great Britain

The objective of this paper is to consider why lessees lease and to demonstrate how little the existing academic literature has done to help us understand lessee behavior. Writing several years ago, Myers, Dill, and Bautista [10] introduced a paper by saying "leasing has attracted so much scholarly attention that it is impossible to say anything totally new about it." Such a statement is justified only to the extent that one is content to remain within the narrow confines of researching for appropriate lessee valuation models, and even there unsolved problems remain. If one wishes to address the question of lessee motivation per se, as Myers and his colleagues do, there are many fruitful areas for research that have as yet received practically no scholarly attention.

In order to substantiate this claim, the existing state of the art in developing valuation models will be reviewed in the next section. This theoretical literature suggests that savings of taxes is the dominant reason for leasing, and so the second section is devoted to a comparison of leasing in different countries in an attempt to see whether national tax differences might account for material differences in leasing behavior. The reader is warned now that the results are

227

inconclusive (but suggestive) and indicate that this in itself is an area needing much more careful research. The third section proposes that research on lessee motivation might usefully commence, paradoxically, with a study of lessor behavior, and it reports in outline the results of a recent study of the U.K. leasing market [12].

The fourth section reviews the results of a number of postal surveys and interview studies that have been undertaken in order to identify lessee motivation and concludes that these tell us very little and that a different emphasis in research methodology is needed if progress is to be made. The fifth section then provides evidence of various financial and risk factors that have been found to influence lessee behavior. These factors indicate that existing valuation models are of very limited use for *large-scale* international leases.

Right at the outset it is made clear that this paper does not offer a rigorous analysis of any decision situation. It has the modest aim of trying to direct scholarly attention to under-researched aspects of leasing operations.

LEASING VALUATION MODELS

There have, of course, been numerous papers published on equipment leasing, but for purposes of this paper the state of the art in theory development is taken to be the three articles published in the June 1976 issue of the *Journal of Finance* (that is, the papers by Miller and Upton [9], Lewellen, Long, and McConnell [8], and Myers, Dill, and Bautista [10]), and a later paper by Weston and Dann [13].

All these authors employ lease valuation models, but develop them within a perfect market context. The general conclusion of all the authors is the same — namely, that in perfect markets there is no financial advantage to be achieved by leasing even under conditions of uncertainty. It is, of course, important that someone lay a rigorous theoretical basis so that the basic analysis itself can gradually be extended to incorporate real-world market imperfections, but the result will hardly surprise those who have studied earlier literature in the finance field. The "rigorous perfect market model basis" is therefore vital, but it is nowhere near sufficient if leasing activities are to be understood. In the United Kingdom now, leasing is used to finance about 9 percent of U.K. investment in plant and machinery, ships, vehicles, and aircraft, and Clark [2] has estimated that this represents about 25 percent of externally funded investment. In the United States, leasing apparently accounts for about 20 percent of total investment in these types of assets. This in itself must suggest that existing models indicating indifference results do little to explain reality. There is an obvious need to identify which market imperfections make leasing more or less attractive than other financing methods and also the degree of imperfection needed to justify the reality observed. The American authors referred to above have made a start on this task. Miller and Upton [9] focus on the tax asymmetries and conclude:

> What destroys the symmetry is not the way rentals and interest payments are treated for tax purposes, . . . but rather the fact that user firms may not always be able to take full advantage of some of the tax subsidies to hardware that Congress bestows.

Also they say that manufacturers may defer taxes on profits by leasing their own sales products. Similarly, Myers, Dill, and Bautista conclude:

> In efficient and competitive markets the lease vs. borrow problem would be a toss-up, apart from tax considerations.

These authors suggest that saving taxes is the only obvious and substantial factor encouraging leasing. However, Lewellen, Long, and McConnell seem to go much further, for, as well as saying that

> . . . in an identical competitive milieu, a reliable rationale for leasing attractiveness cannot reasonably be maintained,

they recognize that taxes could create advantages to leasing but, for various reasons, they raise doubts about the extent to which this accounts for much of the leasing business written.

Myers and his colleagues and Lewellen and his do, however, call for research into the empirical prevalence of market imperfections that might lead to advantages in leasing. This plea is also supported by Weston and Dann [13].

It is important to stress that it is *empirical* work on the industry and lessee motivation that is required. Another way forward would be to incorporate into valuation models "hypothesized imperfections" (or often quoted ones) and to deduce their effect. However, such an approach can lead to highly misleading results if the selected "imperfection" is not itself one that exists in reality or that is perceived to be important by lessors or lessees. For example, Miller and Upton conclude that tax exempt or "loss carry-forward" organizations might prefer to buy, rather than lease, assets, but their conclusion depends wholly on their assumption that net present value of lessor subsidies cannot exceed the net present value of taxes paid on lessor rental incomes. If a U.K. writer were to adopt such an assumption, the result could be immediately discarded as totally irrelevant to understanding real-world leasing activities, as such an assumption would be well known by lessors to be invalid. Moreover, it is suspected that the assumption may often also be invalid in the United States, where the combination of the investment tax credit and accelerated depreciation allowances probably has a similar value to the U.K. 100 percent immediate capital outlay write-off. However, whether Miller and Upton's assumption is an accurate reflection of reality or not is of little importance per se. What is important is to recognize that a fairly close knowledge of institutional and market realities is required; otherwise, academics are likely to use much energy pursuing (or modeling) phantasmagoric market features. They should first ground their theories in reality [8]. At least as far as leasing is concerned, it is proposed that there should be a major effort diverted toward understanding how the market operates and what motivates the various parties and that this is probably a prerequisite to building normative models that are useful to practitioners. The rest of the paper is directed toward looking for evidence of why lessees lease. It is suggested that the reasons for leasing are often more complicated than suggested in existing literature and that clear results will not come from just one paper or even two or three studies. Nevertheless, it is hoped that this paper will indicate some fruitful research paths.

LEASING ACTIVITY IN DIFFERENT COUNTRIES

Insofar as the effects of imperfections have been examined at all, it is clear from references already quoted that tax saving provides a strong potential reason for leasing. Moreover, the major tax factors are the way in which depreciation is treated for tax purposes, whether the lessor can shield profits from other businesses by purchasing assets, and whether the lessee is liable to tax or able to defer liability. Tax regimes throughout Europe are quite different, and, in particular, the potential tax benefits through leasing in the United Kingdom are far greater than those in Scandinavia, Germany, Spain, and France. In addition, the lessor is not entitled to depreciate equipment for tax purposes in the Netherlands. Consequently, a comparative examination of leasing activity in each country together with the tax treatment should yield some evidence on the degree to which tax is the major factor encouraging leasing.

Some figures are presented in Tables 1 and 2, and it soon becomes clear that such a study would be far from straightforward. To begin with, there is considerable difficulty getting the required statistics on leasing in each country. Leaseurope is involved in collecting statistics, but no comprehensive and authoritative figures have yet been issued. Figures for both Tables 1 and 2 are based upon a paper given by S. Errington [4], and these have been supplemented by other data supplied privately by a U.K. lessor. The immediate problem becoming apparent is one of legal definition. For example, in France there is no developed hire-purchase market, and so one wonders whether the figures for France are comparable with those of the United Kingdom, which relate only to finance leases. Nevertheless, despite these problems, one may form a *prima facie* hypoth-

Table 1. Leasing and Investment in Machinery and Equipment, Europe and the United States, 1976

	(a) Leased Equipment in 1976[a] (In Millions of U.S. Dollars)	(b) Investment in Machinery and Equipment in 1976 (In Millions of U.S. Dollars)	$\frac{a}{b}$ %
Belgium	133	5,400	2
France	2,103	34,900	6
Germany	800	42,900	2
Italy	428	13,100	3
Netherlands	353	7,500	5
Spain	119	6,200	2
Sweden	109	6,300	2
Switzerland	79	6,300	1
U.K.	716	17,600	4
Total Europe	4,972[b]	150,200[b]	3
U.S.	16,100	104,700	15

Sources: Based on extracts from S. Errington [4]. Errington's figures are based on estimates provided by national leasing associations and OECD National Accounts Year Books.

[a]It is estimated that these figures represent between 80 to 100 percent of the total leasing market in each country. France is the only country in which 100 percent coverage was achieved. The U.K. figure relates to finance leases only; total U.K. leasing, including operating leasing in 1976, has been estimated by the Department of Industry at 1034 million U.S. dollars.

[b]Includes estimates for Austria, Denmark, Ireland, Luxembourg, Norway, and Finland individually having less than 50 million U.S. dollars leasing.

esis from Table 1—namely, that there is more to leasing motivation than tax alone. The Netherlands and France show a larger proportion of investment financed by leasing than the United Kingdom in 1976. However, the United Kingdom is substantially behind the United States in these terms, and this cannot be accounted for in terms of much greater tax benefits in the United States. Next, looking at Table 2, one sees substantially different growth rates not only from year to year, but also from country to country. It is theoretically possible that this was due to differing tax situations varying not only across countries, but also frequently through time; however, that seems too simple an explanation. Moreover, some of the very high growth rates may merely reflect that leasing was being introduced from a fairly small basis, but the 1972–1976 growth figures do not seem to correlate well with the years leasing commenced. Finally, it is interesting to note that leasing commenced on a significant scale in the

Table 2.   The Growth of Leasing in Europe and the United States

	Year Commenced Leasing	Growth in Leased Equipment Purchases per Year[a]		
		1972–1976	1976–1977	1977–1978
Belgium	1962	48%	n.a.[c]	n.a.
France[b]	1961	83%	−26%	42%
Germany	1962	80%	21%	n.a.
Italy	1961	1,612%	101%	18%
Netherlands	1963	89%	n.a.	n.a.
Spain	1965	148%	n.a.	7%
Sweden	1964	354%	28%	49%
Switzerland	1964	25%	n.a.	n.a.
U.K.	1960	224%	60% (50%)[e]	80% (67%)[e]
Total Europe	–	115%[d]	n.a.	n.a.
U.S.	1952	87%	n.a.	n.a.

Sources: S. Errington [4] provides details of the year in which leasing commenced and figures from which growth rates 1972–1976 have been calculated. Growth rates for 1976–1977 and 1977–1978 were made from figures made available to us privately by a leading lessor. The U.K. figure is publicly available; we are not sure about other countries.

[a]Figures were *not* adjusted for inflation before measuring growth. Figures include those for cars, but not for real estate.

[b]There are widely differing estimates in existence of leasing figures in France for 1976, 1977, and 1978.

[c]N.a. indicates not readily available to the authors of this paper. Also the 1976, 1977, and 1978 data used for the last two columns cannot be linked easily with data for previous columns because figures are expressed in different currencies and prepared by different sources, and it is not clear what exchange rates or adjustment for market coverage is appropriate to make the figures comparable.

[d]Including estimates for countries with less than 50 million U.S. dollars in 1976.

[e]U.K. figures in parentheses are after adjustment for new membership each year of the Equipment Leasing Association.

United States in 1952; it would be interesting to know why it took eight years to cross the Atlantic—it is doubted whether this can be explained solely in tax terms.

The conclusions that can be drawn from Tables 1 and 2 are obviously very tentative. Indeed, some may say no conclusions can be drawn. There seems to be sufficient evidence, however, to point to the benefit that could be derived from a properly conducted comparative country study that attempts to isolate comparable statistics and major events that could account for different activity and growth. Such a study would be very difficult to launch and requires institutional, tax, and legal knowledge of each country involved. However, it might be done on a collaborative basis by researchers in different countries. Also, research into why lessees lease need not initially focus upon lessee motivation directly, for some initial evidence can be obtained from a comparative study of the structure of the leasing markets in different countries. A study has just been completed of the U.K. market structure and is described in the next section.

THE U.K. LEASING MARKET

Initially the authors of the U.K. leasing market study [12] were interested in investigating why lessees lease. However, it was thought that before this question was tackled directly some insight could be gained and knowledge about leasing improved by studying lessor behavior. The U.K. leasing market is far more concentrated than the U.S. market, with only thirty-four members (in 1977) in the Equipment Leasing Association (ELA) whose members claimed about 90-95 percent of U.K. finance leasing business at the time of our inquiry. Very extensive questionnaires, relating mainly to factual data, were issued through the ELA to all its members, but only seventeen companies completed them. Nevertheless, our sample covered 62 percent of the leasing industry in 1976 by volume of leases written. Afterward, extended interviews (the longest lasted about five hours and the shortest about two hours) were conducted with lessors to discuss features emerging from the questionnaires and also with some lessors who were prepared to give interviews even though they were unable to complete the questionnaire. The parts of the results most appropriate to this paper concern the structure of the industry, cost conditions, barriers to entry, profitability, and performance of lessors. By examining these facets of leasing, one gets some indication of the extent to which the leasing market is competitive, thereby indicating the extent to which financial advantages achieved by leasing are shared by the lessor with the lessee and to what extent the market is segmented, indicating, in turn, different client characteristics and perhaps underlying differences in motivation to lease.

Market Concentration

The U.K. leasing industry was found to have a high degree of concentration. Whatever measure of concentration was used [12], the top three lessors had over 40 percent of the leasing market, and about 80 percent was held by the top ten. Moreover, the market shares were extremely stable through time, with rank correlation coefficients mostly over 0.9 for different measures of size. This indicates an oligopolistic market with an apparent scope for agreed market sharing and lease pricing. Therefore, there is unlikely to be severe price competition, and the extent to which the lessee can share in any asymmetric tax or other benefits will depend upon the degree to which the lessee market is organized. Given that leasing is undertaken by most industries, it would appear that, up to 1976, lessors would be retaining the greater part of any tax benefits generated through leasing. There are now (in 1979) signs that competition has greatly increased in the industry and that leasing rates are falling partly due to new entrants to the industry.

Segmentation in the Market

Having examined the competition in the industry in a very general manner, the next step was to see whether variables that segmented the market could be identified. Obviously, if all lessors tend to be specialized and to serve particular parts of the market, the degree of competition is reduced. The following were used as possible segmenting variables: type of lessor parent, size of lease, primary period of lease, type of equipment, customers served, location of assets, riskiness of business written. The full details of this analysis are contained in Tomkins, Lowe, and Morgan [12, Chapter 3]; only a brief summary can be given here.

First, as regards lease size, there was some suggestion of specialization of lessors with different parent types in leases of different sizes. Leasing subsidiaries of investment banks tended to have higher average size of leases than arms of the joint stock banks, which in turn had larger leases than lessors that were independent or subsidiaries of nonbank institutions. However, the relationship was not clean-cut, and lessors could be grouped far more neatly by reference directly to the distributions of lease sizes irrespective of parentage. Three groups were formed: Group I (four lessors with average lease size written in 1976 of £834,000), Group II (seven lessors with average lease size £45,000), Group III (three lessors with average lease size £853). Only fourteen lessors were able to give full-size distributions of leases written and outstanding.

It transpired that lease size proved to be the best segmenting variable. Grouping lessors by length of primary period of leases written in 1976 was not so useful, although any different grouping tended to follow lease-size groupings. Of all leases written in 1976, 83 percent had a primary period of between three and five years. Only Group I companies wrote more than 5 percent of their leases for longer periods, although they had 27 percent over five years, with 11 percent over eight years, and some beyond twelve. Grouping by equipment leased was also less definite, but tended to follow lease size. Groups I and II were hardly distinguishable, seemingly being prepared to lease any type of asset, but Group III clearly specialized in offices, shops, and hotel equipment. Leasing companies supplied, on average, eleven industries from a possible nineteen industrial groups, and their primary industry accounted for approximately 37 percent of the total value of leases written, compared with 9 percent if their activities had been evenly spread. But only two could be classed as specialists— that is, with over 50 percent of leasing activity confined to one industrial class. In addition, both Groups I and II had 42 percent and 27 percent of the value of leases written in 1976 with the public sector. But Group III had only 9 percent. In terms of regional pattern, from questionnaires and interviews the markets were obviously national in terms of competition from other lessors, but a majority of leases were written for customers in the south of England. Attitudes toward risks were also examined across all lessors. In discussions it seemed that all lessors were very cautious, making customer creditworthiness a prime criterion to be observed in writing a lease. Because the majority of the lease business investigated was full-payout leasing adequately insured against disaster, lessors saw little risk inherent in most types of assets—although occasions were discovered where particularly hazardous equipment was refused. However, there were differences between Groups I and II, on the one hand, and Group III, on the other, in their use of variation clauses. Most leases in Groups I and II carried tax or interest variation clauses, but the small leases of Group III rarely did. Although bad debts were generally low, Group III also provided bad debts provisions about four times as high, in terms of a percentage of rentals, than did Groups I and II.

It may be concluded, therefore, that there is a clear distinction between lease size. Class I (big ticket lessors) had significantly different characteristics from Class III (small ticket lessors). Class II tended in some way to be similar to Class I, but was nevertheless distinguishable. Class II lessors tended to have more widespread distributions of lease size, and so further research might attempt to split the leasing activity of each lessor in that class into different sizes of lease before measuring other characteristics. Nevertheless, enough had been achieved to indicate that the leasing market is not homogeneous in terms of all lessors operating across all types of lease, and so this grouping was used to explore profitability and performance in the industry. However, before looking at those results, it is interesting to examine cost conditions and barriers to entering the industry.

Cost Conditions and Barriers to Entry

Average operating costs of lessors (i.e., excluding depreciation) were also found to be at least twice as high in the case of Group III lessors as in the case of Group I and II lessors. When interest (80 percent of operating costs) was also excluded, Group III costs were eight times higher per £1 of business outstanding. The small ticket/large ticket split in the market seems to be a dominant feature of the industry. By measuring economies of scale, further corroboration was obtained. Using cross-section data, an average cost curve was drawn for 1976 per £1 of leases outstanding at original cost. The expected L-shaped cost curve emerged, but, whether one included or excluded interest, cost per £1 of lease outstanding was constant above a portfolio size of about £20 million, indicating that only Group III lessors were likely to operate below this level; aggregate portfolio values of Group II lessors were somewhat higher than those of Group I lessors, but Group III lessors averaged only about £25 million.

Economies of scale are also, of course, an indication of the limitation on entering an industry. It would appear that minimum costs are reached at a very low level of business. Other aspects of barriers to entry were also examined, including absolute cost advantages of financial access to funds and taxable capacity. The only major barrier in evidence was taxable capacity. There was evidence of some parents charging leasing subsidiaries subsidized interest charges, and yet those lessors not benefiting from this were still able to compete successfully and to survive. Foreign banks clearly wanted to enter the U.K. industry, but had not been able to do so on any significant scale because they had no U.K. taxable capacity to gain the benefit of the 100 percent first-year allowance. On the other hand, nonfinancial commerical consumers and private persons having taxable capacity had not entered the market on a scale to challenge the banks by 1976. There is newspaper evidence of significant entry into the market by such lessors in the current year (1979), but the dominant position of the banks is still not threatened in the sense that they are not losing business.

Deferring Tax Liability as a Lessor Motivator

The importance of recognizing the small ticket/big ticket segmentation also became clear after attempting to measure the profitability of alternative market segments. First, it had to be recognized that an attempt to measure profitability in any precise fashion from the accounts of leasing companies is a particularly difficult task. The usual problems associated with assessing economic performance from records constructed according to accounting conventions are severely exacerbated when dealing with accounts of leasing companies in an industry subject to rapid and unstable annual growth. These difficulties are discussed fully in Tomkins, Lowe, and Morgan [12], but despite these problems, clear differences in profitability of the small and large ticket market segments did emerge. Some City commentators had been observing that many lessors were earning only very low profits. As Table 3 shows, our investigation indicated that small ticket operators (Group III) were clearly more profitable than middle ticket lessors, which were in turn more profitable than big ticket lessors when defining profitability in terms of accounting-based net profits over capital employed. Moreover, a similar analysis based upon alternative definitions of "profit" (namely, taken before depreciation and also before both depreciation and interest in order to allow for differing company practices in depreciation and interest-charging policy) revealed the same very clear distinction between groups. However, as also shown in Table 3, when one allowed for the change in deferred tax balances by adding that element to the net profit numerator, there was a rather dramatic change of group profitability rankings, with the larger ticket operators appearing to be more profitable. Of course, incorporating the deferred tax charge within "profitability" does *not* give a good indication of absolute percentage profitability for the year 1976, but assuming that this tax balance can be deferred for a number of years (or even forever), the measure incorporating the deferred tax change indicates which company groups are likely to be contributing most to their parent companies, assuming that deferred tax balances are efficiently reinvested. Other market segmentation definitions were also used and examined for comparable profitability, but the most clear segmentation occurred with companies classified according to average lease size as just described.

Table 3. Lease Type and Profitability in the United Kingdom, 1976

		$\dfrac{Net\ Profit}{Capital\ Employed}\ \%$	$\dfrac{Net\ profit + \Delta\ in\ deferred\ tax}{Capital\ Employed}\ \%$
Big ticket	Mean	1.2	23.5
	Range	−2.6 / 4.5	9.2 / 45.3
Middle ticket	Mean	5.3	25.8
	Range	2.4 / 10.5	7.4 / 52.4
Small ticket	Mean	6.4	14.9
	Range	−2.1 / 17.4	12.9 / 17.9

Source: Tomkins, Lowe, and Morgan [12], Tables 6.3 and 6.6.

Summary of the Study of the Leasing Industry

It is exceedingly difficult to summarize a book with about fifty detailed tables in a few pages. However, the results of the analysis of the U.K. leasing market lead to one main indication for purposes of this presentation. The market is *not* one homogeneous unit. A main difference emerges between lessors dealing with larger, as opposed to small, ticket leases. The former seem to be in the market very much for the benefits they can obtain from tax-shielding parent banks' profits, while the small ticket and sales/aid lessors are able to survive and to earn modest profits without major tax-shielding potential. This market classification is also reflected in differences in average overhead costs, bad debts incurred, and so on. This clear segmentation at least suggests strongly that lessee motivation to lease is somewhat different in these two elements of the market. It also needs to be remembered that we were only able to obtain figures on profitability, costs, and so on, on a total company basis and to allocate each company to the relevant segment according to its *average* lease size. The middle ticket leasing companies, although covering the "middle market," also operate at large and small ticket levels, and one very large "middle ticket lessor" assured us that a subsidiary analysis of "middle ticket" company figures for separate ticket sizes would probably make the results more clear-cut. In addition, one or two lessors have suggested that our level of market segmentation was very broad and that, if company figures could be broken down, the broad segmentation features we have identified would contain important "subsegments," which again suggest differences in lessee motivation to lease. A justification for an attempt to subsegment at least the big ticket lease group is offered later in this paper.

A REVIEW OF PREVIOUS SURVEYS ON LESSEE MOTIVATION

Several surveys have been conducted in Europe in recent years in an attempt to discover why lessees lease. All these have used postal questionnaires, and one or two have supplemented this method with interviews. Just the outline of these studies will be referred to here.

First, Fawthrop and Terry [5] gained information from fifty-four U.K. corporations, and their main results are reproduced in Table 4. The survey was conducted in early 1974. The interesting points in this table are the twenty-five out of thirty-eight who said that they did *not* use leasing to gain the effective transfer of 100 percent first-year allowances and the seventeen out of forty-one who said that leasing was very relevant as part of a planned finance mix. However, although it was possibly a pioneering effort to gain some insight into lease

Table 4. Results of Fawthrop's and Terry's Analysis: If your company used, uses, or will use leasing, do any or all of the following factors apply?

	Very Relevant	Relevant	Irrelevant
The need was/is/will be urgent, no other funds being available (emergency finance).	7	4	28
Leasing is part of a planned financing mix.	17	12	12
Leasing is spillover financing (covers deficiencies in planning).	7	6	25
Leasing is off-balance sheet finance and so			
(1) does not affect borrowing capacity.	8	15	18
(2) improves apparent return on capital employed.	4	14	19
Leasing is used for the transfer of the benefits of 100 percent first-year tax allowances from lessors.	8	5	25

Source: Fawthrop and Terry [5].

motivation, one can raise severe qualifications about the study. Leasing may well have been adopted by lessees because it seemed cheap, without a clear recognition by them that it was due to tax reasons; also there is no analysis in the paper [5] that indicates clearly what corporate officials meant by a planned financing mix. The usefulness of the study is therefore open to considerable question.

Another U.K. study was undertaken by Sykes [11] in 1976; he issued postal questionnaires to 202 corporations. Sykes included reasons for hire-purchase activity, as well as leasing, and separated his analysis of taxation from "other reasons." Sykes's results are included in Tables 5 and 6.

Dietz [3] also conducted a postal survey among customers of his own lessor company in Germany and an associated one in Switzerland. His results are shown in Table 7. Dietz asked each respondent which of a number of reasons were "very important," and the percentages in the table indicate the proportion

Table 5. Sykes: Advantages of Leasing as Source of Funds

	Hire-Purchase (%)	Finance Leases (%)	Operating Leases (%)
Provision of source of funds that does not use existing working capital	67	76	67
100% financing permissible	23	37	29
No dilution of equity, no dependence on solvency	22	28	22
Off-balance sheet financing	–	29	23
Maximum loss potential reduced	–	21	23
Size of sample	193	185	175

Source: Sykes [11].

Table 6. Sykes: The Budgetary Advantages of Leasing

	Hire-Purchase (%)	Finance Leases (%)	Operating Leases (%)
Smoothing of cash flows	45	48	41
Hedge against inflation	19	22	17
Budgeting accuracy	17	21	22
Stability (independence of market conditions and government policy)	15	17	15
Flexibility of contract (suit needs of lessee)	–	30	21
Size of sample	193	185	175

Source: Sykes [11].

Table 7. Results of Surveys Reported by Dietz [3]

Reasons for Leasing	Switzerland (%)	W. Germany (%)
1. Matching of terms Liquidity	75 (1)[b]	
2. 100% finance	72 (3)	74 (1)
3. Credit links remaining open	74 (2)	66 (3)
4. Capital freed	—	65 (4)
5. Protection against obsolescence	48 (6)	55 (7)
6. Fixed costs	58 (5)	72 (2)
7. Tax advantages	47 (8)	63 (5/6)
8. Parallel between costs and return	59 (4)	63 (5/6)
9. AFA reduction[a]	47 (7)	—
10. Cheaper than other credit	—	49 (8)
11. Balance sheet neutrality	42 (10)	46 (9)
12. Effect as regards inflation	44 (9)	32 (10)

[a] Official scale for depreciation in Switzerland.
[b] Figures in parentheses indicate ranking of importance.

of those replying who thought each reason was very important. Dietz says the interesting thing is that reasons 5, 7, and 11 are relatively lowly ranked. Considerable care should be exercised with the interpretation of such responses because even the lower-ranked reasons in Germany (the off-balance sheet argument) have 42 percent of respondents calling them very important.

A similar U.S. study is being undertaken by Anderson and Martin [1]; by postal survey, they asked 180 U.S. corporations to score forty possible reasons for leasing. Their results are shown in Table 8. The full results of the study were not available to the authors when writing this paper, but the interim results show a similar picture to the European studies, with the tax-credit reason lowly ranked at number 8.

All these studies are of relatively little value in terms of a real understanding of the leasing market. In addition to the criticisms already levied, the European studies (and perhaps the U.S. one as well) took no account of possible segmentation of the leasing market. Furthermore, one has all the problems associated with trying to elucidate reasons for decision making by postal questionnaire perhaps from persons not primarily involved in making the decision and certainly long after the decision was made. The postal questionnaire is of extremely limited use for identifying lessee motivation. Nevertheless, at least one very

Table 8. Anderson and Martin: Rank Order of Ten Highest Weighted Agreement Scores for Why U.S. Lessees Lease

---

1. Leasing provides 100 percent deductibility of costs.
2. Leasing provides long-term finance without diluting control.
3. Leasing frees working capital for other uses.
4. Leasing avoids problems of disposing of secondhand equipment.
5. Leasing allows piecemeal financing of small items of equipment.
6. Leasing protects company against obsolescence.
7. Leasing has a lower after-tax cost than equity finance.
8. Leasing enables the lessor to pass on tax credits.
9. The tax deductibility of lease payments improves cash flow.
10. Leasing leaves normal lines of credit undisturbed.

Source: Anderson and Martin [1].

broad conclusion does emerge from all these surveys: Tax is not the only factor in motivating lessees to lease. They do therefore suggest the need for a much closer empirical examination of lessee behavior and decision processes. It is probable that this can only be successfully achieved by identifying a classification of leases by type and then following through the lease negotiations with each party either during the negotiation process or soon after the deal is completed. It may then transpire that some reasons identified for leasing are "irrational" from the viewpoint of modern finance theory. But at least this will provide a practically useful and directly relevant focus for theoretical modeling.

STRATEGIC FACTORS IN BIG TICKET LEASING

Believing that significant progress in the study of leasing can only come after empirical inquiries relating to specific leases written, the authors have commenced discussions with three large company lessees and a large ticket lessor with a view to identifying what decision factors are really involved. Already some features have emerged that indicate that the big ticket market should itself be segmented. In particular, at the *very big* ticket end of the market, the capital allowance tax argument is only one of many other factors that may be relevant. Moreover, with such deals usually involving equipment of at least 30 million U.S. dollars, and often much more, which also has international finance connotations, the lessees insisted that each deal is unique, with its own mix of strategic and financial prerequisites. What follows is merely a catalog of reasons given by the lessees and the lessor; most were linked directly to specific leases written by them, although some relate to other known practices. Also, in the opinion of one senior finance executive, the demand for big ticket leases "has not anywhere near peaked"; he sees a growing number of very large international projects coming onto the drawing board involving multiple parties with different financing abilities and tax positions, so that the need to understand such complicated deals will become even more important than it is now.

Off-Balance Sheet Financing

Perhaps the most often mentioned reason for leasing, other than the tax benefit, is that although leasing is not capitalized in the lessee's balance sheet, it enables the lessee to show a higher rate of return on capital employed and a lower financial leverage. In the United States, FASB 13 has made lease capitalization mandatory, and so one can now discount that reason for U.S. lessees. Also, Hughes and Oldfield [7] concluded that before FASB 13 was issued, investors were cognizant of lease commitments and took them into account in stock market price evaluations. However, it is by no means a worldwide requirement to capitalize leases, and so this form of motivation may be important in some countries, but certainly there is strong resistance to capitalization by lessors in several European countries.

Apart from the general argument, there is one specific situation where the failure to capitalize has a clear impact on the decision whether to lease or to buy. Terms for government contracts can take various forms, and in the United Kingdom some Ministry of Defence contracts allow a "normal" rate of return on capital employed, while others are based upon contract costs plus a profit percentage. One company explained that leasing would mean a lower-reported capital-employed base in the balance sheet, and so the government, applying its "normal" rate of return percentage, would pay the company less. On the other hand, for "production cost plus" contracts, leasing would usually mean higher costs because leases were written for periods less than the life over which they would be depreciated if purchased, and hence the government would pay larger sums of money earlier in the contract. Since the government insists on the calculations being based upon accepted accounting principles, the U.K. company has the freedom to adopt capitalization or not, although once it decides to capitalize it will be difficult to change back. Until such time as an FASB 13 equivalent is introduced into the United Kingdom, companies may take a view on the type of government contracts they are likely to receive in future, and this may influence the decision in terms of accounting presentation and leasing practice.

"Budget Busting"

Another widely held reason for leasing is that it helps managers of subsidiaries or corporate divisions to avoid capital expenditure limits imposed by parent companies or head offices. The authors thought that most sophisticated companies would have been wise to do this by now and would have inserted leasing rules within the capital budgeting procedures. Evidence was obtained from the lessor of one major U.K. company recently writing a lease where this was the main motivation to lease. The lessor stated that this was not an isolated phenomenon. He thought that there were still financial directors who did not recognize the problem and that directors were often too busy to delve into the problem of providing operational definitions for operating leasing and financial leasing — the former being very similar to straight renting and very much within normal divisional autonomy. In addition, the lessor said that in Europe and Asia, few companies include leasing expenditure within capital expenditure controls, except for subsidiaries of a few sophisticated U.S. companies. Moreover, the lessor also explained that, in his experience, corporate head offices of divisionalized groups often believed in considerable divisional autonomy and did not want to be involved in questions regarding acquisition of computers or complex contract arrangements (such as those mentioned regarding government contracts) and, for this reason, were often prepared to overlook avoidance of capital budgeting rules by leasing, provided it was not practiced on a large scale.

This lessor also indicated that "budget busting" was not always confined to the private sector. Large leases had been written by U.K. lessors for government departments in Poland and the U.S.S.R. who wished to overcome constraints on spending in their prescribed five-year capital programs.

NULLIFYING GOVERNMENT AND
CENTRAL BANK REGULATIONS

In the mid-1970s, the Bank of England told U.K. subsidiaries of certain foreign companies that they had reached the limit of loan finance and had to increase equity investment in the United Kingdom. Instead of doing that, some leased equipment, which, oddly perhaps, was acceptable. This does not apply in the United Kingdom now, where borrowing limits have been lifted, but it still applies in many overseas countries. In a number of countries (South Africa is one example), there is a maximum local borrowing ratio (often as low as 25 percent), which does not include leasing within the definition of "borrowing." Consequently, companies may lease locally and effectively ignore the requirement. Obviously, such countries are still awaiting an equivalent of FASB 13.

Situations can also arise in which companies have accumulated cash from earnings in countries from which withdrawal is blocked. Turkey is a good example. Such countries often have severe foreign exchange problems, and companies with such surpluses have the choice of investing in local financial institutions (which often effectively means the central bank) at very low rates of interest or investing in new projects in that country. Examples were given of companies that did not want to build up further operating activities within such a country and decided to lease assets to other companies that did wish to invest there, but that had been told by the foreign government that they would not be allowed to raise local borrowing. This enabled the lessee to avoid taking on foreign exchange risks, while the lessor was able to reinvest funds blocked abroad in a profitable way without a major extension of operating personnel, production activity, and so on. Also, some countries would only allow the owner of the blocked funds to use them for 50 percent of the new investment, requiring him to raise the rest abroad. Then the leasing arrangement enables the lessor to avoid contributing further funds to the country in question in order to earn a decent rate of return.

A variation of that process has occurred occasionally when the Bank of England has required companies to bring cash surpluses back to the United Kingdom (where not blocked). If the company reinvested such surpluses abroad in bonds, the Bank of England would "see through this" and, as the investment was liquid, would still require repatriation of funds. However, use of funds to lease abroad was often lost in operating activities, absorbed cash surpluses, and meant that the assets were not easily liquidated. Consequently, leasing was a means of keeping cash abroad for future business expansion plans. If the cash had been remitted to the United Kingdom and then later back abroad for investment, the investment dollar premium would then have been payable.

Other government restrictions may involve physical import controls. While these are not applied in the United Kingom now, a lessor stated that leasing was a method of overcoming such measures because leased assets were viewed as a short-term import and not a permanent one.

One company provided another interesting recent example of how leasing can overcome foreign government regulations. A foreign subsidiary of the company wanted to import about 5 million U.S. dollars worth of computer equipment, using its own local cash generation and borrowing to buy the equipment. The foreign government refused, saying that the import license would be refused unless the parent company raised the finance abroad. The company did not wish to commit further capital to this country, but offered to lease through an offshore company. Rather ironically, the host government's central bank accepted this arrangement, even though the lease payments were payable in local currency. This may have been due to the avoidance of a large capital sum being paid at once, while use of the asset was obviously available immediately. Moreover, the offshore lessor was not raising local foreign debt.

A Unique Source of Finance

The lessor interviewed argued that lessors had now been in business in the United Kingdom for seven years or so and had reached the stage of generating cash surpluses, so that they could now undertake ten-year fixed-term leasing without risk of interest rate changes on borrowing that was previously needed to finance this investment. "Banks," he said, "cannot afford to lend at fixed terms like this unless it can match fixed-term lending and borrowing and this is difficult." He conceded that one could argue that the leasing subsidiary's parent bank could siphon off leasing earnings and use them for financing fixed-term lending operations, but U.K. banks simply do not look at things in such a coordinated way. Banks encourage autonomy in their leasing arms and say they must prove themselves as financial operations using their own funds if they want to expand—at least for the time being. Of course, the leasing subsidiary incurs an opportunity cost if interest rates rise and it is locked into a fixed-term lease, but, in the eyes of the lessor being interviewed, that is not so serious as the possibility of having to *report* accounting losses through leasing at fixed rates financed by variable interest rate borrowing. Despite the doubtful economic logic, it is clear that some leasing has actually been provided by this lessor for fixed rates over long terms when such arrangements could not be found by means of straight debt. It is, of course, impossible without much further research to see how important an implication this is, whether other lessors share the same attitude, and whether the uniqueness of leasing in offering fixed terms for some financing duration applies in different countries.

Some companies also find that leasing is the only source of finance for other reasons. One of the multinationals interviewed stated that it had a growing number of joint ventures in its mineral business. Often partners in joint ventures were rapidly growing but financially weak and unable to raise the 30 percent equity stake that must normally be found, given that banks will only normally lend 70 percent of the asset cost. In such circumstances, leasing was the only answer for them. Lessors were prepared to provide 100 percent finance because of the security in the asset itself. The multinational representative stated that in his view this was more of a psychological argument because repossession (especially for large assets held abroad) of leased assets was just as difficult as exercising possession rights associated with changes on assets fixed by debt, even if major financial institutions did seem to sleep easier at night knowing they owned the asset. When faced with this argument later on, the lessor involved in the study stated that in some cases the reasoning was more than psychological and indicated that, in the United States, a lessor can repossess an aircraft under lease but cannot repossess an aircraft under mortgage.[1] Moreover, in some underdeveloped countries mortgages and charges cannot even be registered. The authors know of an example of a manufacturer who leased abroad for that reason, rather than sell on credit.

The practice of hiving off autonomous corporate activities appeared important once more when discussing leasing as possibly the only source of finance. One multinational said it practiced the policy of setting up new ventures as completely separate units having to prove their worth by getting started with very limited financial support from the parent. If the subunit was initially successful, it might enter a rapid growth stage, be short of funds, but still be in a stage where the parent was not yet ready to recognize the development as permanent and to provide further funds. Moreover, the parent would often be reluctant to issue guarantees or borrowings at this stage of the business. In such circumstances, the new development might well use leasing.

Handling Political Risks

In many foreign investments, the main political risks are attached to the owner of assets rather than the operator of those assets. One of the multinationals gave a very clear example of the way it had used leasing for protection against political risk. The company in question had wanted to undertake a reasonably large investment in a developing country, but feared the possibility of nationalization. It therefore leased the asset from an American bank that had numerous other financing arrangements in the country in question and that the developing country government would almost certainly not provoke to exercise cross-default mechanisms on other financial arrangements. Such "deterrent muscle" arrangements were likely to become even more important.

Similarly, another U.K. company is known to prefer leasing to some developing countries through a third party because if its equipment is faulty, the country cannot make deductions from loan or rental payments due to that manufacturer. Presumably, the lease payments would be stopped and the lessor would resort to the manufacturer, but this could be handled back within the U.K. legal jurisdiction.

On the other hand, the lessor participating in these discussions indicated that a shipping lease had nearly fallen through because the potential lessee was concerned that it was better to own ships to avoid some of the risks associated with accidents (and the resulting pollution) of ships operated by *other* lessees. The country polluted might seize another ship belonging to the same lessor, in which case the innocent lessee of the *second* lease suffers. Would-be lessees of just one or two ships might not be prepared to take such risks even if insured, as the company name would be brought into international disputes, and, even if corporate reputation is not paramount, it takes a long time to settle international legal wrangles of this sort.

Government Risk Insurance and Subsidies

Most developed countries offer some form of political risk insurance for investment in developing countries, but the insurance can only be obtained for owners of the equipment if they are resident in the country of the government offering the insurance. There may be very good reasons why a U.K. company might want to locate the ownership of the assets in, say, the United States—for tax reasons or for subsidy reasons (see below)—and then it seems reasonable also to obtain U.S. political risk insurance. However, if the U.K. company set up a subsidiary in the United States, the U.S. government would see through the arrangement, say the real beneficiary is in the United Kingdom, and not insure the risk. However, the U.K. company can lease the asset from an American owner, and the risk insurance is given. This could, in theory, be done solely to obtain foreign political risk insurance where one's own country's scheme was not so generous, but the U.K. company in question never did this.

The United States is, however, a good example of providing reliefs from which non-U.S. companies can benefit by leasing. The U.S. government provides a conventional form of subsidy to accelerate shipbuilding in the United States however it is financed. This scheme has several elements to it. First, there is the possibility of obtaining a Title 11 U.S. government guarantee in respect of bonds issued by a borrower whose credit as far as the lenders are concerned is then irrelevant, and to get that, the ship must be built in a U.S. shipyard by a 51 percent U.S. owner to be run by a U.S. crew sailing under a U.S. flag. Also, in exchange for those prerequisites, the U.S. government recognizes that construction and crewing subsidies must be provided because costs are lower in other countries. However, if non-U.S. companies wish to have ships built in the United States for technological reasons, they can also indirectly get the benefit of American subsidies by leasing from a U.S. owner rather than building in the United States itself—thereby making the whole package more attractive. The leasing is therefore directly linked to the technological argument as, so the company said, it would not be worth building in the United States for the subsidies alone.

Another similar arrangement, which as yet has not been exploited to any great extent, is the U.S. capital cost fund (CCF) system. If an American owner

is willing to open a special fund in which he is prepared to deposit the depreciation provisions of his ships, the earnings of that fund will be completely free of
U.S. income tax, provided he applies the fund's cash and earnings to finance
further U.S. ship construction. Also, the earnings of the new ship can be put into
a fund to pay off debt used to finance the shipbuilding, and then no tax is payable on those earnings. Consequently, it would pay a non-U.S. company to lease
from a U.S. owner rather than build there themselves if that owner was prepared
to use the CCF scheme. Only about six major institutions have CCFs (Bankers
Trust, Citibank, Bank of America, Chase Manhattan, Ford Motor Company,
GEC). The benefits are quite significant because running lease earnings through
the CCF earnings account is apparently equivalent to 1½ percentage points off
the interest cost. In the past, few non-U.S. companies knew much about this
scheme, and the CCF holders "kept the goodies to themselves," rather than
passing them through in lower rentals. However, from now on, at least one
major lessee wants to see the U.S. lessor's benefits from CCF "on the table" and
to have some discussion about sharing those benefits.

The Impact of Residual Values

While this paper is concerned with financial leasing, it is quite obvious that
sound economic reasons can be found for the existence of operating leasing
without resorting to tax arguments. Lessors may be able to take advantage of
economies of scale in purchasing and maintenance and also their specialized
knowledge of secondhand equipment values. With full payout leases involving
single asset acquisition by nontechnical lessors like bankers, such benefits dis-
appear, and this accounts for the major part of the domestic U.K. leasing market. However, in the United States, leases only get investment tax credits if the
asset is leased for less than a specified percentage of the asset's life. Consequently, there is likely to be a residual value to the asset at the completion of
the lease and, if they want to be regarded as owners for tax purposes, U.S. lessors are not allowed to give the lessee a rebate of rentals (or a secondary lease
with only nominal rentals), as is practiced in the United Kingdom. Consequently,
a lessor with special knowledge of asset values or a different risk attitude may be
able to reflect this in lower rentals to the benefit of the lessee. Several lessors in
the United Kingdom have indicated that this is bound to come in the United
Kingdom before long. If it does, there is the possibility of valid economic reasons for financial leasing apart from tax or other motives mentioned already. In
addition, the benefit of special knowledge about the life of the asset can lead to
lower rentals than the cost of writing off the asset by a nonspecialized-knowledge
lessee even under full payout leasing. Benefits to lessees could therefore accrue if

manufacturers start to enter the full payout leasing market without the banks as intermediaries.

A related problem concerns not the obsolescence rate, but fluctuations in demand and supply for the services rendered by assets owned or leased. In times of *unexpected* increases in business, the only way to obtain assets may be by leasing (e.g., with various forms of transport, containers, and tankers), at least until there is time to build or to acquire new assets for ownership. This argument probably relates more to operating leasing and ship chartering, but it could also apply to full-payout leasing.

Learning to Lease

One company provided an example of a proposal to invest in a developing country that was met with a refusal. However, the company was told that it could invest if it leased the asset through a local lessor. It soon transpired that the lessor knew very little about leasing, and the company said that it was a means by which the foreign government helped its financial institution learn about Western financial techniques—although it also earned a healthy commission and the ultimate ownership of the lessor was not questioned!

A multinational company located in the United Kingdom also said that it was sometimes willing to enter into lease negotiations even though the deal was only marginally attractive in order to keep abreast of modern financing techniques and practices. A lessor commenting on this statement emphasized that large and complex leasing deals can take several months to complete, and where new types of clauses and provisions are involved with lessees/lessors in new environments, the lead time can be very lengthy. It may, therefore, pay the really major lessors to write leases from time to time containing some new aspects, so that it has this expertise and knowledge "on tap" should it be needed quickly in order to be competitive if a possibility of a big deal arises. He likened this to a manufacturer's experimenting with new equipment in order to be up to date.

Raising Massive Sums of Money

Companies in certain industries are now having to face expenditures on a massive scale for new foreign developments involving sums even as large as 8 billion to 10 billion U.S. dollars on one project with costs incurred over five to six years' construction time. Financing on such a scale must be spread around for several reasons. First, a multinational said that if you try to place massive sums with just one or two institutions, they will cause problems for you. By spreading the package around, a finance executive stated that you can "soften the edge of competition" from the financial institutions. The same executive also said that a real problem in the United States in very large deals was the legal limitation on the amount that could be lent to one customer. However, if there were difficulties of this type, he had been able to overcome them in the past by bank's lending to a leasing company, which then leased the assets to his company.

Similarly, a bank may have its full quota of a particular country risk in its lending portfolio, but it could lend to another bank that had some spare capacity to undertake such risks, which in turn lent or leased to the customer of the original bank. Such interbank movements could apply to straight lending, as well as leasing, but on occasions a bank's leasing affiliate had been the readily available linkup.

CONCLUSIONS

This paper has presented firm evidence that the U.K. financial leasing is segmented, indicating that tax alone is insufficient to explain lessee motivation. A similar initial impression is obtained when examining the figures for leasing in different countries, although the quality of such statistics at present leaves much to be desired. Previous postal and interview data also suggest multiple reasons for leasing; however, the research methodology has in most cases been inadequate to draw firm conclusions. Finally, anecdotal evidence has been presented of a variety of factors that have motivated the writing of some very big international leases. Moreover, these leases should not be ignored on the basis of being relatively unimportant in terms of total value of leases written. One multinational, which had a very large leasing portfolio, estimated that it had 90 percent (by value) of its leasing in the big ticket international leasing category.

The main conclusion can only be that much more systematic empirical work is needed in order to explain leasing activities. Moreover, at least at the very big ticket end of the market, theorists should recognize that investment and leasing decisions are often very much interrelated. In addition, companies may have to consider what the optimal level of leasing in a firm's capital structure is. This is something academics seem to have overlooked, simply assuming that leasing is equivalent to debt in terms of financial risk, which could be a rather naive assumption given the way in which financing cash flows might differ over time and also affect foreign currency and political risks. At this level of the leasing debate, it seems that there is a need for a strategic management approach investigating the impact of leasing upon a whole range of financial parameters that cannot all be captured in the existing valuation models.

Theorists have called for research into imperfections that make it profitable to lease. The quantification of the importance of these imperfections will be a lengthy process.

POSTSCRIPT

Prior to the United Kingdom Finance Act, financial institutions offering full payout leases on cars obtained 100 percent first-year write-off for tax purposes, whereas lessees only obtained 25 percent if they purchased cars themselves. The 1979 Finance Act restricted lessors' relief to 25 percent, which, given the lags in tax payments and short lease periods for cars, meant that tax benefits became minimal or nonexistent. After initial falling off of car leasing after the Finance Act, the market recovered to end the year 1979 with even higher total full-payment car leasing than existed in 1978. It is stressed here that the growth was *after* the Finance Act and not in anticipation of it. Taxation may be very important, but there are "more things in heaven and earth" than tax alone.

NOTES

1. The new U.S. Bankruptcy Act had initially proposed to prevent lessors from repossessing leased assets, but this was changed in the legislation finally drafted.

REFERENCES

[1] Anderson, P., and Martin, J. "Lease vs Purchase or Lease vs Borrow: A reply," privately circulated paper, 1978.
[2] Clark, T. *Leasing*. New York: McGraw-Hill Book Company, 1978.
[3] Dietz, A. "Marketing and Commercial Policy," paper presented to Leaseurope Conference, Oslo, 1977.
[4] Errington, S. "Leasing in Europe," paper presented to Leaseurope Conference, Oslo, 1977.
[5] Fawthrop, R., and Terry, B. "Debt Management and the Use of Leasing Finance in UK Corporate Financing Strategies," *Journal of Business Finance and Accounting* (Autumn 1978).
[6] Glaser, B., and Strauss, A. *The Discovery of Grounded Theory: Strategies for Qualitative Research*. Chicago: Aldine Publishing Company, 1967.
[7] Hughes, J., and Oldfield, G. "An Empirical Assessment of Lessee Disclosure Policy," privately circulated paper, 1978.
[8] Lewellen, W.; Long, M.; and McConnell, J. "Asset Leasing in Competitive Capital Markets," *Journal of Finance* (June 1976), pp. 787–798.

[9]   Miller, M., and Upton, C. "Leasing, Buying and the Cost of Sources," *Journal of Finance* (June 1976), pp. 761–786.

[10] Myers, S.; Dill, D.; and Bautista, A. "Valuation of Financial Lease Contracts," *Journal of Finance* (June 1976), pp. 799–819.

[11] Sykes, A. "The Lease-Buy Decision—a Survey of Current Practice in 202 Companies," *Management Survey Report*, No. 29, B.I.M., 1976.

[12] Tomkins, C.; Lowe, J.; and Morgan, E. *An Economic Analysis of the Financial Leasing Industry*. Saxon House, November 1979.

[13] Weston, J., and Dann, L. "A Framework for the Analysis of Leasing," U.C.L.A., Finance Workshop Paper, October 1977.

14 A PRAGMATIC APPROACH TO THE ESTIMATION PROBLEMS ENCOUNTERED IN LEASE-PURCHASE ANALYSES

John D. Martin
Texas A & M University

Paul F. Anderson
Virginia Polytechnic Institute and State University

Chester L. Allen
Stephen F. Austin State University

The lease-purchase problem has provided the basis for a staggering volume of academic research, with theorists from finance, accounting, and economics each making their respective contributions. The net result of these combined efforts has been the development of a number of very complex models.[1] The primary differences in the more recent models relate to (1) the choice of appropriate discount rates and (2) the treatment accorded the differential leverage effects of leasing versus purchase financing. In this paper, we address a problem shared by all these models. This problem is that of estimation errors related to both cash-flow items and discount rates.

Our objective in this paper is managerial rather than theoretical, with emphasis on the development of a pragmatic aid to decision making. The approach taken involves the use of two forms of sensitivity analysis that have been widely used in the capital budgeting literature. These involve a univariate and a multivariate analysis of the variables in the lease-purchase model that are subject to estimation error.

In the first section, we present an overview of the potential economic advantages associated with lease financing. This discussion is intended to identify those factors involved in the lease-purchase problem that might not agree with the competitive market equilibrium assumptions that have been used to establish indifference theorems regarding the use of financial leases.[2]

The second section introduces the Schall [21] lease-purchase model. This model provides the basis for the sensitivity analysis. However, the Schall model is modified slightly so as to accommodate the risk of insolvency criterion that is used to equate the financial risks of the lease and purchase financing options. In addition, the format of the Schall model is modified so that the impact of the financing and investment components of the analysis can be more easily identified. The third section contains the results of an analysis of a hypothetical lease-purchase problem. This includes both the univariate and multivariate analyses of the investment and financing components of the model. Finally, the fourth section contains concluding remarks and implications of the study for lease-purchase analyses.

POTENTIAL ADVANTAGES OF LEASE FINANCING

The potential economic benefits from lease financing can be separated into two sources: benefits from cash-flow savings and benefits derived from differential expectations regarding salvage values. These benefits have been denied in the recent lease-purchase literature [12, 14, 16] through a set of assumptions that are used to characterize a perfect capital market in competitive equilibrium. Our interest in this section is to briefly overview some of the more important sources of economic benefits to leasing wherein the assumptions underlying a perfect capital market and its resulting general equilibrium conditions are *not* fulfilled.

Benefits from Cash-Flow Savings

There are five sources of cash-flow savings that *may* arise with lease financing. The first such source relates to the acquisition cost faced by the lessor versus the lessee. The lessor may, by virtue of his size and past experience, be able to capture quantity discounts or just price concessions not available to the lessee. One might even argue that where information is costly, the lessor might be willing to acquire the information related to the acquisition decision because of his volume of purchases, whereas the individual lessee would find the acquisition price of the information too high given his needs for that information. A second potential source of an acquisition cost advantage to the lessor relates to the investment tax credit on new equipment purchases. If the lessee already has tax credits that make the investment tax credit useless, then by leasing the asset he (the lessee) may gain some or all of the investment tax credits through a reduced rental fee.

The lessor may be able to provide certain maintenance and other services to the lessee at a cost lower than he could otherwise obtain them. This particular cash-flow benefit is most likely to accrue through lease agreements with manufacturer lessors.

The lessor may be able to depreciate the asset over a shorter period of time than the lessee. For example, the lessor may use the term of the lease as the depreciable life of the asset, whereas the lessee may use the Class Life Assets Depreciation Range method prescribed by the IRS. Under the Class Life ADR method, firms are allowed to choose a range of depreciation lives for each type of asset owned by the firm. However, once a firm has elected to use the ADR system for a particular type of equipment, all assets falling within the guideline class must be depreciated under the ADR system during the year of the election. To the extent that the lease term is less than the ADR period, the lessor's depreciation will exceed that of the lessee.

The lessor may be able to accrue a larger interest tax shelter benefit from a higher use of financial leverage than the lessee. If debt capacity is influenced by the risk of insolvency (either because of the interests of the owners, manager, or creditors), then the asset diversification of the lessor may be such that he can utilize a higher level of financial leverage and thus accrue a higher interest tax shelter benefit.[3]

Finally, the lessor may face a lower tax rate on income than the lessee. Of course, this lower tax rate would also reduce the value of the tax shelter accruing to the owner-lessor.

Benefits from Differential Salvage-Value Expectations

Lessor-lessee expectations regarding both the expected level of any asset salvage value and the risk assessment attached to that salvage value may differ widely. In addition, differences in lessor-lessee risk aversion may lead each to attach different values to a salvage value, even where homogeneous beliefs are shared with regard to the distributional characteristics associated with the salvage value.

This concludes a very brief overview of the potential economic benefits involved with lease financing. In addition to these arguments, there have been a number of "noneconomic" or "noncost saving" benefits associated with lease financing. These include allegations that lessee managers incorrectly assess the costs of leasing, that leasing provides off-balance sheet financing (no longer true in the United States given the reporting requirements of FASB 13), and that leasing preserves working capital since no down payment is required.[4] Finally, managers may lease even when it is more expensive than purchasing if company budget controls allow the manager to enter lease agreements without higher management approval but where a purchase would have to go through a lengthy budget review process.

In the next section, we present the Schall [21] lease-purchase model. This model exemplifies the basic form of the more recently developed models and provides the basis for the sensitivity analysis developed later.

THE LEASE-PURCHASE MODEL

Table 1 contains a complete listing of symbols and definitions to be used throughout this section. Note the use of bars to denote expected values for each of the random variables.

Table 1. Definition of Variables

$NPV(P)$	= the change in shareholder wealth as a consequence of purchasing the asset.
$NPV(L)$	= the change in shareholder wealth as a consequence of leasing the asset.
$\bar{Z}_i$	= the total cash revenues expected to be generated by the asset in year i.
$\bar{C}_i$	= the total pretax cash operating costs expected to be required to operate the asset in year i if it is purchased.
O_i	= total pretax cash operating costs expected to occur in year i if the firm purchases the asset, but not if the asset is leased; this includes such things as insurance, maintenance, and property taxes covered by the lessor.
$\bar{C}_i - O_i$	= the total pretax cash operating costs expected in year i if the asset is leased.
t	= corporate marginal tax rate on ordinary income.
R_i	= lease payment required in year i.
N	= useful economic life of the asset.
r	= the pretax cost of debt or borrowing rate to the firm.
D_i	= depreciation charge for year i allowed for tax purposes.
$\bar{V}_N$	= expected after-tax salvage value of the asset at the end of year N.
I_i	= interest expense for period i.
A_0	= cash purchase price of the asset.
L_i	= annual installment loan note paid in year i.
K_c	= the market-determined rate of return on the unlevered cash flow of the project being evaluated.
K_a	= the market-determined rate of return on the cash flows of a lessee firm.

The Modified Schall Lease-Purchase Model

Schall defines two separate equations to model the lease-purchase problem. The first measures the net present value associated with normal purchase financing, NPV(P):

$$NPV(P) = \sum_{i=1}^{N} \frac{(\bar{Z}_i - \bar{C}_i)(1-t) + tD_i + V_N}{(1+k_c)^i} + \sum_{i=1}^{N} \frac{tI_i}{(1+r)^i} - A_0. \qquad (1)$$

Each of the terms is defined in Table 1. Note that equation (1) is actually a finite life version of the Modigliani-Miller [15] tax-adjusted valuation model. Thus k_c is the market's required return on the project's unlevered cash flows. Note that (1) does not include the basis for determining the size of the interest tax shelter (tI_i) generated by the project. Schall suggests that another assumption must be introduced if all debt financing is not to be optimal. We will utilize a cash-flow adequacy standard to assess the size of the tI_i term. Specifically, we use a risk of insolvency criterion based on before-tax cash flows to assess debt capacity. A similar standard can be readily applied to the lease financing arrangement.

Schall's second equation measures the net present value of the asset if leased, NPV(L):

$$NPV(L) = \sum_{i=1}^{N} \frac{[\bar{Z}_i - (\bar{C}_i - O_i)](1-t)}{(1+k_a)^i} - \sum_{i=1}^{N} \frac{R_i(1-t)}{(1+r)^i} - \sum_{i=1}^{N} \frac{t\delta I_i}{(1+r)^i}, \qquad (2)$$

where $t\delta I_i$ is the interest tax shelter that is lost where the financial risk of 100 percent lease financing exceeds the debt capacity of the asset. The determination of δI_i raises the issue of the financial risks inherent in leasing versus borrowing. We address this problem as an integral part of the debt capacity issue. Again, through the use of sensitivity analysis, the analyst is provided with the basis for assessing the practical significance of the problem of assessing financial risk equivalence between lease and loan financing.

Unfortunately, Schall offers little guidance as to the selection of appropriate discount rates. He suggests the use of a discount rate appropriate to the riskiness of an all-equity firm with cash flows $[(\bar{Z}_i - (\bar{C}_i - O_i)](1-t)$. However, this cash flow differs from an all-equity firm that owns its assets by an amount equal to $[tD_i + \bar{V}_n - O_i(1-t)]$. Thus the appropriate rate of discount for K_a is not the cost of equity for an unlevered firm, K_c.[5]

Making two key assumptions, we can redefine NPV(L) as follows:

$$\text{NPV}(L) = \sum_{i=1}^{N} \frac{(\bar{Z}_i - \bar{C}_i)(1 - t) + tD_i + \bar{V}_n}{(1 + K_c)^i} + \sum_{i=1}^{N} \frac{O_i(1 - t) - tD_i}{(1 + r)^i} - \frac{\bar{V}_n}{(1 + K_c)^n}$$

$$- \sum_{i=1}^{N} \frac{R_i(1 - t)}{(1 + r)^i} - \sum_{i=1}^{N} \frac{t\delta I_i}{(1 + r)^i} . \tag{2a}$$

The first assumption is that both $O_i(1 - t)$ and tD_i are appropriately discounted at the cost of debt. Since the O_i generally consist of insurance premiums that are contractually set and the depreciation tax shelter is known with a high degree of certainty, the borrowing rate is assumed to approximate the discount rates for these cash flows. Second, the unlevered cost of equity, k_c, is used to find the present value of the after-tax salvage value, $\bar{V}_n$. This treatment is consistent with that of the NPV(P) model discussed earlier. Furthermore, where $\bar{V}_n$ is based upon the continued use of the asset in the same application (as opposed to a scrap value), then the use of k_c as a risk-adjusted discount rate is consistent with the discounting of the project's unlevered cash flows using k_c. Therefore, the analyst need only estimate the cost of equity for the unlevered cash flows, k_c, and the loan rate, r, in the proposed framework.

Traditional lease-purchase models have often used a net present value advantage to leasing format. By subtracting (1) from (2a), we define the advantage of lease financing (NAL) as follows:

$$\text{NAL} = A_0 - \frac{\bar{V}_n}{(1 + k_c)^n} - \sum_{i=1}^{N} \frac{tD_i - O_i(1 - t)}{(1 + r)^i} - \sum_{i=1}^{N} \frac{R_i(1 - t) + tI_i + t\delta I_i}{(1 + r)^i} . \tag{3}$$

The NAL model can be used to address the issue of whether to use lease or normal purchase financing, but it does not provide any insight into whether the asset should be acquired via either method of financing. Thus the NAL model provides only a partial solution to the lease-purchase problem. However, we analyze NAL here because of its widespread use and the fact that it highlights the present value advantage (disadvantage) of leasing.

Estimating Project Debt Capacity

Debt financing affects project value through the interest tax shelter terms (i.e., tI_i and $t\delta I_i$). Again, the Schall model does not prescribe the basis for estimating the appropriate financing mix for the project and, consequently, the level of these interest tax shelters.[6] In this paper we utilize the risk of insolvency as the basis for assessing the prudent level of project debt financing. This standard is appealing because it is both intuitive and tractable. A number of alternatives have been suggested in the literature and are summarized in the appendix.

The methodology used in assessing debt capacity has its roots in the pioneering work of Donaldson [6, 7]. However, we extend that analysis to formally consider the impact of project risk on firm risk via portfolio considerations.[7] Specifically, the risk of insolvency criterion for assessing project debt capacity is based on the assumption that a firm's management has a target risk of insolvency that limits its use of debt financing. We will here assume that the firm's target risk of insolvency is reflected in its present use of financial leverage. Thus the added debt capacity created by the acquisition of an asset is that level of new debt that the firm can incur without increasing the firm's present (target) risk of insolvency.

The first step in the estimation of a project's debt capacity involves estimating its annual debt service capacity (DSC). This is the added amount of before-tax annual cash outflow which the firm can incur after the project has been accepted without increasing the firm's overall risk of insolvency beyond its preproject (target) level.

Defining the firm's present risk of insolvency involves estimating the firm's annualized, unencumbered cash flow, $\bar{C}_f$. This cash flow can be defined as the annual equivalent of the following sum $[EBIT + DEPR - I - SF/(1 - t)]$.[8] $\bar{C}_f$ is the annual equivalent of the firm's expected future unencumbered cash flows, EBIT is earnings before interest and taxes, I is the interest expense associated with existing debt, and $SF/(1 - t)$ is the before-tax level of principal or sinking-fund payments on existing debt. If we assume that C_f is normally distributed with mean $\bar{C}_f$ and with variance $\sigma^2_{C_f}$, the firm's preproject risk of insolvency can be defined as follows:

$$P(C_f \leq 0) = P[C_f \leq (\bar{C}_f - z\sigma_{C_f})], \qquad (4)$$

where $z = 0 - \bar{C}_f/\sigma_{C_f}$.

Having estimated the firm's preproject insolvency risk, we must now consider the corresponding postproject risk. We begin by defining the mean of the combined unencumbered cash flow of the firm and the project:

$$\bar{C}'_f = \bar{C}_f + \bar{C}_p, \qquad (5)$$

where $\bar{C}_p$ is the annual equivalent annuity cash flow for the project:

$$\bar{C}_p = \sum_{i=1}^{N} \bar{C}_{pi}/(1 + r)^i \ / \ \sum_{i=1}^{N} \frac{1}{(1 + r)^i}. \qquad (6)$$

$\bar{C}_{pi}$ is the expected project cash flow in the ith year, and r equals the firm's borrowing rate. This rate of interest is used since this is the rate at which the firm can "time-adjust" its cash flows.[9] A similar procedure may also be used to estimate $\bar{C}_f$ on an equivalent annuity basis. The standard deviation of the combined firm and project flows σ'_{C_f} is given by

$$\sigma'_{C_f} = [\sigma^2_{C_f} + 2r_{fp}\, \sigma_{C_f} \sigma_{C_p} + \sigma^2_{C_p}]^{1/2}, \tag{7}$$

where r_{fp} is the coefficient of correlation between firm and project flows and σ_{C_f} and σ_{C_p} equal the standard deviations in firm and project flows, respectively. The presence of r_{fp} in equation (7) demonstrates that the project analysis depends, in part, on portfolio considerations; that is, the debt capacity generated by a given asset will differ depending upon the firm acquiring the asset.

Having estimated the firm's existing risk of insolvency and the parameters of the combined firm-project distribution of unencumbered cash flows, we can now proceed to estimate DSC. Specifically, DSC becomes the amount by which we can reduce $\bar{C}'_f$ before the probability of a zero or less value for C_f exceeds its project level. If C'_f is normally distributed and z_0 is the z-statistic corresponding to a zero or less value for C_f (preproject), then we may determine DSC as follows:

$$z_0 = \frac{\bar{C}'_f - \text{DSC}}{\sigma'_{C_f}}, \tag{8}$$

and hence

$$\text{DSC} = \bar{C}'_f - z_0 \sigma'_{C_f}. \tag{9}$$

Once DSC has been determined, the corresponding debt capacity of the asset can be easily calculated. This level of debt, D, is found by solving for that level of debt whose annual before-tax cost, AC, equals the DSC of the asset. The cost of an installment loan in year i equals the after-tax cost of debt, $L_i - tI_i$, divided by one minus the tax rate. The annualized cost of the debt over its entire life then equals

$$\text{AC} = \sum_{i=1}^{N} \frac{(L_i - tI_i)/(1-t)}{(1+r)^i} \Bigg/ \sum_{i=1}^{N} \frac{1}{(1+r)^i}, \tag{10}$$

where r is used for the same reasons that it was used in (6) above.[10] Note that where L is a level payment, project debt capacity (DC) can be defined as follows:

$$\text{DC} = \text{DSC}(1-t) \sum_{i=1}^{N} \frac{1}{(1+r)^i} + \sum_{i=1}^{N} \frac{tIi}{(1+r)^i}. \tag{11}$$

The debt capacity of the asset then is that level of debt whose AC equals the DSC of the asset.

Thus the analysis of the financing component of NPV(P) in (1) proceeds as follows:

1. Establish the firm's existing (i.e., target) insolvency risk.
2. Estimate the asset's DSC as the annualized cost of debt service that the firm can incur after the asset's acquisition while maintaining the pre-project risk of insolvency.
3. Calculate the debt capacity of the asset as that level of debt financing whose before-tax annualized cost equals the asset's DSC.
4. Compute the interest payments on the asset's debt capacity and enter into the computation of the NPV(P) using equation (1).

The computation of $t\delta I_i$ may proceed in a similar fashion. Recall that δI_i is the interest on that amount of debt, δD, which must be retired (issued) in order to equate the leverage effects of the lease and purchase alternatives. The first step in solving for δD involves the determination of the differential AC, δAC, of the lease versus the purchase alternative. Since the before-tax cost of leasing is simply the rental payment, R,

$$\delta AC = R - DSC. \tag{12}$$

The problem that remains is one of solving for that amount of debt, equal to δD, that can be serviced by δAC. This involves a repetition of the process outlined above. This time, however, AC is equated with δAC and not with DSC. The resultant value of δD serves as the basis for determining the $t\delta I_i$ for use in equations (2) and (3).

This completes the discussion of the lease-purchase model. In the next section, we perform a sensitivity analysis on the lease-purchase model utilizing a hypothetical problem.

SENSITIVITY ANALYSIS

Example Problem

To demonstrate the use of sensitivity analysis on the modified Schall model, an example problem will be used. Pertinent annual cash-flow information for the lease-purchase exercise is contained in Table 2. In addition, the purchase price of the asset is $40,000, and it has an expected after-tax salvage value ($\bar{V}_N$) of $10,000 at the end of its ten-year life. The firm is assumed to face a 50 percent marginal tax rate and estimates its cost of equity if unlevered (K_c) to be 12 percent.

Table 2. Annual Cash-Flow Data for the Lease-Purchase Example Exercise

Year	Total Cash Revenues Z_i	Operating Costs— Purchase C_i	Operating Costs— Covered by Lessor O_i	Depreciation Expense[a] D_i	Lease Expense[b] R_i
1	$13,250	$5,000	$250	$5,454	$6,400
2	13,250	5,000	250	4,909	6,400
3	13,250	5,000	250	4,363	6,400
4	13,250	5,000	250	3,818	6,400
5	13,250	5,000	250	3,273	6,400
6	13,250	5,000	250	2,727	6,400
7	13,250	5,000	250	2,182	6,400
8	13,250	5,000	250	1,636	6,400
9	13,250	5,000	250	1,091	6,400
10	13,250	5,000	250	545	6,400

[a]Sum-of-the-years digits depreciation is used.
[b]Lease payments are paid at year end.

To estimate project debt capacity, the following information is needed: The firm's estimated level of unencumbered cash flow $(\bar{C}_f)$ is $150,000, with a standard deviation (σ_{C_f}) of $75,000. The standard deviation in project cash flows is estimated to be $2000, and the correlation between firm-project cash flows is estimated at .60.

Table 3 contains the results of an analysis of the example problem based on the expected levels of all variables. The project's NPV(P) is calculated to be $2547.44. This indicates that the acquisition of the asset via purchase financing is indeed warranted. An analysis of the present value advantage of leasing (NAL) indicates a positive advantage of $180.17. Thus the asset's services should be acquired via lease financing.

Note that these estimates reflect an estimated before-tax project debt service capacity of $6506.75 per year, which supports $26,639.99 in new debt financing (where the borrowing rate equals 8 percent). Recall that the estimated DSC is one that will leave the firm's risk of insolvency at its preproject (target) level. Note also that the project's pretax DSC actually exceeds the before-tax rental payments by $106.75. Thus, if the asset is leased, the firm can issue new debt equal to $298.90, which can be supported by an annualized before-tax debt service requirement of $106.75.

Recapping the lease-purchase algorithm, we first analyze NPV(P) to determine whether the asset should be acquired via normal purchase financing. If

Table 3.   Lease-Purchase Analysis of the Example Problem

Analysis of Purchase Alternative:

$$\text{NPV}(P) = \sum_{i=1}^{N} \frac{(Z_i - C_i)(1 - t) + tD_i}{(1 + k_c)^i} + \frac{V_N}{(1 + K_c)^N} + \sum_{i=1}^{N} \frac{tI_i}{(1 + r)^i} - A_0$$

$$= \$34{,}522.07 + 3{,}219.74 + 4{,}805.64 - 40{,}000$$

$$= \$2{,}547.44.$$

Analysis of the Lease Alternative:

$$\text{NAL} = A_0 - \frac{V_N}{(1 + K_c)^N} - \sum_{i=1}^{N} \frac{tD_i - D_i(1 - t)}{(1 + r)^i} - \sum_{i=1}^{N} \frac{R_i(1 - t) + tI_i + t\delta I_i}{(1 + r)^i}$$

$$= \$40{,}000 - 3{,}219.74 - 10{,}376.12 - 26{,}223.97$$

$$= \$180.17.$$

Additional Solution Data:

Project DSC = $6,506.75.
Project debt capacity = $26,636.05.
Differential annualized cost of leasing (δAC) = $6,400 - 6,506.75
    = -$106.75.
Debt retirement (issuance) with leasing = -$298.90

NPV(P) is positive, we still evaluate the advisability of leasing through the NAL equation since leasing may be a more attractive means of financing. If NAL is positive, then the asset should be leased; if it is negative, then the asset should be purchased—given that NPV(P) has already been determined to be positive. Should NPV(P) have been negative, then NAL should still be evaluated since lease financing may offer a present value advantage large enough to offset the negative NPV(P); that is, NPV(L) may be positive even though NPV(P) is negative.

Univariate Sensitivity Analysis

This form of sensitivity analysis involves determining the effect of a single variable on the lease-purchase decision where all other variables are held constant at their expected values. The particular type of analysis utilized here involves a break-even format wherein the analyst seeks that value of the variable being analyzed that will reverse his decision. For example, this means finding that level for the salvage value that will make the purchase option preferred to leasing or that will reverse the decision to acquire the asset's services via purchase or lease.

The NPV(P) equation can be conveniently dichotomized into its investment and financing components as follows:

Investment component:
$$\sum_{i=1}^{N} \frac{[\bar{Z}_i - \bar{C}_i (1 - t) + tD_i + V_N]}{(1 + K_c)^i} - A_0$$

Financing component:
$$\sum_{i=1}^{N} \frac{tI_i}{(1 + r)^i}$$

The key variables involved in a sensitivity analysis of the investment component are $(\bar{Z}_i - \bar{C}_i)$, $\bar{V}_N$, and K_c. The key factors involved in analyzing the financing component (i.e., tI_i) include the estimated values of both firm and project unencumbered cash flows, their respective standard deviations, and the correlation between them.

Both the investment and financing components of NPV(P) are affected by the level of project cash flows $(\bar{Z}_i - \bar{C}_i)$. However, we perform our sensitivity analysis on this crucial variable as it affects the investment component. This is consistent with the greater relative impact of the $(\bar{Z}_i - \bar{C}_i)$ on project worth via the investment component.

An analysis of the net present value of the example problem presented earlier reveals that the present value of the firm's after-tax operating cash flows—that is, the present value of the $(\bar{Z}_i - \bar{C}_i) (1 - t)$—could be as low as 89 percent of their expected value without reducing the positive NPV(P) of $2547.44 to zero. Thus the analyst could overestimate the present value of the true after-tax cash flows from the project by as much as 12.36 percent, and the error would not affect the NPV(P) signal to acquire the asset's services via purchase financing. In addition, the after-tax salvage value could be as little as 21 percent of its estimated $10,000 amount, and the NPV(P) would still offer the same purchase signal. However, the estimated discount rate for the project's unlevered cash flows, K_c, could rise to only 12.81 percent before reversing the purchase signal given by NPV(P). Finally, the present value of the interest tax shelter (tI_i) created by the use of debt financing could fall to 47 percent of its estimated value without reversing the NPV(P) signal. Thus, through the use of this methodology, the analyst can pinpoint those variables whose estimates are most critical to the decision that is to be made. In this example problem, it appears that K_c

is the single most important estimate that must be made in terms of the relative error that can be tolerated before the NPV(P) signal changes from go to no go. Note that we still have not analyzed the lease option via NAL.

We now turn to a detailed analysis of the impact of estimated project debt capacity on the lease-purchase decision both in terms of NPV(P) and NAL. Table 4 contains a set of six values for NPV(P) and NAL. The fifth-row figures are based upon the expected levels of all variables. Each of the remaining values of NPV(P) and NAL corresponds to different values of each of the determinants of project debt capacity. For example, the first row in Table 4 represents a NPV(P) of -$406.48 and a NAL of $204.93. These measures of project worth would result where the standard deviation in project cash flows was as high as $5177.84, or the standard deviation in firm cash flows was as low as $28,970.04, or the level of firm cash flows was as high as $396,543.10. Note that any one of the above would alone account for the level of both NPV(P) and NAL observed in the first row.

A quick comparison of the NPV(P) and NAL values in rows one, two, and six reveals that different decisions are reflected at each of these levels of the debt capacity variables. In row one, NPV(P) is negative, indicating that the asset's services should not be acquired via normal purchase financing. Further, the NAL is positive ($204.93), but not large enough to offset the negative NPV(P)—that is, the NPV(L) is negative but less negative than NPV(P)—and thus the asset should not be leased or purchased. In row two, we have a situation where NPV(P) is negative (-$203.09), but NAL more than offsets this negative NPV(P) so that the asset should be leased. In row six, we see a case where NPV(P) is a very large positive value, but NAL is negative. In this case, the asset should be purchased. This type of exercise allows the decision maker to assess very quickly the sensitivity of the lease-purchase analysis to errors involved in the estimation of the determinants of the financing component of the lease-purchase problem. In the example problem, we saw that the effect of these variables was sufficient to change the decision signal of the model from lease, to purchase, to one of not acquiring the asset using either form of financing. The use of sensitivity analysis again provides the analyst with an estimate of the magnitude (both relative and absolute) of the estimation errors that he can make without altering the signal of the lease-purchase analysis.

Multivariate Sensitivity Analysis

In the sensitivity analysis presented thus far, it has been assumed that all random variables behave independently of one another so that a univariate analysis is appropriate. This, however, is generally not the case, as many of the determi-

Table 4. Sensitivity Analysis of the Determinants of Project Debt Capacity

	NPV(P)	NAL	Standard Deviation		Expected Firm Cash Flows	Project-Firm Correlation	
			Project Cash Flows	Firm Cash Flows			
1	$ -406.48	$ 204.93	$5,177.84	$ 28,970.04	$396,543.10	a	Do not acquire the asset's service.
2	-203.09	204.79	4,963.16	30,222.96	379,580.70	a	
3	.16	204.80	4,747.81	31,593.89	362,618.10	a	Lease the asset.
4	1,428.46	204.93	3,110.44	48,225.55	235,051.50	.95	
5	2,547.44	180.18	2,000.00	75,000.00	150,000.00	.60	
6	3,566.55	-141.97	872.72	171,885.30	64,962.69	.25	Purchase the asset.

[a]This level of NPV(P) and NAL could not occur because of an error in estimating the level of the project-firm correlation in cash flows. The required correlation coefficient would exceed unity.

nants of the final investment outcome tend to hinge on the same factors. Examples of these basic determinants of project success are general economic conditions and competitive conditions. Thus some form of multivariate sensitivity analysis that can account for these interdependencies should be helpful. However, a problem arises in performing such an analysis in that the analyst must now estimate the nature of the assumed interdependencies. One possible solution to this problem would involve simply assuming that all estimated variables were "off" by some fixed fraction. In the example used here, we use 1 percent increments and analyze the effects of joint, adverse estimation errors of up to 10 percent.

Table 5 contains the results of the multivariate sensitivity analysis. Note that adverse estimation errors of up to 5 percent do not reverse the NPV(*P*) signal to purchase the asset. Furthermore, errors greater than 6 percent are required to negate the positive net present value advantage of leasing. Recall that this is a 6 percent adverse estimation error in *all* random variables affecting the lease-purchase analysis. Where estimation errors are not believed to occur uniformly in an adverse direction, then the analysis presented in Table 5 is too severe. However, by combining the univariate and multivariate analyses pre-

Table 5.   Multivariate Sensitivity Analysis

Percent Error[a]	NPV(P)	NAL	DSC[b]	Debt Capacity	δ Debt Capacity[c]	
0%	$2,547.45	$180.18	$6,506.75	$26,636.05	$ -298.90	
1%	2,033.54	271.02	6,368.88	26,071.63	128.35	
2%	1,523.41	336.14	6,230.44	25,504.94	694.99	Lease
3%	1,071.32	400.13	6,091.56	24,937.39	1,262.62	the
4%	514.58	463.28	5,952.25	24,366.13	1,832.91	asset.
5%	15.86	525.20	5,812.50	23,794.06	2,405.00	
6%	-479.19	586.11	5,672.25	23,219.94	2,979.13	
7%	970.45	645.71	5,531.56	22,644.88	3,555.95	Do not
8%	-1,458.52	704.84	5,390.44	22,066.30	4,133.62	acquire
9%	-1,942.86	762.96	5,248.75	21,486.29	4,712.75	the asset's
10%	-2,423.57	819.70	5,106.63	20,905.20	5,295.45	services.

[a]Only adverse estimation errors were considered.

[b]Debt service capacity of the asset being analyzed.

[c]Excess debt capacity displaced by the lease. A negative value indicates that the project supports a higher level of financial leverage than is represented by the lease (i.e., the project's DSC exceeds the lease payment). Note that a 10 percent estimation error means that the asset's acquisition v. .uld require the repayment of $5295.45 in outstanding debt financing to maintain the firm's preproject acceptance level of insolvency risk.

sented here, the analyst can place reasonable bounds on the relative magnitude of the estimation errors that the models will absorb without a reversal in the model's signal.

CONCLUSIONS

The lease-purchase problem has provided the impetus for the development of an extensive literature and an increasingly more complex set of analytical models. Differences in the more recent models relate primarily to the choice of appropriate discount rates and the treatment accorded the financial risks of leasing versus purchasing. However, all lease-purchase models suffer from the difficulties presented by estimation errors. In this paper, we have attempted to develop a pragmatic approach to dealing with the problem of estimation errors via two forms of sensitivity analysis. These included a univariate break-even form of analysis and a multivariate sensitivity analysis. Both methods of analysis were used to assess the relative estimation error that could be tolerated before changing the decision signal of the lease-purchase model.

APPENDIX: ASSESSING THE FINANCIAL RISK OF LEASING

Three basic approaches have been taken in the lease-purchase literature in attempting to evaluate the financial risk of leasing vis-à-vis debt financing. In this appendix, we briefly overview each one in terms of the definition of financial risk upon which it is based and the resulting tradeoff between lease and loan amounts.

To expedite our presentation we define the following terms:

P_0 = loan equivalent of a financial lease;
R_j = lease payment in period;
r = the pretax cost of debt;
r_1 = rate of interest implicit in the lease;
L_j = loan payment in period j;
I_j = the interest component of the jth loan payment;
P_j = the principal component of the jth loan payment ($P_0 = \Sigma_{j=1}^{n} P_j$);
A_0 = the acquisition price of the asset;
$B_0 = \Sigma_{j=1}^{n} [R_j/(1+r)^j]$.

Some of these terms were previously defined in the text of the paper; however, their definitions have been repeated here to facilitate the reading of this appendix.

There are three basic categories of attempts to deal with the financial risk of lease financing. We discuss each in turn.

Category 1: Financial risk is a function of the level of before-tax finance charges faced by the firm.

This approach has been advocated by both Vancil [23] and Ofer [19] and simply defines the financial risk posed by a lease payment R_j as equivalent to an equal loan payment L_j. The resultant "equivalent loan" for a lease then equals

$$P_0 = B_0 = \sum_{j=1}^{n} \frac{R_j}{(1+r)^j}.$$

Note that where $r < r_1$ the equivalent loan will be greater than the acquisition price of the asset (i.e., $P_0 > A_0$). This latter observation led Bower, Herrington, and Williamson [3] to propose a second method for dealing with the financial risk of leasing.

Category 2: The financial risk of a lease is equivalent to a loan equal to the acquisition price of the asset being leased.

This method presumes that the loan equivalent of a lease is A_0. Bower, Herrington, and Williamson arrived at this "conclusion" by adjusting Vancil's [23] equivalent loan payment as follows:

$$L_j' = R_j(A_0/B_0),$$

where L_j' is the new loan payment on the adjusted lease-equivalent loan. Note that this adjusted loan payment (L_j') produces an equivalent loan equal to A_0 or

$$A_0 = \sum_{j=1}^{n} \frac{L_j'}{(1+r)^j}.$$

This particular definition of the financial risk of leasing has also been used by Beechy [2] and is implicit in most of the net advantage of leasing equations presently used in finance textbooks.

Category 3: Financial risk is a function of the after-tax finance charges faced by the firm.

In this particular approach, we define the financial risk of a lease in terms of the after-tax lease payment, $R_j (1 - t)$, and the after-tax loan payment, $P_j + I_j (1 - t)$. Equating these after-tax finance charges produces an equivalent loan of

$$P_0 = \sum_{j=1}^{n} \frac{R_j (1-t)}{[1 + r(1-t)]^j}.$$

This is the particular form of equivalence that we utilized and that was also suggested by Ofer [19] as his second method.

Summary. A brief summary of the three approaches to assessing the financial risk of lease financing is provided below:

	Equivalent Loan	
	Amount (P_0)	Annual Payment (L_j')
Category 1	$P_0 = B_0 = \sum_{j=1}^{n} \frac{R_j}{(1+r)^j}$	$L_j' = R_j$
Category 2	$P_0 = A_0$	$L_j' = R_j(A_0/B_0)$
Category 3	$P_0 = \sum_{j=1}^{n} \frac{R_j(1-t)}{[1+r(1-t)]^j}$	$L_j' = [P_j/(1-t)] + I_j$

Each approach provides a different loan amount, which is considered to be equivalent to the lease. The latter seems most consistent, in the view of the authors, with a correct assessment of the risks of insolvency posed by the lease versus debt financing. Note that we have not discussed the determination of the optimum level of financial risk to which the firm should be exposed. This is the debt capacity issue that we address in terms of a target risk of insolvency in the paper.

NOTES

1. In a recent survey of forty-six Fortune 200 companies, only two were found to be using lease-purchase models developed after 1967 [1]. One reason for this low level of acceptance may relate to the increasing complexity of the more recent models. Still another may be that the refinements of the newer models are viewed as more cosmetic than real. The sensitivity analysis performed here will provide some evidence as to the practical significance of some of the variables that differ among these models.

2. We refer here to the trio of papers by Lewellen, Long, and McConnell [12], Miller and Upton [14], and Myers, Dill, and Bautista [17].

3. The interest tax shelter benefits referred to here are those accruing to the levered firm in the sense of the Modigliani-Miller [15] valuation model.

4. In a recent issue of *Business Week* [4], a number of noncost savings advantages of leasing were cited as underlying the recent boom in lease financing.

5. Since the two cash-flow streams differ by more than a scale factor, it is difficult to accept that $k_a = k_c$, as Schall seems to suggest [21, p. 1209].

6. The literature on this subject is anything but settled, as Chen and Kim [5] point out in their synthesis. From a managerial perspective, we still largely operate through the use of simple rules of thumb. See appendix for further discussion.

7. The methodology used here is a natural extension of Lewellen's [11] theory of financial synergism as later refined by Higgins and Schall [8] and tested by Kim and Mc-Connell [9].

8. In the unlikely event that the sum of these terms would form a level perpetuity, then $\overline{C}_f$ is simply any year's unencumbered cash flow. However, where uneven cash flows are anticipated, it is the annualized equivalent of these cash flows that becomes relevant. We discuss the procedure for finding an annualized equivalent later in conjunction with project cash flows.

9. Donaldson [6, 7] suggested that the analysis be based on recession cash-flow levels; that is, the target risk of insolvency should be based upon the largest such risk faced by the firm, which for most firms corresponds to recession conditions.

10. Generally, we assume that a firm cannot lend at the same rate that it must pay to borrow funds. However, the assessment of $\overline{C}_p$ becomes unnecessarily complex where such a restriction is placed on the analysis.

Furthermore, the impact of the use of r as both a borrowing and a lending rate can be assessed through a sensitivity analysis on $\overline{C}_p$. Finally, note that C_{pn} includes the salvage value of the project. Thus, salvage value is allowed to affect the project's debt carrying capacity through its effect on $\overline{C}_p$.

REFERENCES

[1]   Anderson, Paul F., and Martin, John D. "Lease vs. Purchase Decisions: A Survey of Current Practice," *Financial Management* 6 (Spring 1977).

[2]   Beechy, T.H. "Quasi-Debt Analysis of Financial Leases," *Accounting Review* 41 (April 1966).

[3]   Bower, R.S.; Herrington, F.C.; and Williamson, J.P. "Lease Evaluation," *Accounting Review* 41 (April 1966).

[4]   *Business Week,* "Recession Gives Leasing a Lift" (August 13, 1979).

[5]   Chen, A.H., and Kim, E.H. "Theories of Corporate Debt Policy: A Synthesis," *Journal of Finance* 34 (May 1979).

[6]   Donaldson, Gordon. *Corporate Debt Capacity.* Homewood, Ill.: Richard D. Irwin, 1971.

[7]   Donaldson, Gordon, "Strategy for Financial Emergencies," *Harvard Business Review* 47 (November–December 1969).

[8]   Higgins, Robert C., and Schall, Lawrence D. "Corporate Bankruptcy and Conglomerate Merger," *Journal of Finance* 30 (March 1975).

[9]   Kim, E. Han, and McConnell, John J. "Corporate Merger and the 'Co-Insurance' of Corporate Debt," *Journal of Finance* (May 1977).

[10] Lewellen, Wilbur G. "A Conceptual Reappraisal of the Cost of Capital," *Financial Management* 3 (Winter 1974).

[11] Lewellen, Wilbur G. "A Pure Financial Rationale for the Conglomerate Merger," *Journal of Finance* 26 (May 1971).

[12] Lewellen, Wilbur G.; Long, Michael S.; and McConnell, John J. "Asset Leasing in Competitive Capital Markets," *Journal of Finance* 31 (June 1976).

[13] Martin, John D., and Scott, David F., Jr. "Debt Capacity and the Capital Budgeting Decision," *Financial Management* 5 (Summer 1976).

[14] Miller, M.H., and Upton, C.W. "Leasing, Buying and the Cost of Capital Services," *Journal of Finance* 3 (June 1976).

[15] Modigliani, F.F., and Miller, M.H. "Corporation Income Taxes and the Cost of Capital: A Correction," *American Economic Review* (June 1963).

[16] Myers, Stewart C., "Interactions of Corporate Financing and Investment Decisions — Implications for Capital Budgeting," *Journal of Finance* 29 (March 1974).

[17] Myers, Stewart C.; Dill, David A.; and Bautista, Alberto J. "Valuation of Financial Lease Contracts," *Journal of Finance* 31 (June 1976).

[18] Myers, Stewart C., and Pogue, Gerald A. "A Programming Approach to Corporate Financial Management," *Journal of Finance* 29 (May 1974).

[19] Ofer, A.R. "The Evaluation of Lease versus Purchase Alternatives," *Financial Management* 5 (Summer 1976).

[20] Schall, Lawrence D. "Asset Valuation, Firm Investment, and Firm Diversification," *Journal of Business* 45 (January 1972).

[21] Schall, Lawrence D. "The Lease-or-Buy and Asset Acquisition Decisions," *Journal of Finance* 29 (September 1974).

[22] Scott, James H., Jr. "A Theory of Optimal Capital Structure," *Bell Journal of Economics* 7 (Spring 1976).

[23] Vancil, Richard F. "Lease or Borrow: New Method of Analysis," *Harvard Business Review* 39 (September–October 1961). Reprinted in *Leasing Series*. Boston: Harvard Business Review, n.d.